Essays in Critical Theology

Gregory Baum

Sheed & Ward

Sheed & Ward™ is a service of The National Catholic Reporter Publishing Company.

Library of Congress Cataloguing-in-Publication Data

Baum, Gregory, 1923-
    Essays in critical theology / Gregory Baum.
        p.   cm.
    Includes bibliographical references.
    ISBN: 1-55612-710-3 (alk. paper)
    1. Sociology, Christian (Catholic) 2. Liberation theology.
3. Critical theory. 4. Church and social problems—Catholic Church
5. Catholic Church—North America. I. Title.
    BX1753.B364 1994
    230'.2—dc20   94-19427
                                                                           CIP

Published by: Sheed & Ward
                 115 E. Armour Blvd.
                 P.O. Box 419492
                 Kansas City, MO 64141

To order, call: (800) 333-7373

Contents

Preface vii

Part I: Critical Theology in Dialogue

1. Critical Theology: Replies to Ray Morrow 3
2. David Tracy: Pluralism and Liberation Theology . . . 35
3. For and Against John Milbank 52
4. Postmodern Discourse and Social Responsibility . . . 77
5. Allan Bloom: The Separation of Truth and Love . . . 96
6. Emil Fackenheim and Christianity 108

Part II: Theology and Social Analysis

7. Do We Need a Catholic Sociology? 139
8. Vatican II: Critical Openness to Modernity 171
9. John Paul II on Structural Sin 189
10. Liberal Capitalism:
    Has John Paul II Changed his Mind? 205
11. The Ethical Foundation of Workers' Co-ops 223

Acknowledgments

"David Tracy: Pluralism and Liberation Theology" was first published in *Radical Pluralism and Truth*, eds. W. Jeanrond and J. Rike, New York: Crossroad, 1991, pp. 3-17.

"For and Against John Milbank," expanded version of a paper given at the "Theology and Religion" Symposium at the Presbyterian College of Montreal in May, 1992, to be published in forthcoming proceedings.

"Postmodern Discourse and Social Responsibility" was published under another title in *The Ecumenist*, 29 (Spring, 1991) pp. 4-12.

"Allan Bloom: The Separation of Truth and Love" was published under another title in *The Ecumenist*, 27 (July/August, 1989) pp. 65-70.

"Emil Fackenheim and Christianity" was published in *Fackenheim: German Philosophy and Jewish Thought*, eds. Louis Greenspan and Graeme Nicholson, Toronto: University of Toronto Press, 1992, pp. 176-201.

"Do We Need a Catholic Theology?" was published under another title in *Theological Studies*, 50 (1989) pp. 718-43.

"Vatican Council II: Critical Openness to Modernity," co-authored with Jean-Guy Vaillancourt, was published in *Religion and the Social Order*, vol. 2, ed. Helen Ebough, Greenwhich, CT: J.A.I. Press, 1991, pp. 21-33.

"John Paul II on Structural Sin"—an earlier version, called "Social Sin" was published in *The Logic of Solidarity*, eds. G. Baum and R. Ellsberg, Maryknoll, NY: Orbis, 1989, 110-26.

"Liberal Capitalism: Has John Paul II Changed his Mind?" an expanded version of the article, "Liberal Capitalism," in *The Logic of Solidarity*, pp. 75-89.

"Ethical Foundations of Workers' Co-ops" was published in *Journal of Religion and Culture* (Concordia University, Montreal), vol. 5, Spring 1991, pp. 1-22.

To my friend and colleague
the praxis theologian
Rudi Siebert

Preface

Ever since my studies in sociology at the New School for Social Research from 1969 to 1971, my principal interest in research and writing has been the intersection between theology and sociology, including social ethics, Catholic social teaching, liberation theology and the sociology of religion. Important in my sociological studies was the encounter with Critical Theory associated with the Frankfurt School. I became convinced that this critical approach could be usefully applied in theology as this was already being done by Johann-Baptist Metz and other political theologians. In a book I published after my years at the New School, I used the term 'critical theology' to designate any theology that uses critical social theory to uncover and unfold the emancipatory meaning of the Christian Gospel. Since then I have learnt that critical theology must also listen to the voices of the powerless, including women, who are largely excluded from public discourse. I have pursued this critical approach in several publications and in *The Ecumenist,* a review I edited for the Paulist Press until 1991 and edit again, this time for Sheed & Ward, from the fall of 1993 on. For this venture I express my gratitude to Mr. Robert Heyer, editor-in-chief of Sheed & Ward.

The essays collected in this volume bring critical theology into conversation with social thinkers, theologians, and Catholic social theory. In Part I, I engage in dialogue with several authors, some of whom are concerned with the postmodern thesis, and in Part II, I deal with issues of social analysis and social ethics, mainly in the Catholic tradition.

My move to the Religous Studies Faculty of Montreal's McGill University in 1986 greatly encouraged me in my work as a theologian, in part because the dean, Dr. Donna Runnalls, greatly supported me in this, and in part because the progressive wing of the Catholic Church in Quebec is still a believing, active and productive community. In Montreal I am in conversation with political economy at the Karl Polanyi Institute attached to Concordia University. After my move to this city I wrote *The Church in Quebec*, a book published in Canada, and the forthcoming *Karl Polanyi on Ethics and Economics* and *Protestant Theology in Communist East Germany*, which testify to my ongoing involvement in the Church and my uninterrupted dialogue with critical social science. The present volume, *Essays in Critical Theology*, tells the same story.

Gregory Baum

Part I

Critical Theology in Dialogue

1

Critical Theology:
Replies to Ray Morrow

Raymond Morrow is one of the few critical theorists who have paid attention to contemporary social-justice movements in the Christian churches and, related to this, the development of political theology and liberation theology. At the meeting of the Canadian Learned Societies in June 1991, Ray Morrow presented a paper to the Society for Socialist Studies on Gregory Baum's critical theology with particular reference to his theological method and approach to social criticism. I was greatly honoured by the attention he paid to my writings and the sympathetic interpretation he offered of them. It is not easy for a secular scholar to move into theology. Ray Morrow was quite willing to study the wide-ranging debate among theologians regarding the primacy of practice and the role of social theory in articulating the Christian message. Since he read this literature and my own writings with so much sympathy, I must conclude that he regards critical theologians as allies in the contemporary intellectual debate.

Let me reply that I too regard him—and critical theory in general—as an ally against powerful intellectual trends of the present: the all-pervasive positivism in the natural and social sciences, the neo-conservative agenda reflected in economics and political science, the postmodern rejection of any form of universal reason, and the functionalist approach that protects important human values yet remains insensitive to the dark and destructive side of society.

At the end of his paper Ray Morrow formulated several questions and asked me to reply to them in light of my own critical theology. The issues he raised were profound: each one would deserve a full-length treatment. What I wish to do in the present essay is to offer some reflections on the issues raised by him, following the method of critical theology as I understand it.

Following this method, I always start reflection in response to concrete troubling issues in church or society so that I am unable to jump directly into theoretical considerations. Theoretical debates always reflect the historical context in which they take place. That is why critical theology moves from 'story' to 'theory.' Thus I wish to begin this essay by briefly telling the story of my involvement in critical theology and the entry of this theology into the official discourse of the Catholic Church.

'The Option for the Poor' and Critical Theory

Over the course of the last two decades or so, I have come to think of myself as a community-oriented intellectual. I am a Catholic theologian teaching at a university, but I am also involved in a network of church organizations where I communicate with a wider public beyond the academy, made up of people engaged in pastoral and social action. Many theologians think of themselves primarily as university scholars: they do valuable work which I greatly admire. By contrast I think of myself as an intellectual identified with social-justice movements in the Christian churches. I participate in meetings where, listening to others, I learn from their practical experience and insight, and where I am asked to address concrete issues in light of critical theology. At the same time I also write papers addressed to my colleagues at the university, where I am often able to mediate ideas acquired by participating in social-justice networks.

Many years ago in *Religion and Alienation,* I used the term 'critical theology' to designate a theology that uses critical social theory to uncover the emancipatory meaning of the Christian Gospel.[1] The term has not been widely used. In Latin America the theology that draws upon critical social theory is called 'liberation theology' and in Germany 'political theology.' Latin American liberation theology is grounded in the religious experience of base communities that struggle for justice and dignity in conditions of marginalization. German political theology tends to be university-based. Critical theology in North America tries to mediate between the academy and social-justice networks. These various centres, groups, communities and congregations, accompanied by their theologians, constitute a significant movement within the Catholic Church, a movement that is ecumenically connected to similar movements in the Protestant and Anglican Churches.

The Catholic social-justice movement has had a significant impact on the Church's official social teaching. Even if liberation theology was occasionally suppressed by the Vatican, it has nonetheless influenced the Church's public discourse. The reason why I wish to document this influence is to show that critical theologians like myself are not mavericks, but represent positions recognized in the Church.

The Latin American Bishops Conferences of Medellin in 1968 and Puebla in 1979 adopted a new theological term derived from liberation theology: 'the preferential option for the poor.'[2] This option, we are told, is a contemporary form of discipleship; it is a dimension of Christian faith. It is founded upon the life of Jesus and incarnates the spirit of the entire biblical message. How is this option defined? The preferential option consists of a twofold commitment: first, to read society and its texts from the perspective of the poor and oppressed, and second, to give public witness of one's solidarity with their struggle for liberation. The first commitment has hermeneutical implications and the second activist ones.

The documents of Medellin and Puebla describe the historical conditions of Latin America from the perspective of the poor and oppressed—the great majority—and they announce the Church's solidarity with their struggle for liberation. The documents recognize that to do this the Church must undergo a spiritual conversion. In light of the Gospel as presently understood, the Church must review its own institutions, pastoral practice and secular connections.

While this radical social-justice movement provoked strong opposition within the Catholic Church, it did receive support in a series of Vatican documents, especially Pope John Paul II's encyclical, *Laborem exercens* (1981).[3] The Canadian Catholic bishops, seconded by the Christian social-justice networks in Canada, produced several pastoral statements that endorsed the preferential option for the poor in the Canadian context. They offered critical analyses of the present economic system and its cultural and human consequences. Remarkable is their formulation of a pastoral methodology, involving a number of steps:[4]

   a) being present with and listening to the experiences of the poor, the marginalized, the oppressed in our society,

   b) developing a critical analysis of the economic, political and social structures that cause human suffering,

   c) making judgements in the light of Christian principles concerning social values and priorities,

   d) stimulating creative thought and action regarding alternative visions and models for social and economic development, and

   e) acting in solidarity with popular groups in their struggles to transform economic, political and social structures that cause social and economic injustice.

While the preferential option is emphasized in these and several other ecclesiastical documents, only a minority of Catholics allow themselves to be affected by this. They realize that most of the bishops who sign these documents are themselves not deeply committed to what they proclaim, and that the radical statements of Pope John Paul II are contradicted by his practical politics and his conservative stance on ecclesiastical issues. Still, the progressive church documents protect the global network of the Catholic Left, assure for these groups some episcopal support, lend a certain authority to their critical theology, and encourage them to act in solidarity with Protestant networks, labour organizations and popular movements representing the marginalized.

The preferential option for the poor, I wish to argue, has a certain affinity with Frankfurt School Critical Theory. (When I speak of critical theory in this essay, I refer to the critical ideas of the original Frankfurt School, founded in the early 20s, and not, as some authors do, to Jürgen Habermas's more recent social theory.) Let me mention five implications of the preferential option and critical theology that reveal an affinity with critical theory.

1) *The primacy of action.* Critical theology demands that the preferential option for the poor precede any effort to understand the biblical texts, the Christian tradition and the situation of the world. The truth of society and its texts is accessible only from the perspective of its victims. Here the ordinary meaning of objectivity is no longer valid. Required for the acquistion of knowledge and the search for truth is an emancipatory commitment. Critical theology recognizes that researchers always have a social location and a particular perspective, even when they believe they are detached, objective and engaged in value-neutral science. In that case, they are unlikely to be aware of their identification with the cultural mainstream. Critical theology stands against positivism and every effort to assimilate social science to the natural sciences.

2) *Thinking begins with negation.* Having opted for the perspective of the victims, the knowledge of society and its texts begins by detecting structures that produce their victimhood. Knowledge begins with the critique of society and its ideologies. This is in keeping with the biblical perspective where God's Word is judgement before it is new life: God reveals the hidden human sins before forgiving them and renewing the human spirit. Critical theology subjects to an *ideology critique* not only society and its secular culture but also and especially the Christian tradition, the source of its own inspiration. Critical theology does this with confidence, without any fear that it will invalidate its own foundation. The reason for this faith is that the biblical stories to which this theology assigns central importance were themselves written from the perspective of the victims: the Exodus, the rescue of the Israelites from Pharaonic oppression, the Exile, the compulsory immigration of the Israelites to Babylon, and the Crucifixion, the condemnation of Jesus by his religious institution and the Roman Empire.

The Hegelian term 'negation,' adopted by the Frankfurt School, is derived from the classical theological tradition. The entry into all theology is *via negativa*, through negation. Why? Because God is 'infinite' and therefore 'other' and incomprehensible, every predicate assigned to God is false and must first be negated. To speak of God in univocal terms is simply impossible. Only after the negation does theology turn to analogous or metaphorical meanings that can be assigned to discourse about God. But even then, every statement about God remains in need of correction since its inappropriate implications must be negated. God-talk has no last word: human intelligence finds rest only in paradox.

3) *Truth is transformative.* According to critical theology, truth is not the mind's conformity to a given reality nor the mind's fidelity to its cognitive procedures, even if these two modes of testing thought play a role in acquiring knowledge. For critical theology, truth saves or rescues. Truth rescues the poor, truth makes them see their situation in a new light and gives them access to the power that renews them and transforms their social condition. Since thinking begins with negation, truth reveals the contradictions of society and renders transformative action possible. Truth is always non-identical: it does not stabilize the knowing subject nor the object known, but continues to transform them both.

In the Christian tradition truth and love were seen as inseparable. "He who does not love does not know God. . . . He who hates his brother is in the darkness and walks in the darkness."(1 John, 4:8; 2:11). Critical theology laments the split between science and ethics that has come to dominate the intellectual life of modern society. The widely-held myth of objectivity disguises the insight that important truths can be discovered only from an engaged perspective and that in turn these truths expand the heart's capacity to love.

4) *The end of innocent critique* or the negation of the negation. Critical theology recognizes that its own critique of society and its texts is never a final judgement. For built into this critique are hidden biases that will reveal their destructive power only in the future. No critique is perfectly innocent. A negation, however

valid, calls for the negation of the negation. In critical theology it is the preferential option for the poor that plays this dynamic role.

In the late 60s, the Latin American liberation theologians focused almost exclusively on the continent's economic exploitation and its cultural consequences. A decade later, after many debates and new listening, they recognized that their own analysis of oppression was still marked by racist and sexist biases inherited from their culture. Following the preferential option, they modified their critique of society. Critical theology questions its own critiques not only in regard to remnants of past prejudice, but also regarding the possibility that under changed social conditions of the future these critiques could become ideological defenses of new marginalizing structures. The option for the poor is a transcendent principle since after a radical social transformation, this option does not defend the new order but demands instead that one listen to the newly marginalized.

5) *The retrieval of emancipatory reason.* Critical theology stands with critical theory in denouncing the dialectic of the Enlightenment, that is to say the collapse of reason into pure instrumentality—initiating an age of inhumanity. But with critical theory, critical theology refuses to abandon the Enlightenment and turn to the irrational, as was done in the 20s by romantics (and fascists) and is being done in the 90s by postmodern thinkers. With critical theory, critical theology wants to de-centre instrumental reason and 'retrieve' the practical, ethical, emancipatory reason present in the original Enlightenment project.

In the Catholic tradition, faith and reason have not been seen as opposites but as dialectically interrelated, correcting and empowering each other. For critical theologians, the 'retrieval' after the 'negation' reaches much further back than Kant's practical reason or the ethical claims of other Enlightenment thinkers. After the negation, critical theologians retrieve their own religious inheritance by re-reading Scripture and tradition and uncovering their liberative meaning and power. In doing this, critical theology makes use of critical theory. At the same time, the return to the religious inheritance reveals the great difference between critical theology and critical theory.

After this brief reflection on the affinity between critical theology and Frankfurt School critical theory, let me turn to Ray Morrow's questions.

Question 1: Does Critical Theory Need Theology?

The five characteristics given above reveal how deeply critical theory dwells within critical theology. Critical theology depends on critical theory in one form or another. This leads us to Morrow's first question. Is critical theory also in need of theology? Must critical theory faithful to itself eventually raise the theological issue?

I find this a troublesome question. To reply with a simple 'Yes' would sound triumphalist in my ears. Today Catholics question the manner in which the Church announced the universality of its truth. They recognize that the promotion of the one true religion was often associated with cultural, social and political domination. In contemporary theology an important debate deals with the Church's acceptance of religious and secular pluralism and the reinterpretation of its mission in the world. Conscious of the ambiguity of their religious tradition, theologians do not tell their secular friends that they should become believers. Is belief in God always helpful? In Northern Ireland and parts of the former Yugoslavia, the churches are full.

At the same time, I am unable to reply with a simple 'No' to Ray Morrow's question because I am firmly convinced that we cannot understand the human reality without reference to God. What I shall do, since I cannot say 'Yes' or 'No,' is to explain how critical theology sees the shortcomings of the secular commitment implicit in Frankfurt School critical theory. Let me begin with a text I wrote several years ago.

> The Frankfurt School thinkers did not take the retrieval of ethical reason seriously enough. They did not ask the question how values are generated, sustained and communicated. They tried to overcome 'liberal' reason by a more solitary form of rationality, and hence retained the Enlightenment suspicion of the non-rational elements in community, ethnic

heritage and religious tradition. They had few words in which to express their ethical concern and no rites and symbols to celebrate it.[5]

Critical theory is not grounded in a network of communities, hence it does not speak to ordinary people. Because of this, critical theory remains the prisoner of the university and fails to influence the thinking and acting of the wider population. Critical theory has no historical subject.

Secondly, critical theory is not the heir of a rich value tradition. Its retrieval of the ethical dimension, largely with the help of Kantian practical reason, is important; but because it is highly rational it does not generate a rhetoric capable of forcing solidarity and creating a community of friends. Critical theory enables us to see that the biblical values of love, forgiveness and peace can be (mis)used ideologically to bolster an unjust social order, but critical theory is unable to retrieve the liberative meaning of these bibical values, communicate them through stories of witnesses and saints, and celebrate them as precious gifts to humankind.

Critical theory does not understand that human justice, however perfect, is not enough to build the good society. Since we start out from a situation of sin and inequality, justice must be achieved through a historical struggle. But if the achievement of justice is not tempered by mercy and forgiveness, it creates resentments that will become the starting point for future conflicts.

Critical theory, finally, is unable to give a reason for the hope that dwells within it. When postmodern thinkers non-dialectically negate modernity and universal rationality, critical theorists find it difficult to explain why they continue to trust in the empancipatory power of reason. In today's troubled world it is only too easy to get stuck in the negative phase and lose confidence in the positive, i.e. the retrieval of ethics and the struggle for emancipation. A secular humanistic belief may not survive the Holocaust and other massive crimes against humanity. Despite these horrors, believers in biblical religion continue to have hope, a hope grounded in God's promise of rescue.

The conclusion is that the secular commitment implicit in critical theory has its shortcomings. Conversely, since the religious traditions (including Christianity) are by no means innocent, I am prepared to argue that the world religions need the critiques of non-believers to remain honest. Since religious traditions bear the marks of ideological distortion and not infrequently cause internal and external violence, believers often ask themselves whether it is really possible to reinterpret and reshape their tradition and renew the spiritual power to heal and transform people and society. Because of the patriarchal pattern of biblical religion, critical Jewish and Christian women often wonder whether they should remain identified with their religious inheritance. Many Christian women have remained in the phase of negation and given up on the possibility of retrieval: they have chosen to be Christians no longer.

The Christian discourse of God's creation and redemption can be so intertwined with symbols of privilege and inequality that rejecting this discourse may well be prompted by fidelity to God. In other words, there are Christian reasons for disaffiliating oneself from the Christian Church. That is why I am unwilling to tell my secular friends that their critical theory ought to open itself to the religious question. The *via negativa* they have chosen may be the right place for them.

At the same time, if 'innocent critique' must be overcome, then it must be admitted that the critique of divine transcendence and a purely secular interpretation of human self-making can also become an ideology that imprisons people and damages the free development of their lives.

These reflections reveal why I am unable to give a simple, unequivocal answer to Raymond Morrow's first question.

Question 2 : The Demise of the Subject

Raymond Morrow's second question deals with deconstructionist thinkers who announce the demise of the human subject, as person, as community and as humankind. If these thinkers were right, their philosophy would invalidate critical theory and critical theology, since both of them presuppose human subjectivity and wish to enhance and liberate it. The freedom affirmed by critical theory and critical theology is not the 'liberal freedom' from external restraint that allows people to please themselves and do what they wish, but rather the 'liberative freedom' that enables people to assume responsibility for their social existence and create a fully emancipated society. Critical theory relies here on the Enlightenment idea of humanity's rational destiny, while critical theology bases its hope on God's redemptive power which releases humans from their many prisons and undergirds their call to become rational subjects. In the past, human subjectivity was denied by determinists and positivists of the right and the left. Today it is being denied, for very different reasons, by deconstructionists.

Deconstructionist thinkers take the negation of critical theory to an extreme where it interprets all of reality as ideological construction. Nothing is given; everything is constructed by particular cultures to maintain their power. Human subjectivity is thus simply a projection of modernity: the human subject exists only as a constructed text that allows Western culture to defend its universality and regard other cultures as inferior. Since nothing is given, since there is no human nature and no universal reason, nothing can be retrieved. The negation here collapses critical theory itself.

This argument, subsequently strengthened by postmodern thought, profoundly challenges critical theory. Since critical theory shies away from metaphysics, it now finds it difficult to defend the human being as subject.

It is hard to avoid the impression that deconstructionist theory reflects the historical experience of former Marxists, at one time convinced that society could be transformed but more recently propelled into despair. This new situation was created by the crisis of Marxism, the collapse of communism, the decline of the political left, the victory of capitalism and the globalization of the economy. In this situation social change seems altogether impossible. The postmodern philosopher J.-F. Lyotard interprets contemporary capitalism as a cybernetic system steered by engineers and managers in a detached, scientific manner to maintain and improve its performance.[6] The world economy, Lyotard argues, no longer has a historical subject. No person, no group of persons, no government is able to assume responsibility for its orientation. Within the iron cage of the economy, reasonably well-off people are able to find happiness by exploring their personal talents and inclinations, but they are not subjects of their history.

This analysis of the present, even though highly problematic, appeals to many disappointed intellectuals. It is for them that Lyotard's message is conceived. If, by contrast, the deconstructionist message of the death of the subject were offered to Blacks of South Africa or Natives in North America, people forcefully excluded from the scene of history, this message would be rejected as an ideology of Western empire. Thinkers identified with the formerly colonized nations argue that poor people cannot afford to be nihilists: nihilism is the privilege of the advantaged.

Still, the question remains whether it is possible to defend human subjectivity on metaphysical grounds. Critical theory hesitates to do this. Yet critical theology welcomes the metaphysics of the Scriptures with their focus on the poor and readily acknowledges the spiritual status of human beings. Since God is partial to the poor, men and women who are marginal, despised or deserted—and by extension all human beings—have a high destiny. Critical theology is suspicious of approaches to metaphysics that are philosophical since they tend to reflect aristocratic or elitist prejudice. Philosophical metaphysics is acceptable to critical theology only if it proceeds from the preferential option for the poor. The idea that a philosopher could discover the spirit and enter into wisdom while remaining indifferent to the suffering of the excluded, would be unacceptable to critical theologians.

I wish to propose an argument, akin to Kant's practical reason, that in today's world the enormous threats to human personal and social existence, especially that of the poor, demand that we affirm and defend the metaphysical status of human beings and the rights that flow from this. I am tempted to go even further and offer an argument that has theological connotation. In contemporary culture, largely defined by capitalism, global competition and the struggle for survival, the metaphysical status of human beings and the rights derived from this dignity will not be effectively defended against the logic of the market unless this dignity be recognized as sacred and hence untouchable; that is to say, as grounded in the divine transcendent. Similarly, I am tempted to propose that in contemporary culture, marked by individualism and utilitarianism, the self-restraint and social sacrifices necessary for protecting the global ecology will not be made unless universal human solidarity, embracing the generations still to come, be recognized as a sacred value, derived from the divine transcendent.

Critical theologians argue passionately, with more vigour than critical theorists, against the philosophers who announce the death of the subject. At the same time, critical theologians would quickly calm down if they could be persuaded that the death proclaimed refers only to the demise of the Kantian, *cognitional* subject, supposedly universal. Critical theologians do not accept the Kantian subject because they recognize both the self's embeddedness in culture and community and it's grounding in God's creative action.

Question 3: The Postmodern Debate

Raymond Morrow's third question invokes the postmodern debate.[7] Again, one wonders whether this is not a debate confined to the university. Whenever I discuss issues raised by postmodern thinkers with non-academics in the activist circles to which I belong, the participants judge them as unrelated to their practical concerns. What characterizes postmodern thought is the attack against reason. Here the negation of critical theory is pushed even further to deconstruct not only the subject but rationality itself whenever it lays claim to universality.

Undoubtedly there are historical experiences behind the postmodern stance. When French Marxists woke up to the massive crimes of Stalinist rule to which they had closed their eyes, they sought the roots of totalitarianism not only in the political will to dominate but also in the very idea of a truth that has universal validity, including reason itself. These thinkers proclaimed the end of all 'grands récits,' all stories of world transformation. They rejected especially the projects of the Enlightement (in the liberal and Marxist versions) and by implication the biblical story of redemption extended to the ends of the earth. Even though Frankfurt School critical theory offered a critique of the Enlightenment and denounced its collapse into instrumentality and inhumanity, the postmodern thinkers repudiated critical theory because it sought to retrieve the original—presently repressed—ethical and emancipatory dimension of reason affirmed by the Enlightenment. The affirmation of context-transcending reason straining toward universality is, according to postmodern thought, totalitarianism *in nuce*.

According to postmodern thought (and 19th-century Romanticism) Enlightenment reason pushes aside and represses feelings, intuitions, symbols, and non-conceptual forms of knowledge as mediated in poetry and stories. Enlightement reason, the postmoderns argue, marginalizes and undermines cultures that claim to be and want to remain different. Reason, they suggest, cannot tolerate difference and otherness: reason does violence to 'the others' by understanding them and interpreting their action in terms of its own logic.

The postmoderns passionately affirm difference and pluralism. According to them, there is no meta-truth, no culture-transcending reason, no common values, no human nature, no humanity. People are constructed by the cultural networks and communities to which they belong: their discourse and their knowledge allow them to communicate only with their own collectivity. Conversation across the boundary is impossible: there is no common ground. For this reason, postmodern thought regards dialogue as the great modern illusion. Dialogues that aim at cooperation, greater understanding and enlarging the common ground are in reality veiled attacks on the others, undermining their own self-definitions.

What postmodern thinkers affirm is difference and irrationality. While they do not join political movements for social change, they think of themselves as resisters against the rational establishment that refuses to respect difference and imposes uniformity. There are cheerful postmoderns who rejoice in exploring the imagination and encourage whatever is artistic, playful, mystical and religious (except for monothetism which is deemed intrinsically totalitarian). And there are bitter postmoderns who are deeply disturbed by the repression and violence they find implicit in language, knowledge and culture. Since language and knowledge are ways of controling the prison called society, these postmodern thinkers regard even truth as a child of violence.

Critical theory and critical theology must resist the postmodern proposal. What intellectual strategies should be adopted by theologians?

The English theologian John Milbank has become fully convinced by the postmodern deconstruction of truth, reason and science and thus accepts the proposal that every sphere of discourse, including the scientific, is constructed on the basis of a myth or story that reflects the practice of the community in question. Milbank agrees with the bitter postmoderns that the practice of all cultures is marked by domination and violence, but he claims that there is one truly different practice, namely the practice of love, forgiveness and peace introduced by Jesus. The myth and the message encoded in the practice of Jesus, Milbank argues, cannot be rejected by an appeal to reason or science because these discourses are themselves constructed and have no validity beyond the community whose practice they reflect and legitimate. In this postmodern age, Milbank argues, the one available choice is between nihilism and Jesus.[8]

I disagree with Milbank's theological approach. Against Milbank and the postmoderns I wish to defend common values and universal solidarity. Yet I gladly admit that we have much to learn from postmodern thought, especially two points: (1) the attention to non-conceptual knowledge communicated in poetry and stories; (2) the emphasis on difference and pluralism. But even as critical theologians and critical theorists become more sensitive to truth communicated in non-conceptual terms, as they overcome their ethnocentrism and become more open to cultural pluralism, they must continue to rescue reason in the contemporary debate.

Let me explain what I mean by the previous sentence. The sins of omission committed by critical theology and critical theory have not been identical. Critical theology grounded in the

Christian tradition has always been sensitive to point(1), non-conceptual knowledge expressed in stories and symbols. Critical theologians greatly appreciate, for instance, the emancipatory message celebrated in the eucharistic liturgy. In this pascal rite, Christians remember the passover meal related to the rescue of God's people from the land of bondage. More directly they commemorate the last supper before the capital punishment of Jesus as troublemaker as well as his resurrection which anticipated the rehabilitation of all victims in history. Christians are immersed in stories and symbols. Where the Christian and in particular the Catholic tradition has sinned is its reluctance to recognize difference and pluralism.

The sins of the Enlightenment tradition were different. In its early phase it was dominated by a rationalism that had no respect for non-conceptual forms of knowledge. The Romantic movement reacted against this. But in a later phase, beginning toward the end of the 19th century, a new appreciation of symbols and emotions by many sociologists, anthropologists and psychologists sought to correct the early Enlightenment's one-sided rationalistic prejudice. Where the Frankfurt School stood in regard to this self-correction is not easy to answer.

What about the relation of critical theory to pluralism and difference? Since these critical thinkers assigned a central place to the Western philosophical tradition, they failed to appreciate the cultural pluralism in the world. They also resisted—with good reason—the value relativism associated with the positivistic social sciences. I am prepared to argue that both critical theorists and critical theologians have a great deal to learn from the postmodern protest. But even as we shift to forms of communication associated with symbols, stories and poetry and hear the voices coming from communities to which we formerly refused to listen, we must still protect human reason. Surrender to the irrational produces gullibility, chaos and eventually violence.

The Catholic tradition has always defended human reason as part of God's gift of creation. This trust in reason was criticized by the Protestant Reformation which emphasized man's original sin and recognized the harm done by this sin to human intelligence. Today, a more nuanced Catholic position, shared by many Protestants, clearly acknowledges first, that sin, power and ideology distort God's gift of human reason, and second, that God's redemptive grace, operative in people as they struggle for truth and justice, enables them to transcend the distortions and become open to the light of reason.

I resist the postmodern view that cross-cultural dialogue is a modern illusion, that the defense of universal values is implicitly totalitarian and that we honour 'the others' as truly other only when we abandon the belief in a common 'ratio.'

What historical experiences stand behind these postmodern convictions? The breakdown of dialogue and comunity has alas become widespread in contemporary society. In France, the home of postmodern thought, we have witnessed the rise of ethnic tensions, the emergence of a new Islamic consciousness and the growing popularity of Le Pen's right-wing political movement. These cultural developments are parallelled in other countries. Is the non-communication and break-up of Yugoslavia the symbol of humanity's earthly destiny?

In my opinion these developments, however painful and worrisome, do not support the postmodern claim that there is no common 'ratio' in humanity. Humans are by nature dialogical creatures. Being addressed and responding is the way we enter upon language and consciousness. Language is derived from others and speech is addressed to others. Speech remains essentially other-oriented. In speaking to others we presuppose that however different they may be, they are capable of understanding us. Otherwise we would not open our mouth. We assume that everyone shares a common ratio. The reason we think so is that we do many of the same things, beginning with loving our own children. We realize that we have common needs and aspirations, and around these we move toward expanding the common ground. This is true even for the postmodern thinkers: they address us, presupposing that we are able to understand them. One famous postmodern thinker tells us that for the author of a book readers are a nuisance, and that writing a book is like putting a message into a bottle and throwing it into the ocean.[9] But who will believe such bragging! An author writes books and invents provocative images to be heard. The very act of communication makes an implicit affirmation of a common 'ratio' that subsequent denials cannot invalidate.

Instead of expanding the philosophical argument in defense of trans-cultural truth and values, I wish to report important experiences I have shared with others, experiences that demonstrated to us that dialogue across boundaries is possible and that respecting others as others implicitly acknowledges a common bond.

In the 20th century, dialogue has revealed itself as a powerful dynamics in the Christian churches, first in the ecumenical movement among the separated Christian confessions and later in the conversation of Christians with members of other religious traditions. In this process we discovered that dialogue is not a simple exchange of information nor a polite conversation avoiding serious disagreement. We realized that dialogue actually demands a high price: listening to 'the others' we have to sacrifice many of our preconceptions, be ready to learn unpleasant truths about ourselves and be willing to enter into a new self-understanding. Dialogue produces a new hermeneutics for reading and assimilating one's own tradition. In many instances dialogue produces a *metanoia* or conversion, not a conversion to the tradition of the partner but a new awareness that demands a re-interpretation of one's own tradition. Dialogue actually transforms both parties in conversation.

Dialogue demands great trust. For only as we trust 'the other' do we dare to abandon our own defensive stance, acknowledge the dark side of our tradition and reveal our own self-critical reflections? And only if we are trusted by 'the other' do we dare to raise questions that touch upon the dark side of the other's tradition. Through mutual trust both partners are made ready to admit that their religious traditions are ambiguous historical realities and that their communities have not always lived up to the best of their potential.

As a Catholic theologian I find it important to listen to Enlightenment thought, especially its critique of religion and society, even if few secular thinkers—Ray Morrow is here an exception—have engaged in dialogue with theology. Thanks to this listening, as I mentioned earlier, I came to define 'critical theology' as a theology that uses critical social theory to unfold the emancipatory meaning of the Christian Gospel.

Against the postmodern objection to dialogue across boundaries, I offer my own experience shared by many others. In this defense of dialogue I actually vindicate my entire life, my work as a theologian and everything I stand for. The recognition of 'the other' has guided my theological efforts to correct the exclusivist trend in the Catholic tradition, whether 'the other' be Protestants, Jews, members of other religions or secular humanists. I had the good fortune to work as a theologian in the Secretariate for Christian Unity at the Second Vatican Council (1962-1965). The Secretariat's principal task was preparing of draft documents for the entire council of bishops that would acknowledge and honour the diverse confessions within Christianity, the Jewish religious tradition, the plurality of the world religions and the secular humanist tradition. At the Vatican Council, the Catholic Church underwent a conversion to a new openness,[10] even if the Vatican regrets this today and offers the narrowest possible interpretation of the conciliar documents.

In the 70s, I became involved in the movement within the Church, defined by the option for the poor, where 'the others' whom we sought to recognize, honour and hear were the oppressed, the marginal, the excluded. 'The others' also included women. Relying on the practice and message of Jesus, we wanted the Church to enter into solidarity with those whom society, economics, culture and religion had made into 'non-persons' and who were now struggling to become human subjects in the full sense.

We can recognize and affirm 'the others' as other precisely as we discover that they share a common humanity with us. Recent church debates reveal that looking upon homosexuals as 'other' is easy enough and allows us to exclude or look down on them. We will welcome the otherness of gay men and lesbians only as we discover that they are human, the same as we are. They are honoured by respect and wounded by contempt. Accepting the despised 'other' as other often calls for a conversion. The postmoderns overlook the paradox that there is no recognition of the otherness of others without the affirmation of their sameness. Pluralism does not mean that humans have nothing in common or that they are necessarily strangers to one another's truth.

Question 4: The Possibility of a Universal Ethics

Ray Morrow's fourth question deals with the possibility of a universal ethics. The postmodern emphasis on difference and pluralism denies this possibility. To affirm a value as context-transcending is here seen as incipiently authoritarian.

The Enlightenment thinkers believed that a common ethics for humanity was possible. Some of them defined human beings in terms of the struggle for freedom and thus believed that their own emancipatory values, such as personal or collective autonomy, had universal validity. Others preferred to define human beings in terms of the struggle for self-preservation and thus believed that utilitarian ethics could come to be universally recognized. Critical theory argued against the instrumentalism implicit in utilitarianism but supported the emancipatory commitment as a precious Enlightenment legacy for all times. If critical theory wants to serve the liberation and pacification of humankind, it must uphold the possibility of a universal ethical consensus.

The Catholic tradition, relying on the classical inheritance of Stoic, Platonic and Aristotelian thought, has always defended the existence of universal ethical norms that could be discovered by human reason reflecting on 'human nature.' Reason was thought capable of discovering 'the natural law' inscribed in the human heart. The Protestant Reformation, stressing the distortion of reason due to sin, repudiated the natural law tradition and affirmed the Gospel as the only valid source of ethics. Taking the Protestant critique into account, Catholic theologians in the 20th century have adopted a more nuanced version of natural law theory. This version recognizes that people's natural orientation toward the good is partially distorted by ideology and cultural prejudice and hence comes to be recognized only through historical struggles of men and women, supported by divine grace. For instance, that slavery was intrinsically wrong, ignored by Greek wisdom and biblical teaching, came to be recognized by Christians only in the 18th century, after the impact of the cultural and political movement against slavery, inspired by humanists and Quakers. The ethical revulsion against slavery is today universal. While slavery still exists in a variety of forms, the men engaged in it refuse to call it this, thereby acknowledging the universality of the ethical taboo.

Even though the Catholic natural law theory has a bad name, having been used to defend conservative positions on the role of women and the meaning of sexual intercourse, I wish to uphold the natural law tradition if it is understood in the dynamic way hinted at above. Since culture often disguises human nature, the content of natural law is revealed through cultural and political struggles that sometimes demand great personal sacrifice. The different human rights, personal and collective, approved by current Catholic teaching as belonging to the natural law, were rejected in the past and achieved public recognition and ecclesiastical blessing only after long historical struggles. Some contemporary theologians, reflecting on the witness of homosexuals to their ethical vocation—witness available on a wide scale only in recent decades—conclude that homosexual love is in keeping with natural law.

If human beings are by nature oriented toward the good—a philosophical position accepted today only by people who believe in God's creation—then it is possible to relativize the differences among ethical norms in various cultures and look forward to norms of universal validity emerging from the joint effort of people to live on this earth in peace and dignity. Respect for pluralism does not imply we should accept female genital circumcision practiced in certain cultures. Here too an historical struggle will eventually produce a cultural transformation and the recognition of a more universal norm.

A modern philosophical effort to uphold the possibility of a universal ethics in the pluralism of our global society has been made the German social thinker Jürgen Habermas, who mediates the concerns of critical theory in his communicative ethics. Because of their traditional concern for universal values, Catholic theologians have taken great interest in his work. Recognizing the radical pluralism of traditions and hence the impossibility of finding a common ground for a universal ethics, Habermas proposes that common ethical norms could be worked out in the future if people representing different communities were able to communicate free of distortion or domination introduced by structured inequalities. Habermas believes that perfect dialogue, where partners patiently learn from one another and where the better argument prevails, will arrive at a consensus on matters of justice and peace.

Such an ideal speech situation, as he calls it, has existed at certain moments when partners from different traditions came together on the basis of equality. But the ideal speech situation does not exist at the global level. Far from it. Oppression and inequality render an open, trusting conversation almost impossible. Yet Habermas argues that implicit in true conversation is the wish for distortion-free communication. Habermas believes that in a domination-free conversation men and women of all backgrounds could agree on values that allowed them to live together in peace and harmony. This common ethics is not yet available to us, but according to Habermas it is anticipated in the turn to dialogue and cooperation.

Catholic theologians have been excited by this theory. But neither they nor social theorists agree on what precisely Habermas means by the ideal speech situation. Some say that its significance is purely epistemological, allowing Habermas to defend universal values. Others prefer to see here a link between theory and practice: for creating the ideal speech situation and universal consensus demands political and cultural struggles to overcome domination. Here a political dynamic is built into the search for truth. Other commentators are skeptical of Habermas's proposal of rational communication, either because they believe that dialogue involves, beyond accepting the better argument, a true conversion of the mind; or because they suspect that Habermas defines the good society in purely rational terms, neglecting the bonds of friendship and solidarity.

Christian commentators wonder about 'the faith' implicit in Habermas's social theory. Is this wish for the perfect speech situation (implicit in every conversation) and the subjective orientation toward it, enough evidence to prove that such a situation could actually come into existence? Or is there in Habermas's proposal an element of hope beyond the competence of reason? Nicholas Lash thinks that such a hope is unfounded and irrational unless one believes, as Christians do, that God is the reconciling Transcendent present in history, moving the plural cultural and religious traditions toward a consensus on the principles of justice, conviviality and peace.[11]

Rather than calling upon theistic faith, I prefer to argue that implicit in Habermas's communicative ethics is an unacknowledged foundational element: a common human nature. Because we know what human beings are and are meant to be, we anticipate that domination-free communication will produce a universal ethics assuring the reconciliation and pacification of the human family.

Habermas's communicative ethics allows me therefore to return to the natural law tradition. Why is this so important? The answer goes back to a famous debate in Christian theology that has continued among secular philosophers. Is ethics a set of ideals imposed on us by God, reason or society, that we must follow whether we like it or not? Or is ethics a set of ideals that reveals our deepest inclinations, calls us to be converted from superficiality to depth, and points the way to our happiness? There are passages in the Bible where God appears as law-giver demanding our obedience; but there are other places where God appears as the One who touches our hearts and makes us yearn for the good. For Plato the ethical norms perceived by reason had to be imposed on the unwilling body, while for Aristotle ethical norms flowed from the inclination of human nature and led to personal fulfilment in the community. For Kant ethical rules, rationally discovered, had to be put into practice by will power, while for the utilitarians ethical rules expressed people's enlighted material self-interest. I uphold the position—echoing Augustine and Thomas Aquinas—that the good life—the life of love, peace and self-forgetfulness—corresponds to the inclination of human nature, even if this ethic can only be discovered through a series of conversions. Ethical principles, including the option for the poor, are not imposed on us as a burden (even if it sometimes appears as such), but proposed as a liberating message that rescues us from distorted self-understanding and allows us to discover our human vocation. I fear that a purely rational ethical theory, including Habermas's brilliant effort, tends to frighten people because they think they will have to swallow hard to do the right thing, while an ethic grounded in being or grounded on a gift—I speak as a theologian—draws people from within their own experience.

Habermas's communicative ethics, I would argue, could be expanded so as to include what we have called the primacy of practice. Habermas's ethical theory would be more acceptable if the perfect speech situation were understood as presupposing certain practices: (a) that cultural and political struggles have created the possibility of the domination-free conversation; (b) that the partners in conversation bring with them a consciousness already largely formed by these antecedent practices; and (c) that the partners are willing to become friends, trust one another, acquire a self-critical spirit and hear the others with an intelligence guided by affection.

Question 5: The Collapse of Utopia

Ray Morrow's fifth question deals with the collapse of utopia. The image of an alternative society (utopia) as a guide for political action implies that people are the subject of their history and hence responsible creators of their future. But this is denied by deconstructionists and postmodern thinkers. For them utopias belong to the dangerous heritage of the Enlightenment, leading to authoritarian imposition of social rules and eventually to totalitarianism.

This critique of the Enlightenment, as we have seen, is not new. Max Weber argued that modernity spelled the end of utopia because the dominance of instrumental reason transformed all efforts to create the good society into bureaucratic dictatorship. Frankfurt School critical theory did not abandon the utopia of a domination-free society, but it articulated this utopia only through negations, *via negativa*, by specifying what the good society is not. It has been argued that this fidelity to the *via negativa* was a heritage from biblical religion where God, the ever incomprehensible One, was characterized only *via negativa*, by saying what God is not. Jews even refused to pronounce the divine name. There is no doubt that the relentless critiques of culture and society produced by the Frankfurt School were not inspired by *skepsis* or cultural pessimism but rather by a passionate conviction of what should be in terms of a utopian image that could only be described as 'other,' other than what we know in the present.

Critical theology was strongly influenced by Ernst Bloch's reflection on utopia.[12] This unusual Marxist philosopher believed that political revolution begins in the imagination. He distinguished between an 'abstract utopia,' the image of an alternative society that could never be and was therefore politically problematic, and a 'concrete utopia,' the image of an alternative society close enough to as yet unrealized possibilies of the present to make it a historical possibility. Without a concrete utopia, Bloch argued, there can be no sustained critique of the existing society, no passionate support for a radical political movement and no revolutionary transformation of society. This Blochian idea was later adopted in one of Pope Paul VI's encyclicals.[13] Disagreeing with the Frankfurt School, then, critical theology affirmed—with many socialists and other radicals—the need for a social utopia.

Still, in agreement with the Frankfurt School, critical theology worried that a utopia spelled out in scientific or ideological terms could become an instrument of oppression. In theological language, a utopia could become an idol or a false god in the name of which human beings would be sacrified. How can Christians support a liberation movement guided by a utopia, yet at the same time guard against making this utopia a sacred icon?

Gustavo Gutierrez replied to this question.[14] He insisted that the *regnum Dei*, the reign of God proclaimed by Jesus, which dwells in the minds of Christians and makes them question all existing societies, is not and never can be a concrete utopia. Gutierrez warned against all forms of political messianism. The promised *regnum* is beyond the possibilities of history as we know it. God's reign can only be presented *via negativa*, by describing what it is not.

By contrast, the concrete utopia, necessary for a liberation movement, is an imaginative construct reflecting emancipatory values (signs of the *regnum*) as well as the contingent conditions derived from the historical context. Hence a concrete utopia is finite and provisional. If the historical circumstances change, the utopia may have to be rethought or even abandoned. What enables Christians in a liberation movement to abstain from sacralizing their utopia and, if circumstances change, to reshape it, is their faith in the promised *regnum* that reveals the ambiguity of all historical societies. Critical theology refers to this as 'the eschatological proviso.'[15] Seen in the light of what is promised for the end (*eschaton*), even the best on earth reveals its dark side.

Overcoming the theoretical opposition to utopia offered by modern and postmodern critics does not, of course, resolve the more difficult question whether there exists a concrete utopia for people dedicated to social justice today. The crisis of Marxism, the collapse of Eastern European communism, the abandonment of Keynesian welfarism, the hegemony of economic liberalism, the globalization of the economy and the decline of radicalism in the Third World have created a situation where the utopias of the 60s and 70s have lost their power. Commenting on the contemporary situation after the Gulf War, I concluded that we have entered a new historical phase, different from the last thirty years, where significant social change on a large scale has become impossible.[16] Today we live in what I call 'the wilderness.' Still, while there is no concrete utopia on the horizon, we witness many solidarity movements in society. We also note that many Christians who endorse the preferential option prefer to define their practice as resistance rather than liberation. But this takes us to the next question.

Question 6: What is to be done?

Ray Morrow's final question asks what is to be done now. What is the practice summoned forth by a secular emancipatory commitment or a Christian preferential option? How does critical theology reply to this question?

In the Christian groups in which I participate this question is discussed constantly. Several years ago, many of us developed a critical analysis that guided our involvement. Since then we have become confused again. After the globalization of the economy revealed its social consequences and especially after the Gulf War, we were forced to ask ourselves new questions. In the following pages I wish briefly to present two critical reflections, the first on the emergence of new social movements, the second on the conditions created by the globalization of the economy.

1. One of the reasons why Marxist theory entered a crisis was the realization that the division of society between bourgeoisie and proletariate no longer described the conflicts occurring in capitalist society. First, the working class became increasingly divided between unionized labour enjoying a certain economic security, and non-unionized labour, badly paid, precariously employed, including a large percentage of women and people of colour. Second, the contradictions of the established system became so massive that serious damage was inflicted on people of all classes and their natural habitat. As a result, we have seen the emergence of new social movements that demanded radical social change: the ecological movement, the peace movement, the women's movement, the movement for alternative models of economic development and citizens' movements of various kinds. Marxist analysis could not deal with this phenomenon.

Sociologists like Alain Touraine interpreted the emergence of these social movements as a sign that we were moving into a new type of society, a 'post-industrial' society, where the class struggle of workers against owners was being replaced by the multiple struggles of civil society against the established bureaucracies. I find the term 'post-industrial' misleading. The industries and the contradictions they generate continue to shape the structure of present-day society, and organzied labour, even if challenged by government policies and sometimes by the new social movements, continues to play an important role as an agent of social change.

In Canada, many progressive voices have called for a new solidarity among social movements and labour organizations. In their book, *The Other Macdonald Report*, Daniel Drache and Duncan Cameron document that there exists a considerable consensus regarding Canada's social and economic development in the so-called 'popular sector' representing trade unions, women's groups, farmers' associations, progressive churches, Native people's councils, racial minority associations and agencies speaking for the disadvantaged, the precariously employed and welfare recipients. "In a period when Canadian society is supposedly shifting to the right, the authors write, there are more forces ready for social change than either the general public or the left have recognized."[17] The same solidarity was recommended by the Canadian Catholic bishops.[18] In 1987 a working committee for social solidarity, representing the popular sector, produced a declaration entitled 'A Time to Stand Together,' which outlined the agreement on alternative social and economic policies and advocated the creation of a nation-wide solidarity movement that would stem the tide of present government policies and struggle for the creation of a more cooperative society.

This was a difficult task. Since the different social justice movements tend to have slightly differing analyses of the oppressive structures in society, depending on their own experience, they are inclined to postpone joint action untill they can agree on the analysis. I have argued that this is a mistake.[19] Solidarity and cooperation, even if limited in scope, affect the consciousness of the participants and prompt them to look at society from the same perspective. Agreement on the analysis is not the starting point but the the outcome of joint action.

2. This still somewhat hopeful picture has been disturbed by the effects of the increasing globalization of the economy, not yet analysed by Touraine's earlier sociology. This globalization, stepped up after the collapse of communism and the victory of the Gulf War, forces every country to adopt 'structural adjustment policies' to make its economy competitive on the world market. The powerful economic actors are more than ever the giant transnational corporations that oblige national governments to offer them favourable conditions and, if not fully satisfied, relocate their industries in parts of the world where labour is cheap, unions are illegal, taxes are low and few laws exist protecting the environment. Even socialist and social democratic

governments are forced by the global market to adopt neo-conservative economic policies.

In the wealthy capitalist countries of the North, the globalization of the economy, coupled with an increasingly sophisticated technology, is producing a growing 'tertiary sector,' made up of the unemployed, underpaid workers, the precariously employed and part-time workers—the poor, in other words—who experience social disintegration in their urban neighbourhoods and rural environments. We are witnessing the creation a new, modified class gap, somewhat different than the gap described by Touraine, between people who have a decent income or work for a decent salary with some security (and this includes certain sectors of working people) and the tertiary sector of the excluded who may never again find employment in the industrial system.

In the poorer South, structural adjustment policies are imposed by the international financial institutions, forcing governments to make their economies competitive, that is to to produce goods for export rather than satisfying the needs of their own people. As a result, misery reaches ever wider sectors of the population.

The globalization of the economy, I wish to argue, produces two important trends in society. The first, caused by the spread of poverty in Asian, African and Latin American countries, is the massive migration of peoples to other parts of the world, including the Western industrialized countries, on a scale that is likely to eliminate, probably for good, the existence of ethnically and culturally homogeneous societies.

The globalization of the economy in the industrialized countries generates another trend that influences people's daily lives. Since national governments such as Ottawa and Washington are unable to protect people from drifting into poverty and social disintegration, we see the emergence of regionalisms or nationalisms that create a new solidarity among people, urge regional governments to act on their behalf, and spur cooperative efforts to produce alternative economic projects. This is the context of Quebec's present-day nationalism. Yet regionalist movements exist also in other Canadian provinces and states of the American republic where under pressure of their people, even premiers and governors demand a new autonomy for their regions.

Regionalism and nationalism are ambiguous developments. On the positive side, they enable people to transcend individualism, become cooperative and engage in alternative economic developments—think of the Mondragon Cooperatives in the Basque country or the Desjardin Cooperatives in Quebec. On the negative side, such movements are capable of provoking suspicion and hostility towards those whom they define as outsiders or regard as responsible for their present plight. The unemployed are tempted to be resentful toward immigrants and women in the erroneous belief that they have taken jobs and opportunties. The overlapping of these two trends, the influx of refugees and immigrants and the emergence of regionalism, is presently reviving cultural and political forces that aim to protect people's collective identities and cement inherited boundaries, encouraging ethnic and racist antagonisms and fundamentalism in religion.

Society is becoming increasingly fragmented. Even social movements that resist established powers have become more divided. The pluralism of heteromorphic networks and communities, unable to communicate with one another, does describe the present situation. But whereas postmodern thought legitimates this situation, critical theory and critical theology denounce and challenge it. Yet at this time people guided by an emancipatory commitment do not see clearly where and how to involve themselves. We are living in 'the wilderness.' Good people continue to support good causes, but there is no common strategy for reconstructing society.

What impresses many of us, especially among the Catholic left in Quebec, is the creativity found in the tertiary sector, in the declining outlying regions and the poor neighbourhoods in the city, where people in growing numbers involve themselves in various forms of economic development. They provide useful services in the community, repair apartments, build houses, provide recreation, protect the environment or engage in small-scale production. These groups receive some financial support from institutions in sympathy with their effort, among them labour unions, church organizations, municipalities and sometimes governments. In these groups the new regionalism, provoked by the globalization of the economy, reveals its positive, creative dimension. Characteristic of these cooperative efforts is that their aim is not only economic but also and especially social. Working together, people become friends, create community and are thus rescued from depression and loneliness.

Since there is no major movement to transform existing society, Christian social-justice networks support these collective efforts to nurture alternative forms of economic development. As more and more people find themselves excluded, cooperative self-help movements are likely to become stronger and more inventive across a growing sector of society. This may even lay the foundation for the renewal of society as a whole.

Notes

1. G. Baum, *Religion and Alienation*, New York: Paulist Press, 1975, pp. 193-226.

2. Puebla, The Final Document, nn 1134-1140, *Puebla and Beyond*, eds. J. Eagleson and P. Scharper, Maryknoll, NY: Orbis, 1979, p. 264.

3. For the text of *Laborem exercens* and commentary, see G. Baum, *The Priority of Labor*, New York: Paulist Press, 1982.

4. "Ethical Reflections on Canada's Socio-Economic Order." *Do Justice! The Social Teaching of the Canadian Bishops*, ed. E.F. Sheridan, Toronto: Jesuit Centre for Faith and Justice, 1987, pp. 411-432, 412.

5. G. Baum, *Theology and Society*, New York: Paulist Press, 1987, p. 224.

6. See pp. 80-81 of this volume.

7. See pp. 77-95 of this volume.

8. See p. 62 of this volume.

9. See below, p. 94, note #9.

10. See pp. 178-79 of this volume.

11. Nicholas Lash, "Conversation in Gethsemane," *Radical Pluralism and Truth*, eds W. Jeanrond and J. Rilke, New York: Crossroads, 1991, pp. 51-61.

12. "Christian theology will one day have to thank Ernst Bloch's philosophy of hope for giving it the courage to recover in the full sense its central category of eschatology." Wolfhart Pannenberg, *Basic Questions in Theology*, 2:237-238.

13. Paul VI, *Octogesima adveniens* (1971), no. 37.

14. Gustavo Gutierrez, *A Theology of Liberation*, Maryknoll, NY: Orbis, 1973, pp. 213-239.

15. This widely-used expression is taken from J.-B. Metz, *Theology of the World*, New York: Seabury Press, 1973, p. 114.

16. G. Baum, *The Ecumenist*, 29 (Spring 1991) pp. 1-3.

17. *The Other MacDonald Report*, eds. Daniel Drache and Duncan Cameron, Toronto: Lorimer, 1985, p. ix.

18. G. Baum, "Toward a Canadian Catholic Social Theory," *Theology and Society*, New York: Paulist Press, 1987, pp. 66-87, 81.

19. G. Baum, "The Catholic Left in Quebec," *Culture and Social Change*, eds. C. Leys and M. Mendell, Montreal: Black Rose, 1992, pp. 140-154, 151.

2

David Tracy: Pluralism and Liberation Theology

David Tracy's theory of pluralism enables him, in *The Analogical Imagination*, to make a brilliant defense of liberation and political theologies, persuasive even to those reluctant to agree.[1] While he himself follows a different trajectory in his own original theological proposal, he understands liberation theology to be an important corrective for ecclesiastical traditions and their theological teachings which, through uncritical practice, have become too closely identified with the interests of the dominant class. The category of 'corrective' is, as we shall see, a key to his general theological approach. It enables him to offer positive interpretations of theological and philosophical trends with which he otherwise disagrees, and to make room for theologies that diverge from his own. In developing his own critical theology, Tracy reveals his intellectual humility by remaining open to correctives uttered by persons with different historical experiences or groups caught in different historical situations.

What does Tracy mean by pluralism? First, we shall examine his theory of 'the *pluralism-of-traditions*.' Tracy appreciates and defends the pluralism of theologies within the Catholic Church, the pluralism of the wider Christian traditions, and the pluralism of the great world religions. He also offers a positive interpretation of the variety of philosophical schools. Since behind the pluralism of traditions stands a faith in a transcendent reconciling power, Tracy's theory implies a theology of history and an ethical summons to dialogue and cooperation.

Second, we shall examine Tracy's idea of 'radical pluralism,' which in my opinion is only indirectly related to his pluralism of traditions. More than most theological authors, Tracy is overwhelmed by the diversity of interpretations which contemporary thinkers give of the present cultural crisis. For a number of reasons, among them the Holocaust, all the inherited certainties have been dissolved. The resulting confusion and uncertainty, according to Tracy, constitutes 'the uncanny' of the present moment.

Finally, we shall examine these two ideas of pluralism from the perspective of liberation theology.

The Pluralism of Traditions

The rich concept of the pluralism of traditions is contained in *The Analogical Imagination*. Tracy argues that great traditions, grounded and supported by classical events and classical texts, are living, creative, self-correcting spiritual movements. Because classics transcend their historical period, have surplus meaning and exercise universal appeal, great religious and philosophical traditions are open to new historical experiences and capable of responding to them creatively. Because the classics have a certain break-through power, they are able to generate new perspectives and spark revisionist trends within the great traditions. For Tracy, religious and intellectual traditions are plural, dynamic, self-renewing historical phenomena.

Tracy applies this concept to the internally diversified Christian tradition—to the many Catholic theologies and Christian confessions. They all merit respect, they all deserve a hearing, and they all contribute to the creative conversation out of which Christians encounter their classical texts and through which they constitute their living tradition.

Introducing the notion of 'corrective,' Tracy is able to interpret in a positive way even passionate, one-sided theological points of view. If interpreted as expressions reaching out for the whole, these viewpoints appear defective. But if they are seen as correctives, as warnings shouted at a community that has dangerously narrowed its perception of the whole, then one-sided emphases play a positive role. Even when examining the plurality in the New Testament itself, Tracy regards 'the eschatological' and 'the doctrinal' as important correctives serving the church's primary mission of proclamation, correctives that have retained their importance throughout history.[2] 'The eschatological' pronounces God's judgement on a community comfortably reconciled with the powerful, and 'the doctrinal' offers conceptual clarity to a community confused and divided over the words in which to proclaim Jesus Christ. These one-sided elements can make their positive contribution only in the back-and-forth of the plural churches' ongoing conversation reaching out for the whole.

These forces become a danger to the Christian tradition when no one is listening, when the conversation stops, when a narrow perception of wholeness is endorsed as the final norm or when correctives become the full message. But Christians, like all human beings, are summoned to wholeness and depth. The pluralism of which Tracy speaks calls for openness, willingness to be addressed, humility, eagerness to learn, and readiness to redefine one's tradition in fidelity to past and present.

This pluralism, Tracy believes, should also inform the interaction of Christianity with other world religions. The self-affirmation of colonized peoples and the subsequent collapse of political colonialism have taught Christians an important lesson. Having come to acknowledge with repentance that the Christian claim to absoluteness has been used to legitimate colonial domination, Christians are now ready to respect the great world religions, enter into conversation with them, and discover the spiritual treasures contained within them. Addressed by the wisdom in these religions, Christians are compelled to reread their own classics and reinterpret their own traditions. Here, too, the many-sided conversation enters into the self-constituting, historical dynamics of Christianity and the other religious traditions.

We note that this pluralism of traditions, from one point of view new and daring, is, from another, conservative in the best sense of the word. It is not a relativistic pluralism that considers all religions equally true, nor all Christian confessions equally reliable witnesses of God's revealed word. Tracy's call for openness, humility and ongoing conversation does not necessarily invalidate the self-understanding of a church that regards itself as an orthodox and unique witness to divine revelation. All that is asked of such a church is the commitment to depth and wholeness: the church must be willing to enter into dialogue, permit itself to be seriously challenged, and then be ready to be addressed again by its own classics and in response to them move forward to a more adequate self-understanding. What Tracy demands from such a church—his own, in particular—is to recognize its own tradition as a vital, dynamic, self-constituting process, not free of ambiguity, in which conversation with others must play an essential part.

As a Catholic, Tracy gladly listens to Luther, Calvin and Thomas Muenzer; yet what he learns from them he wants to introduce to the Catholic theological conversation and thus make fruitful for the dynamic process of Catholic renewal. And, I suppose, he expects the heirs of the Reformation to let themselves be challenged by the Catholic tradition and to react creatively by renewing their own Protestant traditions. Such a conservative proposal does not merit the title of 'radical pluralism.' What Tracy has in mind is actually a world-wide 'ecumenism' of religious traditions and their theologies.

What follows is that for Tracy the pluralism of traditions is not a given, does not express a state of affairs, but rather refers to something to be done, a universal human task. Tracy's pluralism outlines an historical project. It proposes procedures for inter-religious and ecumenical dialogue and developing confessional theologies, and it looks forward to the transformations these procedures will generate in the various religious traditions. The engagement in these procedures, Tracy believes, is inspired and carried by a transcendent reconciling power. Tracy's proposal of the pluralism-of-traditons implies a believing commitment in a divinely-grounded, world-wide historical process.

David Tracy's understanding of the pluralism of traditions differs from the prevailing pluralism, widely endorsed in our society, that confines itself to praising the right of individuals to follow their own truth and choose their own values. This is the pluralism of the shopping mall. If people do not hear the call to depth and wholeness, they are likely to be content with personal opinions. That this individualism-cum-relativism has become the dominant trend in present-day American culture has been documented in Robert Bellah's *Habits of the Heart.* With Bellah, Tracy laments the pluralism produced by arbitrary options and lazy thinking, unwilling to be challenged intellectually. Tracy recognizes the ideological use made of this pluralism in contemporary society where significant conflicts are drowned in a sea of personal opinions. For Tracy, as for Tocqueville and many other thinkers, an unrooted person, a person not identified with a religious or secular wisdom tradition, is a prisoner of public opinion and hence unfree.

Tracy recognizes the hostility of modern culture to his own pluralism of traditions. What he fails to do, however, is to inquire into the historical forces that have produced this modern culture.

But even in the churches and the world religions, this pluralism has its enemies. Even in the sphere of religion pluralism is vulnerable and needs defense. Tracy suggests there are four 'sins' that damage the pluralism of traditions: against openness (the refusal to listen to the other); against depth (the acceptance of reductionist explanations); against justice (the unwillingness to recognize the ideological role played by religion); and against compassion (the indifference to the suffering caused by religious conflicts).

Tracy mentions these threats to pluralism throughout *The Analogical Imagination,* but he does not explore them in any detail. Nor does he ask what historical forces promote these sins. He prefers not to dwell on evil.

In my judgement, Tracy's pluralism of traditions is a magnificant proposal that merits fullest support, even if the dynamics operative in the self-constitution of the religious traditions deserve to be looked at more critically. I shall return to this point below.

In his early *Blessed Rage for Order,* Tracy appears to affirm a similar pluralism of philosophical traditions. What he argues concretely is that Christian fundamental theology, charged with examining the openness of contemporary thought to the divine, must engage in conversation with several distinct philosophical traditions, including transcendental Thomism, process thought, linguistic analysis, phenomenology, and the philosophy of praxis. These philosophical traditions constitute themselves through an ongoing, critical, self-reflective intellectual conversation. Tracy's own perceptive analysis shows that these philosophies, by relying on their classical texts, have reviewed their inherited ideas and judgements, deepened their insights into the human condition, and in some instances recognized 'limit situations' in secular experience that call for religious interpretation. Tracy concludes therefore that God-talk is not a foreign language but has decipherable meaning for the modern philosophies in which contemporary society achieves its self-understanding.

In the Catholic context, this was an exciting conclusion. In the past, Catholic theologians relied almost exclusively on the Aristotelian-Thomistic tradition and believed—or were told—that modern philosophies were not appropriate partners for dialogue. Tracy's work urged Catholic theologians to appreciate the pluralism of philosophical traditions, each one alive with an inner dynamism that allows it to transcend the secularity of its origin and be open to the God-question.

But do the philosophical traditions Tracy examines really represent the intellectual life of contemporary society? Do they actually provide the ideas and values that shape decisions made by important political, economic, and cultural institutions? It seems to me that in modern capitalist society, especially in the Anglo-American world, there exists a venerable, empiricist intellectual tradition—influential to this day—with classical authors such as Hobbes, Locke and Hume; turning more utilitarian with Bentham and Mill and more scientific with contemporary philosophers; an intellectual tradition that has consistently posited an atomistic and mechanistic understanding of human beings without soul and without solidarity, and acted as the theoretical ally of capitalism with its implicit anthropology of man as utility-maximizer. It seems to me that this positivistic empiricism is the prevailing philosophy guiding the major institutions of our society, the bureaucracies of government and industry and certain sectors of the university.

David Tracy would probably argue that the classical authors of this tradition offered important correctives in their day and vindicated human rights against arbitrary aristocratic rule, but that the lesser representatives of this tradition were not seriously committed to depth and wholeness. Tracy does not deny that positivism and utilitarianism are the powerful ideas of contemporary society. But if these are the prevailing ideas, then his pluralism of philosophical traditions seems to paint an excessively hopeful picture of current thinking.

Radical Pluralism

We now turn to another pluralism that plays an important role in Tracy's later theology. Already in *The Analogical Imagination* Tracy speaks of 'radical pluralism' and the 'radically pluralistic present.'[3] For him there is something unique about the contemporary situation: it is radically plural, confused, riddled and incomprehensible; and at the same time it demands attention, makes us uncover the hidden, and opens us to otherness. Radical pluralism has negative and positive connotations. Tracy calls it 'the uncanny' of the present age. The uncanny is a translation of *'das Unheimliche,'* a German word refering to something that produces uncertainty and fear and yet suggests the possibility that behind the puzzling, threatening circumstance a gracious surprise lies waiting.

Tracy develops the uniqueness of the present situation along several lines. He repeatedly refers to the horrifying, death-dealing events of the 20th century, for which there are no parallels in the past. The Holocaust has destroyed the Enlightenment hope in progress and the Renaissance faith in humanity. Mass destruction of human beings now belongs to the order of the day. Even if the atomic bomb has been used so far "only" in one war, the continuing production of nuclear arms and the ongoing perfection of conventional weapons reveal that mass destruction of human beings has become an element of rational planning that governments undertake in preparing for the future. What is new is that we now possess the technology to destroy the whole of humanity.

There is, moreover, the disturbing discovery of the limits of nature and the frightening recognition that pollution and destruction of the environment by modern industrial development have damaged the earth to such an extent that the survival of human beings is by no means assured. What is new in the present situation is that we can survive only if we so choose, only if we turn to sustainable development and create an ecologically responsible society.

A third death-dealing power is the increasing spread of hunger in the poor countries of the South. The famines, often of genocidal proportions, are related to the global economic system that reaches from the industrialized centre of the North to the outlying regions of the South, creating hinterlands that serve the centre with labour and natural resources and in doing so undergo involuntary urbanization, suffer cultural disintegration and lose the ability to produce food for their own needs.

These death-dealing powers make us, the privileged, question our own age. But we cannot agree among ourselves about what is going on in society. What is new, according to Tracy, is that we are unable to name our own age.[4] Is society still a rational project on the way to Enlightenment progress? Or was the Enlightenment a misguided historical interlude after which society is now trying to return to a more communal, value-committed culture? Or are we entering an altogether new phase where the certainties of the past, whether they were rational and scientific or mediated by inherited values, have become meaningless, and where all we can do in the circle of our friends is to explore our own experiences?

Of course, every age is a riddle to itself. In every age, people have been deeply divided in their interpretation of what was happening and where they were going. This was startlingly true in Western society of the 19th century when people wrestled with one another over conservative, liberal, socialist or anarchist interpretations of the historical moment. We are also well aware that conflicts of this kind characterized the culture of the Palestine we encounter in the New Testament when Pharisees, Sadducees,

Zealots, Herodians, and the disciples of Jesus offered quite different interpretations of their historical situation.

The ambiguity of the present moment, Tracy argues, is quite different. He develops especially two themes. First, there exist critiques of culture produced by the masters of suspicion— Marx, Nietzsche and Freud, to name the most famous—which question our thoughts, feelings and actions and reveal the ambiguity of all cultural self-expressions. Because people struggle to protect their vulnerable, constructed self-identities and in doing so introduce distortions in their consciousness, the culture they produce, whatever it may be, is incapable of understanding itself. More than that, the same critiques of culture render problematic the classical traditions, be they religious or secular. All traditions are flawed. Tracy speaks of our new homelessness.

This homelessness strongly affects Christian thinkers. Tracy argues that a distinguishing mark of our situation is the present conflictual pluralism on what are 'the worthwhile fundamental questions' that should be asked. When Tracy proposed his model of theological pluralism, he recognized that what distinguishes various theologies from one another are not simply different sets of concepts but especially different worthwhile fundamental questions emerging from the historical context. Tracy clearly affirms the contextual character of theology. Theology wrestles with the central salvational issues as they are perceived by people in their historical situations. But what is the worthwhile fundamental question in the present crisis? 'Radical pluralism,' as Tracy defines it, makes it impossible to give an answer.

But there is more. Radical pluralism also means that we have learned to listen to groups and peoples who in the past were excluded from the conversation of the educated elite. We have discovered that even the sciences, despite their emphasis on objectivity, carried the bias of scientists who invented and produced them, males of a certain class and culture. Society cannot attain self-knowledge unless it is willing to listen to the voices of its low-status members and it subjugated groups. Society must listen to women. Those engaged in this conversation affirm 'radical pluralism' as a positive moment: they consequently resist the temptation to create a rational synthesis of the many voices, as if reason had the power to reconcile the diverse perspectives. Reason itself has lost its innocence.

Radical pluralism also means that we have to listen to non-Western cultures, societies and religions. This aspect of radical pluralism is related to Tracy's pluralism of traditions. While in the past comparative studies in religion and culture often tended to look upon the others from the standpoint of the Western religious or intellectual traditions, the pluralism advocated by Tracy recognizes the pluri-centric character of the world. There is no one centre. As among the gallaxies, there are many centres. Tracy only hints what this insight might mean for Christian theology. Again, it would be a betrayal of radical pluralism if one wished to produce a new theory that would integrate the different traditions and their various perpectives. We have to learn to respect 'the otherness' of the world religions and of non-Western cultures.

Radical pluralism, this 'uncanny' of the present, is frightening because it undermines our certainties and questions our assumption of a common humanity; but this 'uncanny' also suggests—hopefully—that behind the confusion and lack of coherence stands an as yet unnameable newness, destined to reveal itself as gracious reconciling power.

Pluralism and Liberation Theology

Let us now consider Tracy's notion of pluralism from the viewpoint of liberation theology. 'Liberation theology' names a field of theologies based on what is called 'the preferential option for the poor.' The preferential option includes two commitments: first, to read society and its texts from the perspective of the poor and powerless; second, to give public witness of one's solidarity with their historical struggle for emancipation. The option for the poor has therefore two dimensions, one hermeneutical and the other practical.

This twofoldness constitutes liberation theology as 'a praxis,' which is here defined as the interaction between knowledge and action, oriented toward human emancipation. While all forms of theology recognize the impact of knowledge on practice, liberation theology is keenly aware that there is also an impact of practice on human consciousness and hence on the reading of the social reality and its texts. In ethics and religion, the entry into truth demands an antecedent alternative practice.

From the perspective of liberation theology, Tracy's theological project as outlined in *Blessed Rage for Order* was somewhat puzzling. The distinction he then made among the conversations of theology with three different communities, 'the university,' 'the church' and 'the social order,' created the impression that he regarded the university and the church as outside or above the social order, unaffected by society's cultural, economic or political conflicts. In his later writings, this impression disappears. Tracy came to recognize with increasing clarity that it is impossible to understand the debates at the university and in the church without taking into account the historical condition of society. While Tracy strongly opposes reductionist interpretations of intellectual and religious conflicts, he clearly acknowledges a political dimension in all arguments dealing with ideas or the meaning of religion.

Liberation theology looks with great sympathy at Tracy's pluralism-of-traditions as well as his radical pluralism. Liberation theology sides with Tracy's idea of pluralism against the notion of pluralism advocated by certain American theologians, most outspokenly perhaps Dennis McCann,[5] who try to devise a universally acceptable form of public discourse for the United States. Since American society is made up of a variety of groups and communities, each with their special values and traditions, it would be unjust if the common good were defined by a single group, the heir of power and privilege. The public good should be determined, these authors propose, by an ongoing public conversation, following the rules of democracy, in which each party argues in defense of its own interests and is in principle open to accept the rational compromise that offers proportional satisfaction to all parties, without special privilege to any one of them. What rules the pluralistic society here is the commonly accepted rational discourse.

By contrast, David Tracy is highly suspicious of the commonly accepted rational discourse. He recognizes ideological distortions in the public discourse of any society, created as it is by an elite that had access to power, privilege and formal education. That is why 'interruption' is an important concept in Tracy's theology. An issue of *Concilium* he co-edited is called 'The Holocaust as Interruption.'[6] The normative discourse that a society, be it secular or sacred, creates for its own use excludes sectors suffering oppression, and for this reason such discourse remains essentially ambiguous. That is why moments of interruption must be taken with utmost seriousness. They have a message to which society must listen.

Looked upon from Tracy's perspective, McCann's proposal of pluralism appears as a political ideology that seeks to silence the cries of the poor and the marginalized who are unable or unwilling to use the commonly recognized discourse. The decision to designate the controlled sectors of society, be they women, the poor, or the racially despised, as 'special interest groups' is an effort to disguise the injustice inflicted upon them. By contrast, Tracy insists that the victims must be heard, even if this should explode the inherited rationality.

Still, the perspective of liberation theology also raises some critical questions. As suggested above, Tracy's pluralism of traditions puts the main emphasis on the trusting conversation between these traditions, on listening, learning, gaining new insights and imaginatively expanding one's spiritual and intellectual inheritance. In a paragraph on the enemies of this pluralism, Tracy mentions the sin against justice, which for him means, above all, the refusal to recognize the ideological role played by religion in society. Tracy is aware that the dynamics that widen the distance and create hostility between religious traditions have to do with their entanglement in the structures of political and economic power.

Liberation theology would insist—more than Tracy does—that it is the task of the trusting conversation between traditions to analyze the historical conditions that feed their respective ideological deformations. More than that, liberation theology would have to add that conversation, while precious and important, is not enough. Representatives of the plural traditions must stand together against the historical causes of injustice, especially those from which they have inherited their falsifying biases. What is demanded, from the viewpoint of liberation theology, is an alternative practice, i.e., gestures and acts of solidarity with the people that wrestle against these unjust structures. Such a practice would modify the consciousness of the participants and affect the reading of their own religious tradition. While Tracy's thought is sympathetic to emancipatory political engagement, he did not—until quite recently, as we shall see—call for a new practice as indispensible prerequisite for the quest of theological truth.

The reason for this, it seems to me, is related to Tracy's notion of 'radical pluralism.' This notion, as we saw above, is a collective category that brings together different troubling experiences that undermine the confidence of contemporary thinkers in our inherited science, wisdom, and religious truth. We are overwhelmed by the Holocaust and its continuing presence in other massacres; we are disturbed by the ideological distortions present in the Christian and secular traditions of the West; we are confused by the lack of agreement among contemporary intellectuals regarding the present cultural crisis; we are excited by the possibility of discovering the 'other' religions and the 'other' cultures we have ignored in the past. But is it useful to unite these different factors under the common label of radical pluralism? I do not think so.

In my opinion, this common label tends to undermine the trust in the critical concepts derived from the Enlightenment that could help us to make sense of the society in which we live. Constructing a single category allows the massive crimes committed by our civilization and legitimated or even encouraged by our intellectual traditions to weaken the confidence of our contemporaries in the critical methodology our civilization has also developed. Tracy's 'radical pluralism' is, in my view, an echo of the postmodern idea that the Holocaust and Gulag are arguments demonstrating that every affirmation of a context-transcending normative vision has a built-in orientation toward totalitarianism.

Despite the occasional postmodern rhetoric, Tracy actually defends modern critical theory. Here are two sentences of a long paragraph dealing with the impact of the economic infrastructure on culture and the realm of ideas.

> Only when we understand history as process, humanity as social, as always a result of its own labor, can we understand the profoundly alienating reifications of the socio-economic base hidden and awaiting unmasking in all 'culture.' Only then can we uncover—beyond the fetishism of facts endorsing the status quo and the idealism of philosophers and humanist critics—the actual conflicts of society reflected in all cultural expressions.

The entire paragraph is closer to the Frankfurt School than to the postmodern repudiation of Critical Theory.

It seems to me, therefore, that one might usefully deconstruct the notion of radical pluralism. I wish to distinguish between (A) the shaking of the foundations caused by reflecting on the evils of Western society and the relativizing of the Western religious and philosophical traditions caused by the recognition of the 'other' religions and 'other' cultures; and (B) the confusion caused by the multiple interpretations given of the present cultural crisis. The self-questioning of Western society here designated as (A) is indeed *'unheimlich'* or 'uncanny,' generating remorse, fear and helplessness while at the same time suggesting the possibility of release and new discovery. But the confusion caused by the disagreement of intellectuals, here designated as (B), is not a unique phenomenon. It is puzzling, but not uncanny. Earlier, I recalled the irreconcilable interpretations present in 19th century Europe and 1st century Palestine. What follows from this is that the chorus of discordant voices cannot be used to invalidate the critical theories derived from the Enlightenment and discount them as principles of explanation.

While liberation theology laments the dominance of instrumental reason in society, it does not reject the entire Enlightenment tradition; it still trusts the critical methods capable of uncovering the extent to which economic and other forms of domination are reflected in thought, culture and religion. Liberation theology resists the postmodern proposal that these theories must be rejected because their claims are universal. The above quotation suggests that Tracy also resists the postmodern idea, even if his discourse occasionally reflects postmodern sensibilities. His definition of 'radical pluralism,' I have suggested, is a concession to postmodern thought.

Reflecting on his recent essay, "On Naming the Present,"[7] I conclude that David Tracy's theology has gradually moved into the field of liberation theology. My conclusion is based on two arguments, one related to the evolution of Tracy's thought and the other to a change in the self-understanding of liberation theology.

"On Naming the Present" emphasizes the mystical and political dimension of contemporary Christian existence defined in terms of resistance and hope. Looking back, Tracy points to the 96th issue of *Concilium* (1974), entitled *The Mystical and Political Dimension of Christian Faith*, as a ground-breaking work that prompted many theologians to explore the emancipatory dimension of Christian teaching and spirituality. By concentrating on 'the mystical-political' or, as he prefers to call it, 'the mystical-prophetic,' Tracy has moved into the field of liberation theology. He now calls for an alternative practice, resistance and hope, as the prerequisite the attaining religious truth.

Liberation theology has also moved into a new phase. In this context I can only give the briefest outline of what has taken place. Beginning in the 60s, vast numbers of people on several continents believed that profound social change toward greater justice was a historical possibility in their societies. I recall the liberal optimism of the Kennedy years, the civil rights movement, the opposition to the war in Vietnam, the women's movement, the struggle of the marginalized for public recognition, and among intellectuals the creation of a new political imagination. At the same time there were anti-colonial struggles in Africa, liberation movements in Latin America, and socialist experiments on several continents. It was during this time that Christian people in struggle, aided by their intellectuals, first developed liberation theology. The alternative practice that grounded liberation theology at that time was support for concrete political movements.

Paul Tillich, looking back to the 20s in Germany, designated as *'kairos'* a period of time in which radical social change to greater justice was a historical possibility. The period beginning with the 60s was such a *kairos*. But this period has come to an end.

In the 80s the government-supported shift to liberal or monetarist capitalism, the reorganization of capital around the giant transnational corporations, and the subsequent globalization of the economy have profoundly affected societies in the South and in the North. 'Structural adjustment policies' imposed by the international financial institutions on the Southern nations, unable to pay their debt, forced the governments to neglect their own populations and promote economic activities that served the interests of the developed North. The result has been growing misery and hunger. Liberation movements have been weakened not only by strong-arm policies of governments but even more by the hopelessness of the situation.

Even in the North, governments introduced 'structural adjustment policies' to enable their nations to be competitive in the global market. This meant privatization, deregulation, tax breaks and other advantages granted to transnational corporations, cutting social programs, lowering the salaries of public sector employees, raising the price of public services, humiliating organized labor, and so forth. Even socialist or social democratic governments were forced by the capital market to adopt the neo-liberal or monetarist policies. And the result has been the same everywhere: massive unemployment, job insecurity right into the middle class, the shift of the job market to unskilled, temporary or part-time work, the decline of neighborhoods and misery in the streets.

For many people the Gulf War was the publicly-approved massacre that sealed in blood the new politico-economic order, begun over a decade ago, that seeks to enhance the material well-being of a privileged minority and assign to the margin the rest of the globe's population. Those who refuse to play by the rules are penalized. In the present period there is no historical possibility for deep social change toward greater justice, neither in the South nor the North. The *'kairos'* has come to an end.

The period we have entered—and who knows how long it will last!—may be called 'the wilderness,' another biblical image.

In the wilderness, liberation theology joins David Tracy in defining Christian existence in terms of resistance and hope. The dark night of the soul, often thought to be meaningful only for the few, is becoming a way of life for the many. When Christians pray during a *kairos,* "Thy kingdom come, thy will be done on earth," they expect to see with their own eyes a manifestation of God's justice. But when they utter the same prayer in the wilderness, they hope that God's work among them will be one of preparation. Hope pushes them more deeply into their spiritual resources. They become more aware of their roots where they touch the underground river.

Notes

1. David Tracy, *The Analogical Imagination,* New York: Crossroad, 1981, pp. 390-398.

2. Ibid., pp. 265-268.

3. Ibid., pp. 339-364.

4. Cf. David Tracy, "On Naming the Present," *On the Threshold of the Third Millenium,* special issue of *Concilium,* February 1990, London: SCM Press/Philadelphia: Trinity Press, pp. 66-85.

5. Dennis McCann, *Polity and Praxis,* co-author Charles Strain, Minneapolis: Winston, 1985, and *New Experiments in Democracy,* Kansas City: Sheed & Ward, 1987.

6. *The Holocaust as Interruption,* ed. Elisabeth Schüssler Fiorenza/David Tracy, *Concilium,* vol. 175, Edinburgh: T. & T. Clark, 1984.

7. Cf. note 4 above.

3

For and Against John Milbank

In this essay I wish to engage in critical conversation with the new, orginal theological approach introduced by John Milbank. This learned young Englishman, a postmodern radical theologian, claims with a Barthian vehemence that there is no good society, no valid ethics and no true wisdom apart from the life and message of Jesus Christ. In his book *Theology and Social Theory*,[1] John Milbank repudiates the entire history of freedom associated with the Enlightenment project; repudiates the social sciences in their entirety; repudiates—on Christian, not on Marxist grounds—the capitalist system and its cultural implications; repudiates every form of universal reason, classical and modern, that pretends to define a common humanity;—and all this in the name of Jesus Christ who, with his counter-practice and counter-discourse, interrupted the logic of violence in human history.

Yet Milbank is not Karl Barth *revivivus*. The newness brought by Jesus Christ, according to Milbank, is the practice, not the proclamation, of God's approaching reign. Jesus brought a new praxis of love, forgiveness and peace, a community-creating way of life that saved his followers from the violence implicit in their culture. The new practice generated social actions and cultural expressions that were 'coded'—this is how our postmodern theologian puts it—that bore the imprint of the gospel, a new message that called for articulation and gave rise to attentive reflection. Here praxis precedes *kerygma* and theology. Milbank is an Anabaptist or Mennonite Barth.

A few words about *Theology and Social Theory*. It is an original, brilliant and enormously learned treatise. I spent two weeks reading its tightly-printed 400 pages. From his perspective of the primacy of practice, Milbank re-reads the classical authors, especially Plato and Aristotle, re-reads Augustine and Thomas Aquinas, re-reads the political theorists of the Enlightenment and the sociologists of the 19th and early 20th centuries, re-reads Maurice Blondel and more recent Roman Catholic theologians, re-reads Heidegger, Derrida, Foucault and the postmodern philosophers. The book also offers Milbank's own daring theology. The work is an astounding intellectual achievement, carried through with great passion, conceptual precision, and a difficult but readable prose. The book deeply engaged me. I had great sympathy for Milbank's reading of the classical authors, but because I find his postmodern deconstruction of reason and truth unconvincing, the book also disturbs me. I am writing this article for and against John Milbank.

That Milbank, a member of the Church of England, thinks as an heir to the radical wing of the Reformation, became clear to me only in the book's last section dealing with ecclesiology. My first impression was that Milbank belonged to the Roman Catholic tradition. I had several reasons for this hunch. First, Milbank offers a sympathetic reading of Plato and Aristotle and laments the modern rejection of classical reason. He contrasts classical reason, implicit in the virtues proper to the ideal republic, with modern reason, implicit in the individualism of self-preservation and self-promotion. Only toward the end of the book does Milbank analyze the antinomies of classical reason and attempt to persuade the reader that Christian faith, based on an alternative practice, resolves these antinomies and hence dissolves classical metaphysics.

A second reason for my hunch was Milbank's reticence in regard to classical Protestantism. Since he assigns primacy to the practice (not the message) of Jesus and his followers, salvation is mediated to Christians not *sola fide* but by trusting discipleship; and since the Bible must be read in the context of the practicing community, the claim of *sola scriptura* is seen to misrepresent the manner in which God guides the Church. The third reason for my hunch was Milbank's vehement repudiation of what he calls the 'liberal Protestant meta-narrative' (only loosely related to classical Protestantism) which, according to him, initiated the modern phenomenon of secularization. According to this meta-narrative, spiritual freedom and personal maturity call for the liberation of society from the power of sacred symbols and institutions: in this liberated condition, the sacred survives only as the private motivation in an otherwise secular social existence.

Another reason for my hunch was the fact that Milbank insists on Christian orthodoxy (Incarnation and Trinity as defined by the ecumenical councils), that he finds support for his praxo-theology in St. Augustine of Hippo and the modern Catholic philosopher Maurice Blondel, and that he offers a conservative critique of Karl Rahner and other Catholic theologians influential during and after Vatican Council II.

Only toward the end of the book does it become clear that Milbank distances himself radically from any high church tradition, Roman Catholic or other. Assigning primacy to practice, Milbank conceives of theology first of all as ecclesiology, that is to say, as reflection upon the new, Jesus-inspired and Spirit-empowered social existence of the community. In other words, theology here becomes the sociology of ecclesial discipleship, excluding as sinful distortion all permanently structured inequalities or hierarchies and all canonical legislations capable of overriding the practice of charity. The true Church, for Milbank, is an egalitarian, pacifist community, pacifist not only in the refusal to take up arms but more profoundly in extending love and forgiveness to the perpetrators of evil—an Anabaptist, Mennonite ecclesial project, expressed today in the work of John Yoder and Stanley Hauerwas.

This essay 'for and against John Milbank' shall by necessity be limited to certain aspects of his monumental work. What I wish to do first is to examine Milbank's sweeping rejection of social science and universal values, then enter into dialogue with him regarding his confident affirmation of the supernatural.

The Repudiation of Social Science and Universal Reason

Milbank argues that 'the secular' is an arbitrary construction of modernity. Ordinary human life, he argues, is always and everywhere deeply shaped by symbols and stories that are in some way related to an absolute. Classical philosophy recognized this. For Plato and Aristotle human actions were intrinsically related to a transcendent dimension (the Idea of the Good or the ultimate Telos). The Stoics were the first to confine the religious dimension to the inner life of individuals. With the coming of Christianity, the new coded practice of Jesus Christ, people's daily interactions were again understood as shaped by God's revealed presence. While Augustine's approach to God through the soul's interior journey anticipated the notion of an external world from which God was absent, he himself provided an alternative imagination, especially in his major work, *The City of God.* Only in the Renaissance and the Enlightenment, Milbank argues, did philosophers propose the idea that ordinary, day-to-day human activity was 'secular,' i.e., unrelated to a myth that gave it meaning, and consequently that religion came upon the secular as an *additum,* as brief interruptions in moments of prayer and recollection.

This change of theory, Milbank argues, reflected a change of practice: at the dawn of modernity, people began to understand themselves as defined by the struggle to survive, to promote their own advantage and to do better than their neighbour. As life in modern society increasingly defined itself in terms of personal freedom and scientific rationality, people set aside the religious *additum* altogether. The Comtean proposal of the gradual emancipation of humanity from religious fables was paradigmatic for the orientation of modern society.

For Milbank, the secular designates the sphere of people's historical existence independent of an absolute. To this he adds a further characteristic. What defined secular existence was the 'conatus' of self-preservation, the struggle for survival, security and success, sustained by the desire for freedom from outside interference. Human life was understood apart from its relation to good and evil. Milbank wants to show that secularity is not historical reality, but an arbitrary, anti-theological idea constructed by modern thinkers relying on the myth of secular reason. The concept of the secular reflects the modern meta-narrative of man's emancipatory self-creation through the application of scientific rationality.

Human beings are here defined in opposition to classical and Christian wisdom. According to Milbank, secular reason in the social sciences is founded on a non-demonstrable, anti-Christian stance that cannot make a greater claim to truth than does the supernatural stance revealed in Christ which it sought to replace.

Milbank begins his study of modern scientific thought with the political philosophers of the Enlightenment, for whom human beings are defined by the 'conatus' to survive, protect their life and property, and improve their position in the world. This possessive individualism reflected the practice of the emerging middle class.

But Milbank has no more sympathy for the 19th-century sociologists in the French tradition of Auguste Comte and Emile Durkheim who, reacting against Enlightenment individualism, adopted a collectivist perspective. For them, the individual was embedded in and shaped by society. They held that society steered people's lives through the power of symbols, assigning them their social role for the benefit of the entire body politic. These symbols, Milbank argues, represented a false theology. As these sociologists divinized the finite, they emptied religion of its transcendent meaning and reduced it to the function it supposedly exercised in developing and stabilizing society. The meta-narrative behind their sociological perspective was therefore also the rational orientation of society toward ever greater progress.

Curiously enough, Milbank does not offer a more sympathetic reading of sociologists in the German tradition, Max Weber in particular, even though they rejected the Durkheimian trend of divinizing society and lamented the decline of culture produced by modernity. What Milbank regrets in Max Weber's work is his return to the individualism of the early Enlightenment, his concept of man as defined by the 'conatus' for self-preservation, and his radical separation of sociology from social ethics. When humans are no longer defined by their relation to good and evil, Milbank reasons correctly, then social peace can be conceived only as an unstable compromise between conflicting interests or as an order imposed upon citizens by an all-powerful state.

According to Milbank, sociology in the French and German traditions reflects the practice of modernity, coded by scientific reason—a practice at odds with the counter-practice initiated by Jesus Christ. Milbank repudiates the validity of the social sciences. He refuses to enter into dialogue with sociology; and he scolds contemporary theologians who make critical use of sociological theories in their theology. Milbank admits of course that theologians must offer critiques of church and society, but he believes that such critiques can be derived from the new practice introduced by Jesus Christ and continued by the community of his disciples.

While Milbank calls 'For and Against Hegel' his chapter on the German philosopher and 'For and Against Marx' his chapter on the German revolutionary, he refuses to engage in dialogue 'for and against' the social sciences. Milbank would have my full support if he rejected the positivistic social sciences which suppose that human actions follow scientifically discoverable laws, that these actions are fully determined by antecedent causes and that they are therefore in principle predictable. But Milbank repudiates also the hermeneutical social sciences which recognize only strong trends—not laws—in society, acknowledge only probable causes and understand history as forever open to the unexpected.

To strengthen his case, Milbank offers a reading of Max Weber that does not do him justice. Weber did not define human beings by their 'conatus.' On the contrary, he recognized that human action was prompted by a combination of several motives: (a) conformity to custom; (b) purpose-rationality [the 'conatus' guided by rational self-interest]; (c) value-rationality [personal virtue and social vision]; and (d) strong feelings [religious conviction, social resentment, etc.]. Weber believed that modernity's obsession with purpose-rationality prevented it from reflecting on values and ends, and hence prepared an eventual cultural collapse. While Weber did adopt the Kantian separation of science and ethics, in my opinion Weber still remains a sociologist with whom theologians can engage in fruitful dialogue.

Repudiating dialogue with sociology, Milbank makes the bold proposal that the only valid insights into social developments (insights theology must take seriously) are derived from historical narratives. History, not social science, deserves the attention of theologians. Milbank seems to forget that in organizing their data, historians employ concepts and paradigms derived from their own culture, hence they inevitably make use of thought models culturally mediated from sociology.

John Milbank and other postmodern thinkers—following Emile Durkheim, whom they do not honour—exaggerate the extent to which human beings are constructed by the myth of their society. For these thinkers nothing in human existence is a given: there is no human nature. Human existence is seen as constructed by social and linguistic practices founded upon some meta-narrative. These thinkers overlook (what Weber clearly saw) that human beings live at the intersection of some given orientations and several narratives that affect their minds. For instance, the 'conatus' for self-preservation is a given impulse (not a construction of modernity) that to some degree operates in people's lives, even when they are deeply involved in the religious myth of their society.

Let me give an example of this from the Bible. When the people of Israel, threatened by enemies from the North, asked God for a king to rule over them and protect them, Samuel tried to persuade them to change their mind (cf. I Samuel 8:10-18). What arguments did he use? He did not appeal to their meta-narrative. He did not plead with the people to remain faithful to the egalitarian confederation given to them by God so as to remind them that God alone was their king and to protect their society from becoming another Egypt, a system of structured inequality. Instead, Samuel offered the people a secular argument: he appealed to their 'conatus' of self-preservation. He warned the people that if they had a king set over them, he would force their sons to do burdensome duties as soldiers and labourers, he would oblige their daughters to enter his service as maids and cooks, and he would take away their most valued fields and vine-yards to hand over to his officers.

People never act consistently out of a meta-narrative, unless they are insane. People's lives are complex: they live out of more than one story and are prompted to action by mixed motivations. Max Weber recognized this. But he also acknowledged that some-times people, drawing upon hidden resources or sudden charisms, are able to transcend their culture and create some-thing new.

Samuel's famous speech recorded in Scripture anticipates sociological theory in an intuitive, pre-scientific manner. Why do I say this? Because Samuel applies the theory that monarchies produce class distinction and class exploitation to the particular historical situation of the Israelites. His argument goes farther than simple historical narrative; it includes a certain generaliza-tion, without of course claiming that this establishes a law. Sa-muel regards exploitation as a trend in monarchical regimes that is likely to find historical expression, though he does not deny that this trend may be overcome by an unusual king who loves justice.

Let me add that Milbank occasionally does enter into dia-logue with sociology. When he discusses the work of Norman Gottwald and Wayne Meeks, who applied sociological theory to the interpretation of Scripture (see pp. 111-121), Milbank appre-ciates their research on the social practice of the biblical commu-nity and hence on the meaning of the biblical message. He criti-cizes the conclusions of these scholars only for the element of positivism that remains in them. Because Milbank affirms the openness of history to the unexpected, he expands Gottwald's and Meeks' conclusions by pointing to unpredictable human creativity which, he thinks, the two authors underestimate. Here Milbank involves himself 'for and against sociology.' Why then the categorical repudiation?

Milbank wants to demonstrate that the Church in its prac-tice and proclamation cannot learn anything from sociology and, more generally, from the critiques offered by Enlightenment thinkers. The Church, he argues, has its own sources of self-criti-cism. "Because historical narration is the true mode of social knowledge, theology no longer has any need, like Ricoeur, to concede the foundationalist suspicion of Marx, Freud and sociology, and appropriate this as a supposed mode of the *via negativa*, or as a way of purifying the true subject matter of theology itself" (p. 268.) Milbank, as we shall see, pays a high price for his refusal to listen to the modern critics.

Since Milbank makes the thought of St. Augustine central to his theological proposal, I wish to mention an instance where the pastoral approach of the great African bishop failed tragically because he had no access to sociological theory. His failure is an allegory for many contemporary failures.

In his ongoing struggle against the Donatists, Augustine did not recognize one important reason why these schismatics were so harsh in their judgement of the bishops who had betrayed their faith during the persecution; and why the schismatics refused to recognize these bishops when they repented and were eventually reconciled with the Catholic Church. What was this reason? The Donatists were drawn from the ethnic population of North Africa that had been pushed by the Roman colonists from the fertile stretches of land along the Mediterrenean coast to settle in the mountainous, less fertile regions of the interior. These people refused integration in the culture of the Roman Empire. They stood aloof from the assimilated Christians of North Africa who, like Augustine, spoke Latin and were proud of the best of Roman culture. While the Latinized Christians looked upon the idolatrous surrender to the Emperor in times of persecution as a sin that could be forgiven, the Donatists judged this apostasy as an irreparable break with the Church, pouring into this judgment their historical resentment against the material and cultural oppression inflicted upon them by the Empire. Because he lacked such a social analysis, Augustine was unable to address the Donatists in a manner that acknowledged their suffering.

The Rejection of Universal Reason

Milbank strengthens his rejection of the social sciences by making it part of the wider repudiation of all forms of reason that claim universal validity. Milbank here follows the French de-constructionists and postmodern philosophers who believe that all truth claims are expressions of power within a given society and that universal truth claims are related to an intention of im-perialistic control. Here too practice (the will to power) precedes theory (universal truth.) Milbank agrees with postmodern think-ers that modernity was created by the meta-narratives of the En-lightenment, first the liberal story of continual progress through science, technology and democracy, then the Marxist story, also relying on science and technology, that expected a social revolu-tion to overcome liberal society and man's exploitation of man. What has happened in the present, the postmoderns and Mil-bank argue, is that these meta-narratives have lost their power. Not only have they failed to deliver what they promised, but worse, they have also generated forms of totalitarian rule which, like all stories, claim universal validity.

Milbank thus looks upon reason as an instrument of vio-lence. He applies this not only to modern, secular rationality but also, reluctantly, to classical reason, even though it recognizes the orientation of humans toward the good and expresses the practice of justice in the ideal republic. To show that even classi-cal reason was an instrument of violence, Milbank analyzes the contradiction between the practice of the *'polis,'* defined by jus-tice, and the practice of the *'oikos,'* the household, which was bru-tally exploitative (pp. 364-369). The household, while providing the material basis for the men engaged in the *'polis,'* reduced women, children and slaves to an inferior status. Hence even classical reason offered a legitimation for violence.

According to Milbank, Jesus alone brought a counter-prac-tice of compassion and forgiveness, destined to overcome the re-gimes of violence and transcend the rationalities associated with them.

Milbank's postmodern repudiation of universal reason is not an ideology critique followed by a retrieval in a new key. He specifically disagrees with the philosophers of the Frankfurt School who lamented the collapse of Enlightenment reason into instrumental rationality—'the dialectic of the Enlightenment'—but who still had enough hope to revive and reaffirm the ethical dimension present in the emancipatory project of the Enlightenment. With the postmodern thinkers, Milbank opposes the Frankfurt School because of their continuing trust in context-transcending ethical reason. At this point, as we shall see, I part company with Milbank for reasons that are ultimately theological.

Milbank is not only 'for' postmodern thought, he is also 'against' it. According to his analysis, postmodern philosophies inevitably lead to the deconstruction of all ethical values and the legitimation of arbitrary violence. Milbank offers a passionate argument that the only choice confronting the contemporary generation is between postmodern nihilism and Christian faith.

Against Milbank, I resist those postmodern theorists according to whom a truth claim is always and everywhere an attempt to impose an order on society. They see truth as a child of violence. Yet if we assume that this is so, then the affirmation of their truth is also the child of violence and hence there is no reason why we should trust postmodern reasoning more than the thought they seek to replace. Or again, if truth is always contextual, and if there is no common 'ratio' among different cultural contexts and hence no context-transcending dialogue, then why do postmodern thinkers speak to us? Is not discourse addressed to others always based on the hope that they are capable of understanding it? In my opinion, it can be argued convincingly that human beings are by nature communicators and that implicit in people's cooperative action in transcultural situations is the affirmation of a common ground.

Since Milbank looks at secular reason as an instrument of violence, he discards the critical ideas of Marx, Freud and others which reveal the dark powers operating on a deep and often hidden level in human self-making, personal and social. These critiques, Milbank argues, are part and parcel of the secular project, the construction of a society unrelated to the good and to ultimate meaning; and therefore these critiques contain elements of violence. Milbank also recognizes violence present in the postmodern denial of universal reason and its deconstruction of the great philosophical and ethical traditions. But the question Milbank does not ask is whether the Christian meta-narrative contains grains of violence that might have to be overcome in the Church's history. We shall return to this topic further on.

The Affirmation of the Supernatural

After repudiating social science and universal reason, Milbank strongly affirms the supernatural. He uses this term to refer to the divine revelation brought by Jesus Christ and the gracious transformation it engendered in humanity. Milbank praises the development of 20th-century Roman Catholic theology which has come to acknowledge that God's grace affects the whole of human existence, not only spiritual but also earthly life, not only the individual but also the community. Milbank calls this 'integralism' (not to be confused with '*l'intégrisme*,' the French word for fundamentalism.) Integralist theology acknowledges that the radical newness brought by Christ was a personal and social practice that bore a new message.

Milbank studies two different currents of integralism in Roman Catholic theology. The first considers the supernatural as the Christ-given fulfillment of the natural order that by itself and apart from Christ remains intrinsically frustrated. The second current—less sound, according to Milbank—regards the Christ-event as elevating the whole of human history to the supernatural. The first current is associated with several French theologians, especially Maurice Blondel and Henri de Lubac, as well as Urs von Balthasar, and the second current with Karl Rahner, German political theology and Latin American liberation theology.

Milbank associates himself with the first current. According to his reading, these theologians hold that the human response to the divine initiative takes place in surrender, discipleship and action, which for Milbank means the practice of love, forgiveness and peace. These theologians look upon human nature as essentially frustrated, unable to find fulfillment within the limits of its own powers. Humans overcome this frustration only through the gratuitous encounter with the supernatural. These theologians are critical of scholastic theology which distinguished between two levels of existence, the natural and the supernatural, where

the natural constituted an internally consistent whole and the supernatural appeared as added extrinsically to a fully equipped
human existence. These theologians rejected this 'extrinsicism.'
For them the Christian Gospel was not a complement to human
nature but a way of life and a message that rescued nature from
its contradictions and lifted it to its true vocation.

In a world of competition, power and violence, Milbank
claims the Gospel is the only way to peace. Apart from Jesus,
there is only sin and darkness. Milbank defends an 'exclusivist'
christology. His theology offers an integralist interpretation of
the supernatural, projects the transformation of the entire human situation and hence constitutes a truly social theology; at
the same time, it sets Christians apart from the rest of humanity.
Christians enlivened and enlightened by the supernatural have
nothing significant to learn from outsiders, from people caught
in cultures, religions and philosophical traditions that inevitably
reflect practices of domination. Authentic social theology is
therefore ecclesiology, reflection on the Church's practice. Because Milbank defends this radical thesis with intelligence and
extraordinary learning, I have called him an Anabaptist Barth.

The second current of contemporary Roman Catholic theology, reflecting an 'inclusivist' christology, is severely criticized by
Milbank. Thus, for Karl Rahner, the redemption brought by
Christ assures the presence of divine grace in the community of
believers and in the whole of sinful humanity. Now it is Christ,
and no longer Adam, who defines the situation of all human beings. The divine mercy revealed in Christ is believed, proclaimed
and celebrated only in the Christian Church; but in a hidden
way, the same redeeming grace operates wherever people are, offering them freedom from their sins and supporting their quest
for truth and justice. Because history itself is here seen as lifted
to the supernatural order, the practice of Christians—their faith,
love of neighbour, commitment to justice—does not necessarily
differ from the practice of others who, thanks to God's grace,
have become trusting, loving and justice-oriented.

This theological current also overcomes the 'extrinsicism' of
scholastic thought since here the supernatural is seen as rescu-
ing, elevating and transforming the damaged resources of human

nature. Yet this current of theology differs significantly from the preceding one because it insists that the gift of divine grace creates universal human solidarity and provides the foundation for the cooperation of all in ever-renewed efforts to overcome senseless human suffering and violence.

This second current of integralist theology, Milbank claims, has been taken up by liberation theology and theological approaches influenced by it: here human history itself, not just the Church, is seen as the locus of the supernatural. What Milbank does not mention is that Latin American liberation theology shares with him a strong awareness, stronger than Karl Rahner's, that divine redemption is not yet complete. Here the 'not yet' overpowers the 'always already.' Still, on the basis of their inclusivist christology, liberation theologians do hold that the Gospel summons Christians to practice solidarity with secular social movements struggling for emancipation and to assimilate into their own theology certain Enlightenment insights expressed in these movements. Milbank disapproves of this. Critical solidarity and critical assimilation are not enough: what he calls for is a refusal to cooperate. The content of these solidarity movements, he argues, is totally determined by secular ideas and aspirations, hence cannot be influenced and modified by Christian participants. The only contribution Christians can make to these movements is to provide religious motivation for some of their members. While liberation theology pretends to be a social theology, Milbank argues, it actually turns out to be exclusively personal, revealing its own inner contradiction.

Milbank also criticizes liberation theology because it engages in critical dialogue with Enlightenment thought and intends to purify the Christian tradition with the help of modern critical reflection. Liberation theology uses secular social theory to clarify the Church's mission in the world. It also accepts the secular idea of human autonomy, i.e., the idea that people are meant to be free subjects of their personal and social existence. Milbank claims that liberation theology has accepted the Enlightenment idea of freedom (freedom from foreign interference and for self-determination), which is an 'empty' freedom because the power to create one's own future eventually leads to injustice and violence. Liberation theology, Milbank argues, transfers this 'liberal' idea of freedom to people's struggle against oppression.

Milbanks thus raises three objections against liberation theology:

(1) the use of contemporary social theory,
(2) the reduction of the Christian contribution to personal motivation, and
(3) the adoption of the empty freedom of the Enlightenment.

A critique of liberation theology by a radical Christian social theologian of the stature of John Milbank must be taken seriously. Even if I offer a different reading of liberation theology, I concede that Milbank's objections oblige liberation theologians to clarify some issues they have left relatively unattended.

First, Milbank's claim that liberation theology engages in critical dialogue with Marxism and contemporary social theory is correct. Since this is the theological methodology I am defending throughout this essay, I need not comment on it here. Secondly, Milbank claims that liberation theology does not stand for an ethical vision of its own, but restricts the impact of the Gospel to religious motivation. This raises many issues. Are we sure there exists a specifically Christian ethics? Many theologians argue that because human beings are created and redeemed by the triune God, their nature purified and aided by the redemptive summons moves them in the same direction of faith, hope and love so that Christian ethics echoes the universal moral aspirations of humanity. I do not intend to deal with this question. In reply to Milbank's second objection to liberation theology, I will simply make two remarks, the first affirming the need for modesty in Christian discourse, and the second defending the original Christian ethic on which liberation theology is grounded.

The proclamation that Jesus transforms the human heart and lifts his disciples to a new, Spirit-guided way of life must be formulated with great modesty. For we often encounter people of other religions or secular men and women who have been more deeply transformed by faith, hope and love than we have been. We marvel at this. In my writings I have called this 'the irony of the Gospel.'[2] This experience is theologically illumined by an inclusivist understanding of christology. Christians who join secular emancipatory movements will have much to learn, but—here I agree with Milbank—they will also be able to make specific contributions derived from the Gospels over and above their religious motivation.

Milbank misreads the starting point of liberation theology, which is a practice—a stance Milbank should appreciate—a practice called 'the preferential option for the poor.' This option, understood as a contemporary form of discipleship, implies a double commitment: to look at society from the perspective of its victims and to act in solidarity with their struggle for social justice.

The preferential option based on Christian love is different from a secular emancipatory commitment. Since the commitment to justice does not relativize the summons to love God and neighbour, the preferential option affects the mode of social struggle, the ethics that guide it, the relationship among comrades, and the attitude toward the oppressor. More than that, the preferential option is a transcendent principle that remains valid after the reconstruction of society; here it offers a critical perspective on the new society and nurtures solidarity with the newly marginalized in that society. Thus, after victory in Nicaragua, Christian base communities demanded that forgiveness be shown to Somosa's soldiers.[3]

Let me offer some testimony by a respected Spanish theologian. When Franco was still the ruler of Spain, Father Casiano Floristan exercised his ministry and shared his life with Catholic socialist workers in Madrid. At an editorial meeting of *Concilium*, the international Catholic theological review, to which he and I then belonged, he was asked how his Catholic workers differed from the atheist socialists with whom they shared the same struggle. After a long reflection this was Floristan's reply. First, the Catholic workers had a greater sense of humour because they retained a certain distance from their social engagement. Since ultimate struggle had been won by Jesus Christ, their own historical struggle was only penultimate. Second, the Catholic workers were less crushed by the failure of their common action. Because they evaluated their struggle in terms not of success but of fidelity, they were often able to cheer up their atheist comrades. Third, when their spies in the police force informed them that the next day large numbers of labour activists would be arrested, the Catholic workers gathered at night for the eucharist to celebrate a victory that could not be taken away from them. As they gathered around the holy table singing and playing the guitar, their atheist friends stood in the back because they liked the music.

In this account, the Gospel creates more than personal religious motivation for the common struggle. It creates a mood, an attitude, a culture that will find expression in the practical decisions made by this community.

Milbank wrongly accuses liberation theology of embracing a 'liberal' notion of freedom. Liberation theology is well aware that Christian freedom is not an empty freedom from interference that allows people to please themselves, but a coded freedom that enables people to overcome evil, do good and create conditions of justice. Liberation theology does not use the term 'autonomy' because it is keenly aware of human interdependence. Liberation theologians, moreover, recognize the temptation of the oppressed to envy their oppressor, the wish to conquer him and to put themselves in his place. That is why liberation theology characterizes the new society not in terms of the power exercised by the formerly oppressed (such as the dictatorship of the proletariate) but rather in ethical terms of participation and social and economic justice.

*

Let us now return to the two currents of theology analyzed by Milbank. The first, which he endorses, is based on an 'exclusivist christology' which holds that the supernatural heals, elevates and fulfills the natural only among Christians, only in the Church. The second current, which Milbank rejects and I hold, is based on an 'inclusivist christology,' holding that God's self-communication in Jesus Christ reveals that the summons of divine grace is extended not only to Christians but to people everywhere as they wrestle with issues of truth and justice. It is not my intention to defend this christology, to show that it is rooted in certain biblical texts or in a stream within the Catholic tradition, nor to demonstrate that since Vatican Council II it has been widely accepted in Roman Catholicism. What I wish to do instead is to raise some questions about Milbank's exclusivist christology.

Because of his christology, Milbank looks upon the cultural, religious and philosophical traditions outside the Church in terms of their sin and blindness. This is not done lightly. He offers extended philosophical analyses revealing that these traditions contained myths or meta-narratives that legitimated practices of oppression and thus generated violence. On these terms he discards the secular Enlightenment rationality in sociology and social theory, discards the tradition of classical reason, and discards—with postmodern thinkers—any form of universal reason and any claim of universal truth. The only exception to this is the claim of Jesus Christ, the divine breakthrough in human history, whose message of universal relevance inverts the violence of the world by his unique counter-practice of love, forgiveness and peace.

Yet, as mentioned previously, Milbank and the postmodern thinkers exaggerate the extent to which people's practices and ideas are constructed by the myth implicit in their cultural traditions. This exaggeration is derived from Emile Durkheim's structuralist imagination. In reality people live at the intersection of several orientations, some determined by their nature, others derived from stories and cultural tradition. If we look, for instance, at the practice of hospitality, a virtue widely modeled in many cultures and religions, inspired partly by a sense of mutual interdependence and partly by respect for human beings and compassion before human vulnerability. Elements of legitimate self-interest, cultural conformity, religious conviction and personal generosity (responsing to an inner call) co-exist in this magnificent practice, which Christians cannot but admire. Milbank's approach would oblige us to understand the practice of hospitality as an expression of the culture in which it is embedded and hence as a reflection of the culture's meta-narrative; which means that we would have to understand hospitality outside the Church as an expression of violence. Milbank, I emphasize, misconceives the constructed character of human existence.

What concerns me more is Milbank's practice. I am puzzled by his inability to marvel at goodness found beyond the community of believers. He seems to have no sense of 'the irony of the Gospel.' Like Jonah, John Milbank does not want to believe that God can be merciful to Niniveh.

Basing himself on postmodern theory and his exclusivist christology, Milbank rejects all dialogue across the boundaries of the Church. He regards dialogue accross cultural boundaries as a modern illusion. Why? Because such dialogue wrongly supposes that the partners in conversation share some boundary-transcending 'ratio' in common. In actual fact, the postmoderns argue, the partners belong to differently constructed cultural spheres that are incommensurable. Endorsing the postmodern position, Milbank argues that Christians cannnot act together with non-Christians in defense of a just cause because all practice is coded by the meta-narrative which guides it; hence the practice of non-believers, shaped by their religious or secular culture, will inevitably open the door to violence. Milbank argues that the Church's stance toward world religions should not be dialogue but suspicion.[4] In my opinion, to defend such a position in contemporary England troubled by racial, cultural and religious diversity creates a discourse that encourages violence.

This takes us to Milbank's fateful decision to shield the Church from the critiques of modernity issued by Marx, Freud, Nietzsche and many others. The critiques derived from secular reason, Milbank has argued, perpetuate the violence implicit in the Enlightenment project. What this committed pacifist fails to acknowledge is that Christian practice itself, almost from the beginning, contained dimensions of violence. Hidden at first, these were brought to light in the Church's subsequent history, in part because of outbursts of visible violence and in part because of the Enlightenment's critical rationality.

Symbolic of the dark side of Christian practice was the negation of Jewish existence (in action and theory) associated from the beginning with the proclamation of Jesus as Lord. In her study of Christian origins and the Church's subsequent preaching, Rosemary Ruether has called Christian antisemitism 'the left hand of christology.'[5] The violence present in the Christian meta-narrative escaped the attention of the Churches and their teachers for many centuries. It was only after the Holocaust that the Churches were forced to face the implications of their own linguistic practice about the Jews.

Christian practice and preaching were challenged by the Holocaust and, later, by the protest of nations colonized by Western empires and their Churches. These painful historical experiences revealed the ideology of domination implicit in Christian doctrine as traditionally understood. This unsettling discovery and the subsequent repentance created the spiritual context in which Karl Rahner and many other theologians developed their inclusivist christology. This teaching allowed Christians for the first time to honour Judaism, to respect other world religions, and to free themselves from the dangerous and death-dealing view that God loved only them.

John Milbank, a young man, belongs to a generation born after the Holocaust and, hence, not as profoundly challenged by it as was the older generation of theologians. Milbank's exclusivist christology re-introduces the traditional negation of Jewish existence into Christian theological discourse and interrupts the recent conversion of the Church to universal solidarity.

Throughtout his book Milbank reads history with the old Christian prejudices. When in his long treatment of St. Augustine he compares the Christian virtues with the pagan practices of the Empire, he does not recall the strange irony, often discussed in the literature, that in the year 388, when a Christian mob, led by a bishop, destroyed a synagogue in a city of Mesopotamia, Emperor Theodosius ordered that the synagogue be rebuilt by the bishop—for which he was severely reprimanded and threatened with excommunication by St. Ambrose, who wanted the civil laws protecting Jewish worship annulled.[6] Or again, when Milbank praises the 19th-century Catholic socialists who criticized capitalism on Christian, ethical grounds (and not, as the Marxists did, on grounds of its inner contradictions), he does not mention that the vision of a just, Christian society they entertained generated anti-Jewish resentment among the people who followed them.[7]

Milbank would probably argue that when he uses the word "Church," he has in mind the community that continues the practice of Jesus (the practice of love, forgiveness and peace) and that the Orthodox, Roman Catholic, Anglican and Protestant churches, have on the whole betrayed this practice, except for certain congregations and monasteries within them. Yet I do not accept this as an adequate reply. For the biblical tradition itself, including the books of the New Testament, contains an under-current of violence, of which Christians must become conscious and from which they can be delivered only if they are willing to enter into dialogue with emancipatory secular reason and listen to God's Word addressed to them through the voices of society's victims.

If Milbank had listened to the Enlightenment critics, he would have been forced to deal with a serious question regarding pacifism. Depth psychology has made us aware of the possibility that a self-willed pacifist commitment represses angry and hostile impulses that may eventually return in unexpected ways, especially in the form of paranoia. The ancient Christian hostility to Jewish religion may be a case in point. Milbank suffers from the illusion that it is possible to have a community defined *ad intra* by love and peace, but relates itself to people *ad extra* by distance and non-reception. This illusion is the theme of the novel, *Peace Shall Destroy Many*,[8] by Rudy Wiebe, the Canadian Mennonite author, which examines the harsh indifference of a Mennonite community to the Metis people living near them. To do penance for his own participation in this prejudice, Rudy Wiebe wrote two historical novels celebrating the courage and determination of Native heroes, Big Bear and Louis Riel.[9] The refusal to honour outsiders and the rejection of dialogue are damaging to members of the loving community. This principle has been grasped by the Mennonite Central Committee of Canada and the United States when they extended their ministry of justice and reconciliation to peoples in conflict anywhere in the world.

*

This takes me to my final point. I have the greatest hesitation to follow Milbank in his postmodern (and possibly radical

Protestant) repudiation of any universally shared values. My reasons are drawn not from classical metaphysics or secular reason, but from Christian doctrine and human experience.

According to the doctrine of creation, especially as understood in the Catholic tradition, humanity made in the image of God shares a common nature, not totally destroyed by sin, that is constantly addressed by God's healing and elevating grace. Hence people engaged in cross-cultural dialogue and cooperation should be able to discover common values. Is there any evidence for this?

In my opinion, postmodern thinkers exaggerate the constructed character of human existence, as if nothing were given and hence nothing were shared. Many modern thinkers, Marx included, also exaggerated the malleability of human nature, thinking that it can be radically transformed through revolutionary social change. It is true that infrastructural and cultural factors strongly influence people's behaviour, ideas and dreams, so that mutual understanding across boundaries is difficult. It is also true that attempts in Western civilization to formulate universally valid principles were inspired by a hidden intention of imposing a particular order upon the peoples of the world. Nevertheless, the difficulty of cross-cultural dialogue and the flawed historic search for universal values should not deter present efforts to find trans-cultural values. The inclusivist interpretation of the Gospel encourages Christians to expect that by cooperating with others to relieve human suffering, they will discover features of their common humanity.

This hope is confirmed by many human experiences. At first, outsiders seem strange to us, they seem to violate norms to which we attach great value; but as we engage in conversation and get to know them, we discover them as 'others,' as shaped by a different culture. Yet we can make this discovery only because we have learned to recognize in them spiritual resources of self-making that resemble our own and deserve respect. The recognition of 'otherness' and the respect for pluralism are therefore based on the conviction that we hold something in common. To give a simple example, people come to honour homosexuals as 'different' precisely as they discover the humanity they share with them.

There are reasons why I am not willing to abandon the ancient tradition of 'natural law.' This tradition is capable of transcending its Aristotelian origin. Built into human nature created and redeemed by God (following here an inclusive christology) is a law or orientation toward goodness that, discoverable in principle, is only partly known. This is the concept of natural law proposed by Vatican Council II. It says that in the depth of conscience, listening to an echo of God's voice, people detect a law they do not impose on themselves but which holds them to obedience, a law that summons them to do good and avoid evil and is fulfilled by the love of God and love of neighbour.[10] If I read this proposal correctly, natural law has a supernatural destiny. That is why the Council was able to make the bold assertion that Christians should join with other men and women in the search for ethical norms to solve difficult problems emerging in the lives of individuals and their social relations.

The orientation of human nature is partly known and partly hidden. The virtue of hospitality, so widely practiced in ancient cultures, manifested a sense of mutuality and respect for others that transcended the patterns of domination implicit in these same cultures. This virtue, I would argue, revealed the hidden law of human nature. Very often, the content of this law was discovered through historical struggles that demanded love, courage and sacrifice. Thus, slavery, recognized as a legitimate institution by the greater part of humanity, began to scandalize Quakers and humanitarians in the 18th century, and thanks to the cultural struggle and political action they initiated, modern society and the Christian Churches eventually became convinced that slavery was an abomination, a profoundly unethical institution that contradicted human dignity. I would argue that slavery had always been against the law of human nature, but that economic and cultural factors—in other words, structural sin—blinded people and prevented them from recognizing this. Thus again, it was only after the horrors of World War II that the nations of the world were capable of producing the Universal Declaration of Human Rights, confessing the belief that human dignity demanded the recognition of human rights, personal, collective and socio-economic. (These rights, we note, were not the Lockean rights of the liberal tradition!) Since Pope John XXIII, the Roman Catholic Church has accepted these human rights as part of the natural law. I propose that universal human values—the as yet partially hidden orientation of human nature—are being recognized as different cultures enter into conversation with one another, guided by the option for the poor. Such a joint quest may well be opposed by powerful forces in these cultures. It is possible that a time will come, or will never come, when the subordination of women and the competitive logic of capitalism will be recognized by society as contrary to the natural law.

*

In this essay I have supported several themes in John Milbank's theology: the primacy assigned to practice, the identification of Jesus with a practice of love, forgiveness and peace; the essential Christian orthodoxy (Incarnation and Trinity); the integralist understanding of divine grace; the ethical critique of modernity including capitalist economics; and the spiritual resistance against postmodern nihilism. What I have criticized in Milbank's theology is his exclusivist christology; his postmodern, non-dialectical negation of Enlightenment rationality; and his unsympathetic, I believe mistaken reading, of liberation theology. I insist against Milbank that the Church must be open to its critics, whether they be the victims of society or the modern masters of suspicion, and more than this, that the biblical tradition itself will unfold its full meaning and power only through critical interactions of this kind. But I feel united with John Milbank because I share his conviction that Christian life today demands resistance to society.

Notes

1. John Milbank, *Theology and Social Theory: Beyond Secular Reason*, Oxford, England and Cambridge, MA: Basil Blackwell, 1990, 436 pages.

2. Gregory Baum, *Man Becoming*, New York: Herder and Herder, 1971, p. 67.

3. Cf. James McGinnis, *Solidarity with the People of Nicaragua*, Maryknoll, N.Y.: Orbis Books, 1985, pp. 124-127.

4. John Milbank, "The End of Dialogue," in *Christian Uniqueness Reconsidered,* ed. Gavin D'Costa, Maryknoll, N.Y.: Orbis Books, 1990, pp. 174-191, 190.

5. Rosemary Ruether, *Faith and Fraticide: The Theological Roots of Antisemitism,* New York: Seabury Press, 1974.

6. Edward Flannery, *The Anguish of the Jews,* New York: Paulist Press, 1985, p. 60.

7. Paul Misner, *Social Catholicism in Europe,* New York: Crossroad, 1991, pp. 174, 181, 203, 231, 234-237, 263.

8. Rudy Wiebe, *Peace Shall Destroy Many,* Toronto: McClelland and Stewart, 1962.

9. Rudy Wiebe, *The Temptations of Big Bear,* Toronto: McClelland and Stewart, 1973 and *Scorched Wood People,* Toronto: McClelland and Stewart, 1977.

10. *Guadium et spes,* n. 16, *The Documents of Vatican II,* ed. W.M. Abott, New York: Herder and Herder, 1966, pp. 213-214.

4

Postmodern Discourse and Social Responsibility

Over the last decade and a half, Western society has witnessed many new trends in economic and cultural development. Generally recognized are the new internationalization of capital, the hegemony of the transnational organizations, the widening gap between rich and poor, the mass migrations of refugees, the failure of the communist economies and the crisis of Marxist theory. On the cultural level we observe a deep disappointment among progressive people at one time engaged in political struggles, who now believe that to change the orientation of society is impossible. These people mistrust the government, have no interest in political parties, shy away from supporting labour unions, doubt the validity of current social theories, and express their dissatisfaction with the existing welfare state. People feel powerless, imprisoned in immobile bureaucratic structures. Responding to this situation, many men and women turn to the pursuit of private happiness, to intimacy, art, poetry, religious meditation, and imaginative leisure.

This new situation has been interpreted in a variety of ways. In this article I wish to look at two different interpretations, both of which claim that Western society is moving from modernity to 'postmodernity.' Because I disagree with the 'postmodern' discourse developed by certain French philosophers, I intend to devote the greater part of the article to them. I shall only make a few remarks about the other perception of 'postmodernity,' developed by certain American authors, for which I have a good deal of sympathy. What interests me throughout this inquiry is the ethico-political implications of these theories of postmodernity.

Over sixty years ago Ernst Troeltsch studied the political meaning implicit in the periodization of history.[1] He recognized that the judgement that a certain historical period is over and a new one has begun has far-reaching cultural and societal implications. Why? Because the periodization assigns certain attitudes and approaches to the past and encourages their replacement by an alternative perspective.

Two Meanings of 'Post-industrial'

To illustrate the political implications of the 'post' designation, I wish to mention two distinct meanings which sociologists have given the term 'post-industrial.'

According to Daniel Bell, we are moving toward a 'post-industrial society.'[2] Since the problems of government and management are increasingly becoming matters of science, technology and administrative know-how, we witness a societal process that gives singular power to the emerging 'knowledge class': technical experts, engineers, managers. According to Bell, gone is the old class conflict between owners and workers, gone the endless ideological debate between liberals defending the owners and socialists supporting the workers. He argues that political democracy and welfare capitalism have created a society based on universal consensus that grants all citizens access to material goods and personal dignity. The power of the new 'knowledge class' is not dominative, it does not divide society along class lines, it simply provides technical solutions for the problems of government and industry. Post-industrial society, largely freed from poverty, inequality and conflict—the classless society—will foster the creation of warm human relations and imaginative elevations of the spirit.

Alain Touraine's perspective is different. He agrees that society is gradually becoming 'post-industrial.'[3] Because capital is increasingly invested in services, automation and management, no longer in labour-intensive production, we observe the creation of a new 'knowledge class' and the declining importance of the working class. Touraine agrees with Bell that the new class of technical experts exercises enormous power in society; but according to Touraine this new power, guided by technological reason alone, steers the entire social order toward the 'programmed society,' the ultimate technocratic prison. Touraine here takes up Max Weber's warning that modernity is moving the human community toward 'the iron cage,' and the Frankfurt School's indictment that the domination of instrumental reason pushes us all into the constraints of the 'fully administered society.'

Touraine, unlike Bell, finds no emerging consensus in the present condition. For Touraine the contradictions of contemporary capitalism do not generate the class struggle between owners and workers, as did industrial capitalism. Instead the present contradictions affect people on all levels of society. The giant industrial corporations, run by teams of technocrats, threaten growing crowds of people by the creation of unemployment reaching into the middle class; by arms production and the preparation for war; by the ecological damage they inflict on the earth; and by the patterns of exclusion they generate, marginalizing groups that refuse to conform to technocratic cultural expectations— such as Native peoples, women, artists, religious people, and races that have been so damaged by Western rationality that they are suspicious of technocracy. Touraine argues that the post-industrial social struggle is no longer defined by the working class and the existing political parties—these belonged to industrial society—but by the social movements emerging in civil society, protesting against the rule of the technocrats—such as the movements for alternative economic development, for the emancipation of women, for peace, for nuclear-free space, for ecological balance, for the overcoming of racism and the rights of Native peoples.

It is easy to see that these two theories of 'post-industrial society' reveal distinct political orientations. Bell's theory legitimates contemporary capitalism while Touraine's challenges it and acts as a guide for organized social struggle. As we shall see, these two sociological analyses become paradigmatic for two distinct theories of postmodernity, one defined by French philosophers in line with the ideas of Daniel Bell, the other proposed by American thinkers in line with the perspective of Alain Touraine.

The Post-Modern Condition

Important in the field of philosophy are undoubtedly the learned French theories of postmodernity. They have their equivalent in North America in high philosophy and in sociological reflection. In this article I wish to examine Jean-Francois Lyotard's book *The Postmodern Condition.*[4] (References to this book will be given in the text itself.) To help me understand this original philosophical essay, I have consulted Jean Baudrillard's *In the Shadow of the Silent Majority,*[5] a book to which Lyotard himself refers (p. 90, n. 55); and relied on interpretations offered in the *Canadian Journal of Political and Social Theory.*[6] What interests me especially in reading *The Postmodern Condition* is how the author understands the human condition in the contemporary world.

For Lyotard and Baudrillard, contemporary capitalism has transcended its own history. It has achieved a self-perpetuating stability. Organized in giant transnational corporations, the world economy is guided by management teams that operate on purely technical, value-free, scientific grounds. Science, as we shall see, becomes simply information. What follows is that the world economic system, geared toward maintaining and improving its performance, no longer has an historical subject. No person, no groups of persons, no governments are able to assume responsibility for its orientation. The economy has become subjectless.

'Modern' social thought, the two French philosophers argue, assumed that people were responsible for their society; that humanity had a historical destiny; and that relying on technical and emancipatory reason, people could influence the orientation of their history. Postulating the self-transcendence of capitalism, postmodern thought regards 'society,' 'reason,' and 'history' as 'modern' illusions. They do not exist. The nations and their governments are so caught up in the self-perpetuating economic system that 'societies' have become loosely connected collectivities unable to act in solidarity. Correspondingly, governments have become powerless to make significant decisions regarding the course of their societies.

History too is a modern illusion. The postmodern age spells the end of all the great stories, *les grands récits.* "I define 'post-modern,' " Lyotard writes, "as incredulity toward meta-narratives" (p. xxiv). Discarded is the biblical story revealing the divine destiny of humankind. More directly, Lyotard and Baudrillard attack the two great narratives born of the Enlightenment. First the 'liberal story' of cultural and/or biological evolution. This story, regarded as scientifically verifiable, demanded people's rational cooperation and foretold the movement of history toward ever greater progress. Then came the 'Marxist story' of dialectics and revolution. It also claimed the support of science. This story inspired the trust that the contradictions of society would give birth to new, transcendent forms and thus carry history toward the classless, reconciled society. In particular, Lyotard argues against the Evolutionary Functionalism of Talcot Parsons and Nicholas Luhmann on the right and the Critical Theory of the Frankfurt School on the left (pp. 12-14), including Habermas's universal pragmatics (pp. 60-67). The postmodern condition, Lyotard argues, reveals that not only is there no history, but only one day after another, but also that there is no universal reason.

Why this postmodern hostility toward reason? The French philosophers believe that the Enlightenment, inspired as it was by the power of scientific and emancipatory reason, has brought forth the great totalitarian systems of the 20th century, not only Hitlerism and Stalinism but also the colonial domination of Western reason on non-European peoples and even upon alternative cultural spheres within Europe itself. The claim that reason has universal relevance, they argue, is incipiently totalitarian.

This hostility toward reason makes the philosophical work of these French thinkers difficult to read. In a long conversation between Lyotard and a philosophical colleague, later published as *Just Gaming,* Lyotard says that he does not like to answer questions that ask him to clarify his thought.[7] He feels there is something violent in such questions: they try to foist an intellectual framework on him at odds with his own orientation. Lyotard is suspicious of the 'dialogue' modern thinkers value so highly.

Why? Because dialogue presupposes the 'modern' illusion that the partners are united by a common *ratio*. Lyotard is consistent when he complains that for an author, readers are really a great nuisance.[8] Writing, for Lyotard, is putting a message into a bottle and throwing it into the sea.[9]

A Canadian journal, which since 1984 understands itself as an interpreter of postmodernism, has presented the self-transcendence of capitalism as a tragic event, the great catastrophe.[10] This journal has lamented the loss of 'society,' 'history,' and 'reason.' By contrast, the two French philosophers do not seem to be dejected. They regard the arrival of the postmodern condition as a kind of liberation. The reason for this we shall see further on.

Let us return for a moment to the supposedly self-transcendent capitalism. So great is the cultural power of the forces that sustain our material existence that the nature of science itself has changed. Since science facilitates the smooth operation of the system, science has become purely and simply information. Information enables the teams of experts to make the necessary managerial decisions. Postmodern science no longer asks questions, it no longer argues about appropriate paradigms. It simply feeds the self-transcending system what it needs for its operation. Since computers respond to information only if it has been translated into signs, the task of postmodern science is to deliver signs.

Lyotard and Baudrillard recognize that this information, these signs, are available only to those who can pay for them. Postmodern science is subject to market forces. Under the conditions of postmodernity, the signs that run the great material support system have become commodities.

Conversely, Baudrillard argues, commodities in contemporary society are treasured less for their material benefits than for their sign value. The food we eat, the clothes we wear and the houses we live in do much more than support and protect our bodies, they actually define the standing, the honour, and even the pleasure we enjoy in society. Beer commercials make beer create our happiness. While signs (information) are transformed into commodities, commodities are being transformed into signs.[11]

Because of this fusion it is no longer possible to distinguish between what is real and what is constructed by the imagination. Which of the following alternative is real? The event taking place in a distant country, or its representation on television in our homes? This question touches a theme dear to postmodern thought: the line between fiction and reality is not clearly drawn. Fiction becomes reality.

Irreducible Pluralism of Truth

What happens to the people living in the framework produced by the giant self-transcendent economic system? People are not totally shaped by contemporary commodity culture. Lyotard argues against the claim made by a great number of sociologists that the predominance of the market has turned people into individualists, egotistically concerned with their own satisfaction and self-promotion. Lyotard thinks that under the conditions of postmodernity people actually seek associations and social networks—'clouds of sociality' as he calls them (p. xxiv). What is taking place is a certain re-tribalization of society, except that the boundaries that define these tribes are constantly shifting. As the old loyalties of marriage, family, church and nation break down, new associative patterns are created, unstable in form, generating cultural creativity. Lyotard takes the image of the tribe, I think, not so much from the sphere of ethnic or religious identity, as from the plural world of aesthetic pleasure and creativity. Let a thousand flowers bloom! Cultural pluralism is the promise of postmodernity.

Baudrillard speaks ironically of the stupid and insensitive masses who refuse to listen to rational argument, whether they be offered by the functional rationality characteristic of the capitalist mega-machine or by the critical rationality adopted by the politicians of the left. Yet this 'stupidity', Baudrillard argues, is their glory and the source of their freedom.[12] What the people, the masses, really desire is drama, celebration and conviviality. Football matches and rock festivals involve and excite them more than utilitarian goals and much more than the idea, foisted upon them by the left, that they are the subjects of their history. Post-modern thought liberates people to pursure their dreams and explore their imagination. It gives contemporary builders permission to move from sober, functional, cement-and-glass architecture to baroque structures of playful decorativeness.

In this context we take note that for Lyotard 'scientific knowledge' is not the only form knowledge. He also recognizes what he calls 'narrative knowledge' (pp 18-23). While the great narratives, with their claim to universality, have broken down, there exist a multitude of small narratives generated by the particular experiences of the plural tribes. Each tribe tells its own story, interprets its own world. 'Modern' thought presupposed that these different discourses were related to one another by an underlying *ratio* or *logos*, and that for this reason open dialogue would bring mutual understanding and a certain rational consensus. Postmodern thought recognizes that there is no meta-discourse, no *logos*, no universal reason. The different language games are incommensurable. They share no common ground.

The uninitiated reader will object that since these various discourses refer to a givenness beyond themselves, this given reality should be able to summon forth a certain rational consensus. Yet postmodern thought insists that these multiple language games are self-referential: they do *not* refer to a reality beyond themselves but simply order the world of their own making, facilitate communication between members of the tribe, and remain open to ongoing redefinition. The various language games are hetero-morphic. There is no meta-truth.

Again, the line between truth and fiction is no longer clearly drawn. When a pathological patient complains of pains in his legs and the doctor assures him that nothing is physically wrong with his body, is the pain real or is it fictitious? Or is it both? The piece of world we live in is created by discourse, signs and symbols. For Lyotard, even scientific knowledge is self-referential: it constitutes the piece of world that it knows.

If I understand them correctly, the postmodern thinkers look upon this incommensurable cultural pluralism as a source of human liberation. Freed from the illusion that they are responsible for their society and could affect its orientation, and delivered from the bad conscience that this illusion creates, people are now able to recover their poetic imagination, explore their hidden dreams, transform their tribe into an orchestra, and live their lives creatively—all of this, of course, in the limited, free space left by the subjectless mega-economy.

In this affirmation of pluralism, postmodern thinkers even welcome the return of religion, as long as it is not monotheistic and makes no claim on history. People love the trans-rational and the mysterious, they like rituals and sacred texts, they are attracted by otherness, by whatever transcends the logic of the economic mega-machine. Yet for the postmodern generation, celebrations of the sacred are simply self-referential as is every other language game. Postmodern culture rejoices in polytheism. In this perspective, biblical monotheism appears intrinsically violent: it provides the *ratio* for totalitarian domination.

The shift to the postmodern has been interpreted in various ways. A Quebec social scientist, Daniel Salée, understands the shift as a return to the poets. Deeply disappointed that the historical struggle for self-determination and social solidarity, begun in Quebec's Quiet Revolution, has ended in failure and is now being replaced by economic competition for upward mobility, Quebec intellectuals have lost confidence in political reason. Where will they find inspiration now? Are there resources for spiritual renewal? Postmodern thought, Daniel Salée argues, sends Quebec intellectuals back to the poets.[13]

Temptations for the Church

That the human world is constructed by the meaning we attach to our multiple interactions is a theory elaborated decades ago by a sociological school called Symbolic Interactionism, strongly represented in America. Lyotard refers specifically (p. 90, no. 60) to Erving Goffman's *The Presentation of Self in Everyday Life* (1959). Also comes to mind the well-known book by Peter Berger and Thomas Luckmann, *The Social Construction of Reality* (1966). It is in fact possible to read a later work of Peter Berger, *The Homeless Mind* (1973), as an American sociological theory that has an affinity with French postmodern thought. Berger argues that the economic and political mega-structures of society are here to stay. They follow a scientific logic of their own. Even though the mega-structures treat us in a wholly impersonal way, cause us some agony, and undermine our rootedness in tradition—'the homeless mind'—it would be unrealistic to hope that society could be changed. We are simply stuck with the present mega-system. What people have to do to save their humanity, Berger argues, is to create 'mediating structures' around special interests—Lyotard's tribes with flexible boundaries—where people are able to cultivate interpersonal relations and dedicate themselves to non-utilitarian values such as art, leisure, religion or ethnicity. These mediating structures, fashioned in the interstices of the mega-society, can become islands of happiness and human growth.

Peter Berger, a church-going Christian, recognized that his analysis had important pastoral implications. He argued that in the 60s and 70s the churches, Catholic and Protestant, lost their nerve. They made a major mistake when they emphasized social and economic justice, articulated a critique of capitalism, and urged the faithful to become politically engaged. This pastoral policy, Berger thought, was based on the illusion, encouraged by dreamers of the left, that the mega-structures in which we live could actually be transformed. What the churches should do to respond to people's needs, Berger argues, is to understand their parishes and congregations as 'mediating structures,' as networks of interpersonal relations, that allow people to save and foster their own humanity.[14]

French postmodern theory discussed in this article also has pastoral implications. Postmodern discourse on the return to religion could easily tempt the churches to integrate the new perspective into their pastoral policies. Some Catholic thinkers already argue that the Church's reading of the Gospel as a call to social justice and solidarity with the poor was based on specifically 'modern' presuppositions.[15] Catholic social teaching and liberation theology, it is argued, attached great importance to 'society,' 'history' and 'reason,' and in doing so became a victim of the modern illusion. Instead of weaning Christian people from

their popular pieties and imposing on them a more rational, politically responsible and biblically tested spirituality, the Church
should now welcome the pluralism of devotions and the many
forms of popular religion, even if they do not always share a common theological *ratio*. If Catholicism could sanctify postmodern
polytheism, the churches would fill up again.

Arguments and Refutations

How do I evaluate Lyotard's postmodern theory? What interests me here is the sociological dimension of his proposal. The
reader's first impression is that postmodern theory provides an
ideology defending, neo-conservative economics and culture with
emphasis on aesthetics, intimacy, and spirituality—and its indifference to social inequality and the suffering of others. Postmodern theory has certainly been used to foster the de-politization of
culture. I have just given an example from the theological field.
Yet it would be wrong to think that Lyotard and Baudrillard have
right-wing sympathies and are indifferent to social justice.

In conversation with a philosophical colleague, published
under the title *Just Gaming*, Lyotard confesses his social passion.
He stands against totalitarianism, he defends personal freedom
and collective self-determination. When asked whether 'social justice discourse' is just another language game, he replies in the
negative. He is deeply convinced that social justice required that
the French leave Algeria and the Americans Vietnam. When
asked on what grounds he is so certain, he admits that he cannot
defend his conviction philosophically. He just knows. He speaks
here of 'transcendence,' while refusing to tell us what he means
by this term.[16]

Postmodern theory, I conclude, may not be passed off as an
ideology of the economic right. It deserves to be taken seriously
and to be debated. As I mentioned at the beginning of this article, the postmodern thinkers have put their finger on several new
trends in contemporary society. But do these trends justify the
proclamation of a new age, the postmodern age?

Let me outline several arguments demonstrating that the postmodern theory outlined above is misleading. The reader will note that I limit my critique to Lyotard and Baudrillard's postmodernism since it stands or falls with their specific interpretation of capitalism.

First, trends, even strong trends, do not constitute the entire reality. The two French philosophers exaggerate when they present contemporary capitalism as a subjectless, self-transcending, economic mega-machine. There are in fact qualitative differences between the free-enterprise capitalism of the United States, the social democratic capitalism of the European Economic Community, the government-sponsored capitalism of Japan, and the dependent capitalism of Third World countries. These differences are caused by historical conditions, cultural legacies, and economic and political options made by people individually and collectively. It is not quite true, therefore, that contemporary capitalism is a subjectless world system.

Second, the analysis presented by the French philosophers does not take into account the destabilizing elements of contemporary capitalism. The orientation toward greater automation creates unemployment, impoverishes ever more people, promotes crime and destabilizes society. The deep involvement of capitalism in military production and nuclear weapons fosters the outbreak of armed hostilities. The thrust toward continuing industrial growth exhausts limited natural resources, pollutes the atmosphere and bodies of water, and attacks the ecological conditions of human survival. And since a labour market of low-status people ready to work for low wages is still useful for the development of the economy, capitalism continues to rely on the low status assigned to women and on the subjugation of other races. Postmodern thought pays no attention to these de-stabilizing factors nor to the reactions of peoples who are damaged by the economic mega-machine. This aspect of contemporary capitalism, we recall, was brought out in the work of Alain Touraine. We shall return to this topic.

Third, the French philosophers analyse the present economic order in the most general terms. They show no interest in more detailed, empirical studies to test whether their theory can be falsified. This is all the more curious since the theory that contemporary capitalism has become subjectless holds a central place in their philosophy. The reader has the impression that the two authors have inherited from their Marxist background, despite all disclaimers, a love for grand theory and totalizing explanations. It is somewhat ironic that authors who proclaim the end of universal reason should make such universal claims.

Questionable is also the theory defending the absence of a common *ratio* among the various allegedly postmodern networks and communities. One of the important experiences of the last three or four decades has been the impact of dialogue and cooperation on the creation of a common ground. This experience has been overwhelming for persons involved in the ecumenical movement and inter-religious dialogue. It is true that tensions have recently emerged among cultural, political and religious communities, affecting even the Christian churches, but these tensions are largely caused by factors such as fear, scarcity and the inequality of power. On the material level, collectivities fear that there is not enough land or resources or jobs to go around. And on the cultural and spiritual level, collectivities worry that widening the common ground may weaken their communal identities. These factors distort the dialogue. There is much evidence, however, that dialogue freed of these distortions continues to uncover common ground. This is particularly true when groups of different national, cultural and spiritual origin stand together against the disruptions caused by the dominant system—militarization, ecological damage and the multiple forms of apartheid.

This simple reflection leads us to reject the postmodern theory that the discourses of these communities are simply self-referential and that there is no reality by which they can be tested and found true or false. The theory may be valid for discourses such as poetry, literature, art and music—this is an interesting philosophical question. But the postmodern theory becomes absurd when we apply it to the many dangers which threaten humankind at this time. Here our speech is tested and judged by that to which it refers. Hunger, we note, is a discourse-transcending reality, so is AIDS, so is torture and assassination by death squads.

The postmodern philosophical theory that people create their world, including themselves, simply through discourse, is unconvincing. It appears as a one-sided proposal designed to overcome an earlier one-sided, Marxist proposal that people create their world, including themselves, through labour. Both proposals contain an element of truth. I recognize the power of speech and symbols to constitute universes of meaning. But there are also other, material powers at work. Discourse creates worlds of meaning, but discourse is also judged by its impact on the material conditions of life.

For example, discourse on AIDS has two dimensions, one self-referential, creating a saner universe of meaning for those affected by the virus, and the other political, affecting society and its government. This latter discourse must be judged by whether it promotes or stifles respect, compassion and society's willingness to spend more money on medical research and the care of the sick.

It is ironic that postmodern theory recalls philosophical ideas developed in the 19th-century. Many European thinkers then rejected the rational Enlightenment and wrestled against the universal claim of reason and its power to emancipate human beings. Theologians think here especially of Soren Kierkegaard, who died in 1855. At a later period, an ambiguous philosophical theory called historicism upheld the incommensurability of cultural traditions, the absence of a universal *logos,* and the irrational, voluntaristic origin of values. Ernst Troeltsch, whom I mentioned earlier, criticized this relativistic theory as 'bad historicism' and tried to replace it by a form of historicism that recognized the reconciling power of dialogue and cooperation.[17] Denying the existence of universal norms of justice, 'bad historicism' proposed that the place in history taken by a collectivity depended on its will to power. This historicism belonged to the intellectual background of German fascism.

The French postmodern thinkers, it must be said immediately, oppose the dangerous right-wing movement in contemporary France. Still, their complete rejection of the Enlightenment disturbs me. The Frankfurt School's radical critique of the Enlightenment, offered in the 20s, distinguished between two dimension of the modern emancipatory *ratio:* 'scientific-instrumental reason' and 'ethical-substantive reason.'[18] The Frankfurt School claimed that in the 19th-century, Enlightenment reason collapsed into instrumental reason. The emancipatory project has turned out to be the technological, bureaucratic, de-personalizing society. The paradigm of contemporary Enlightenment thought is domination or mastery. According to the Frankfurt School, the Enlightenment spirit has become an obstacle to humanization and emancipation. The rule of instrumental reason must be rejected.

Yet the Frankfurt philosophers did not reject the original inspiration of the Enlightenment. Emancipation, human rights, participation, equality and fraternity still define the social project for which the oppressed and the marginalized yearn. The Frankfurt School thinkers called for the de-centering of scientific-instrumental reason and the retrieval of repressed or forgotten ethical-substantive reason.

Postmodern thought defines itself against the critical theory of the Frankfurt School. Because Enlightenment culture has been reduced to scientific mastery and technocratic domination, postmodern thinkers mistrust the modern aspirations toward emancipation and participation.

How are we to understand this? For whom are the postmodern thinkers writing their theory? Do they wish to calm down the Native peoples in the Americas? Are they counseling patience and longsuffering to the marginalized in society? No, not at all. These philosophers desire freedom for all men and women. Perhaps we should take literally their claim that tribal discourse is purely self-referential. Postmodern theory may simply be the language game for a network of intellectuals and artists who, deeply disappointed by the failure of the left, create for themselves a non-political world of plural meaning where there is room for their wishes, thoughts and inspirations.

A Different Meaning of Post-modern

At the end of this article I must mention, even if in briefest fashion, another, different theory of postmodernity, one that in my opinion deserves attention and sympathy. This theory recalls the social analysis of Alain Touraine, even though it is mainly proposed—according to the impression I have—by American thinkers who may not be familiar with his writings at all.

In 'industrial society,' Touraine had argued, the contradictions of capitalism generated class conflict between owners and workers. The struggle for emancipation then relied on working class solidarity, labour unions, socialist or social democratic parties, and the interventions of progressive governments. Touraine called present society 'post-industrial' because the contradictions of today's capitalist system adversely affect the population as a whole: centralization, militarization, ecological damage, inflexible bureaucratization, chronic unemployment, the continued need for low-status workers (women, people of colour) willing to work for low wages, etc. In today's struggle for emancipation, the older industrial formations have largely lost their relevance. People struggling for justice have lost interest in political parties, they lament the narrow limits of working class solidarity, and no longer trust the administration of the welfare state.

The new developments, according to Touraine, are the social changes generated by the contradictions of society—movements for peace, for feminism, for ecological balance, for alternative models of economic development, for collective self-determination of colonized people, etc. Here the 'enemy' is not capitalism as such but the rule of technocracy in government and in large, privately-owned corporations. The post-industrial conditions set civil society against the technocrats. In today's world, these social movements bear the promise of emancipation. They are the agents of social change, they may become the levers of history.

What is new in these movements, Touraine argues, is that they create bonds of friendship and solidarity among their members. They free people from the cultural power of technocracy, create community and friendship, and thus exercise a humaniz-

ing function, even if the movements are still far away from transforming society. In a certain sense the social movements are their
own end. They are laying the cultural and spiritual foundation
for a new society.

This analysis points to the 'green' movement in Western society. There are green parties, green lobbies, green philosophies,
and green communal organization. Greens exist in many shades.
But this analysis also points to more recent efforts that promote
alternative economic development in regions suffering from impoverishment.

Several American theologians, sympathetic to the green
movement and an alternative economy, have decided to speak of
the end of modern society and the dawning of the 'postmodern'
age. Let me mention Harvey Cox's *Religion in the Secular City*[19]
with its subtitle, *Toward a Postmodern Theology*,[20] Diogenes Allen's
Christian Belief in a Postmodern World, and Joe Holland's *The Postmodern Cultural Earthquake.*[21] There is no agreed upon definition
of what 'postmodern' means. Yet these authors are convinced
that an important cultural shift is taking place in certain sectors
of contemporary society, a cultural shift related to the human
damage caused by capitalism and state socialism, the oppression
of the bureaucratic state, the false trust in modern rationality,
and the absence of spirituality. They believe that the new culture
being born is open to religion.

We note, however, that these postmodern theologians (as
well as green thinkers and activists) greatly treasure the idea of
emancipation, social transformation and participation. They are
committed to universal solidarity. They wish to mobilize the
population, strengthen new currents, and influence the course of
history. Thus in the terminology of the French postmodernists,
these thinkers are still thoroughly 'modern,' still hold people responsible for their world, still trust some great story of salvation,
and still dream of changing the social order.

In my opinion, serious dialogue with the green movement is
of great importance for social theorists and theologians. Yet I
wonder how useful it is to apply the term 'postmodern' to the
green perspective. The green movement follows a utopian inspiration, appreciates the wisdom of non-Western societies, and lis-

tens to the victims of industrial society; at the same time it also relies on interdisciplinary research involving all the sciences, from sociology and economics to biology and agronomy. To determine whether a certain fertilizer is toxic or not is a scientific task. Is it helpful, then, to call the green movement postmodern?

Notes

1. Ernst Troeltsch, *Der Historismus und seine Probleme*, Tübingen: J.C.B. Mohr, 1922, pp. 730-56.

2. Daniel Bell, *The Coming of Post-Industrial Society*, Harmondsworth: Penguin, 1976.

3. Alain Touraine, *Production de la société*, Paris: Seuil, 1973 (trans. as *The Self-Production of Society*, University of Chicago Press, 1977) and *La voix et le regard*, Paris: Seuil, 1978 (trans. as *The Voice and the Eye*, Cambridge University Press, 1981).

4. Jean-Francois Lyotard, *La condition postmoderne*, Paris: Minuit, 1979 (trans. as *The Postmodern Condition*, Manchester University Press, 1986).

5. Jean Baudrillard, *A l'ombre des majorités silencieuses, ou la fin du social*, Fontenay-sous-bois: Cahiers Utopie 4, 1978, (trans. as *In the Shadow of the Silent Majority*, New York: Semiotexte, 1983.

6. See especially vol. 8 (1984), no. 1-2, and vol. 9 (1985), no. 3.

7. Jean-Francois-Loup Thébaud, *Just Gaming*, University of Minnesota Press, 1985 (orig. *Au juste*, Paris: Christian Bourgeons, 1979) p. 7.

8. Ibid., p. 8.

9. Ibid., p. 5, 6.

10. See especially Charles Levin, Arthur Kroker, "Baudriallard's Challenge," and Andrew Wernick, "Sign and Commodity: Aspects of the Cultural Dynamic of Advanced Capitalism," *Canadian Journal of Political and Social Theory*, 8 (1984), pp. 5-16, 17-34.

11. Jean Baudrillard, *In the Shadow of the Silent Majorities*, pp. 26-27.

12. Ibid., pp. 12-15.

13. Daniel Salée, "Pour une autopsie de l'imaginaire québécois: regards sur la morosité postmoderne," *Canadian Journal of Political and Social Theory*, 10 (1986), pp. 114-123.

14. For a critique of Berger's theory and his theological application, see G. Baum, "Peter Berger's Unfinished Symphony," in G. Baum, ed., *Sociological and Human Destiny*, New York: Seabury, 1980, pp. 110-129.

15. Cf. Jean Remy, "Revalorisation de la religion populaire et recomposition du champ religieux," *Recherches sociologiques*, 18 (no. 2, 1987), 163-83.

16. Cf. *Just Gaming*, pp. 69-71.

17. Cf. G. Baum, "Historical Truth According to Ernst Troeltsch," *The Social Imperative*, New York: Paulist Press, 1979, pp. 231-254, 246.

18. Max Horkheimer & Theodor Adorno, *Dialectic of the Enlightenment*, New York: Herder and Herder, 1972. Also Martin Jay, *The Dialectical Imagination*, Boston: Little, Brown & Comp., 1973, "The Critique of the Enlightenment," pp. 253-280.

19. New York: Simon and Shuster, 1984.

20. Louisville, KY: Westminster/John Knox Press, 1989.

21. Washington, DC: Center of Concern, 1985.

5

Allan Bloom: The Separation of Truth and Love

When Allan Bloom's *The Closing of the American Mind* (New York: Simon & Schuster, 1987) became a best-seller, I was invited by a group of university chaplains to give a lecture on this book, seeing that it dealt with the vocation of the intellectual life and the role of the university in America. I had heard that Bloom was a conservative thinker. When I began to read his book I did find certain conservative themes that on the surface had an affinity with the Catholic tradition. But as I moved into the philosophical centre of the book, the exposition of John Locke's political theory, I realized that Allan Bloom belonged to a rare species of consistent liberals who still defended radical, rational individualism and whose ethics was purely and simply enlightened self-interest.

It is elegantly written in parts. It is clever, sometimes even entertaining. It offers bold interpretations of the great philosophers. The author is often outrageous. Yet while I enjoyed reading the book, I realized that its impact on universities and public culture would be reactionary. Allan Bloom, as I shall show, promotes an elitist intellectualism, opposed to compassion and indifferent to justice. Intelligence militates against solidarity. Thus *The Closing of the American Mind* strengthens the contemporary 'neo-conservative' culture that seeks to reconcile us with inequality and makes us deaf to the voices of those who suffer.

The Theoretical Life

At the outset the book is critical of present-day American universities and the ideas they pass on to their students, ideas still influenced by 'the soft-minded thinkers' who gained power in the 60s. The intellectual imperative is to be 'open.' Students are encouraged to recognize cultural pluralism and accept the relativity of values. Education no longer fosters the search for truth. Truth has become old-fashioned. Truth supposedly prevents one from being open. What education fosters is the collapse of all norms that claim universal validity. The university has come to encourage the view that people live according to values they chose and that different cultures and different life-styles are all equally valid.

Bloom laments the decline of the intellectual life. Students are not initiated into the search for truth. Universities no longer communicate the profound experience of the intellectual adventure. Modern intellectuals, Bloom argues, no longer respect what he calls 'the theoretical life,' i.e., the *'vita contemplativa'* of the classical tradition. Utilitarianism and superficial thinking have come to dominate the academy. Bloom deplores the influence of idealism, the idea that reality is all in the mind, and he rejects the approach to philosophy that begins with epistemology. With the classical tradition he takes for granted that there is an inner and an outer and that knowledge is the bridge that allows us to move from one to the other and understand the given reality.

The growing indifference to truth in university education—'the closing of the American mind'—is accompanied, Bloom argues, by self-centredness and self-indulgence on the part of faculty and students. He holds that a new narcissism pervades the university campus. Visible symbols of this decline are the undisciplined sexual mores of staff and students and the social respectability of the homosexual life-style. Right and wrong are no longer categories that make sense to the current generation of university students and the majority of their professors.

Linked to this decline is the fact that the university no longer introduces students to the classical tradition, to the great thinkers and writers of the past. Even philosophy professors,

Bloom argues, no longer relate their thought to Plato and Aristotle. Studying the classical authors, Bloom believes, would allow students to discover for themselves the exciting adventure of the mind in search of the truth. Students would discover that truth is perennial, that it transcends culture, that it is non-relative, and that its pursuit demands a high price, a life of intellectual discipline.

The Christian reader is greatly impressed by this love of truth. Bloom's lament over the modern university appears to echo an oft-repeated Catholic critique of contemporary intellectual life: the relativism of truth, indifference to the good, abandonment of binding norms, and neglect of the classical philosophical tradition.

Yet one thing puzzles the Christian reader even at the beginning of the book, namely Bloom's totally negative interpretation of the 60s. Bloom writes about the student movement as if it were simply an American phenomenon. While he grudgingly admits that the movement helped the struggle for civil liberties of black Americans, he describes the movement's impact on the university and intellectual life of the nation as irredeemably bad. As a member of an international church, the Christian realizes that questioning authority during the 60s was not simply an American trend but a world-wide phenomenon, anti-colonial, opposing domination, critical of inherited power structures. As we shall see, there is something narrowly American in Bloom's best-seller.

'But what is the truth?' the reader asks. The truth, Bloom argues, is found in the political philosophy of John Locke. John Locke is presented as the greatest modern philosopher who explicated the rational foundation of the Enlightenment. Liberating us from the myths and fables of the past, Locke discovered the truth about human beings, truth on which to build the rational society, that is, a liberal democracy.

Writing not many years later, Jean-Jacques Rousseau voiced a fundamental disagreement with John Locke. From Bloom's point of view, Rousseau betrayed the Enlightenment. He raised new questions about human existence, questions about the irrational, questions that—according to Bloom—have become the source for all the modern errors that undermine rationality and weaken liberal democracy.

John Locke's Theory

Bloom offers the reader a brilliant chapter on Locke. Locke the radical, rejecting all tradition, affirmed and demonstrated that all men were free and equal, and that they enjoyed the right to life, liberty and the pursuit of property. What were Locke's arguments for this?

Bloom reads Locke in line with Hobbes, his predecessor. The first truth is that nature is violent, indifferent and cruel; nature tends to strife and war. This is the hostile world into which man is born. There was no Garden of Eden and there is no God watching over man. Man is simply on his own. He is unprotected, naked, afraid of being robbed and killed. The fear of death in a hostile universe, according to Locke, is the permanent human characteristic. This is the first abiding truth.

Because this truth is so unbearable people have invented myths and philosophical theories which pretended that men were protected by the gods, or that deep down men were really good, that they had a sense of solidarity and were destined to love one another. But these myths did not stop the robbing and the killing. In fact, they made it worse. Because people relied on these fables, they did not use their reason to protect themselves in the hostile environment. Because they trusted one another, wars became almost universal.

Yet reason triumphed in the Enlightenment. The great discovery was that man, gifted with reason, was able to construct a society that would protect him from theft and violence. To do this men had to reject traditional institutions, overcome political tyranny and repudiate paralyzing religious myths; and then, by relying on reason alone, discover the truth about human beings in the state of nature. What is this truth about human beings? Just as rational science discovers that bodies in motion move according to certain laws, rational science is also able to discover the laws according to which human beings move. What is this law? Men seek to protect their lives against violence and overcome the fear of death. Vulnerable humans yearn for self-preservation. If a whole population were willing to face this truth, this enlightenment, then it would be ready to enter into a social contract and constitute a rational society, a liberal democracy, with the task of protecting the civil liberties, personal safety and private property of the citizens.

This is the Enlightenment breakthrough. In liberal regimes human passion and reason are as fully reconciled as mortality permits. Man's universal passion to survive and protect his property is fulfilled in the rationally constructed society.

A new freedom has dawned upon men. The new society is based on rational self-interest, not on Aristotelian virtue. Gone are the repressive regimes of the past that spoke of the common good and created a conflict between private interests and social solidarity. Gone are the old teachings that made people feel guilty. The new society is guided by passion, by enlightened selfishness. By nature each person is his neighbour's enemy, but in liberal society he accepts his neighbour by reason of enlightened self-interest and is thus set free to pursue his own aims and purposes.

The remaining problem in liberal democracy—apart from human mortality—is the scarcity of goods. Mother nature is rich but not generous; she doesn't easily let go. Hence the rational task—self-interested labour—is to conquer nature and rob her of her riches. Those who wrest most from nature, i.e., those who produce most and create great wealth, deserve to be well rewarded. The reward, in turn, will encourage them to continue their efforts in the conquest of nature.

Bloom recognizes the affinity between Locke's political theory and capitalism, but does not dwell on it. Locke assures us that rational self-interest is not against the common good but actually constitutes the foundation of liberal democracy. Scientific reason, Bloom explains, "wipes the slate clean of all the inherited theories and inscribes on this slate contracts calmly made in expectation of profit, involving the kind of relations involved in business." (p. 167) Both Locke's liberal democracy and Adam Smith's capitalism are presented as marvelous breakthrough institutions that transmute human selfishness into protection for universal well-being and thus make virtue a useless inheritance.

Bloom thus identifies himself with Lockean political theory. He regards it as science, as demonstrable truth. What surprises the reader is that Bloom feels no need to ask whether contemporary anthropological research has validated Locke's speculation about man in the state of nature, man before the advent of society, isolated man, naked and unprotected, afraid that his fellow humans will slay him. Has this man ever existed? Or is he a child of the imagination brought forth by the new burghers competing against one another in the marketplace? Anthropological evidence certainly demonstrates that from earliest times humans were communitarian. But Bloom, we note, is not impressed by conclusions derived from anthropology and the other social sciences. In fact, he regards the admission of social sciences to the university as one of the principal causes for the spread of cultural relativism and indifference to truth.

Rousseau's Counter-Theory

Jean-Jacques Rousseau, Bloom claims, undermined the triumph of the Enlightenment. In a brilliant chapter he offers the reader an interpretation of the great French philosopher. Rousseau agrees with Locke that vulnerable man in search of comfort and protection opts for the social contract. However, the rational society does not fulfill man's restless self-concern. Locke erred in thinking that nature and society could be reconciled. According to Rousseau, the security of society and the freedom to accumulate personal property do not fulfill the human passions. Even if men live in the rational society under the most advantageous conditions, they remain restless: they retain memories of nature—the simple joy of youth, the natural sweetness of life, the ecstasy of the senses. In Locke's rational society, people yearn for still greater happiness, for something deeper than security and self-satisfaction. They thus experience a sense of alienation. Only the bourgeois, at home in Locke's society, are incapable of understanding this. People less tamed and more imaginative recognize a longing for nature that society cannot fulfill.

For Locke the abiding characteristic of human beings was the fear of death. Adding to this, Rousseau also recognized the human longing for ecstasy. Rousseau's message was, contrary to Locke, that man was basically good. Allan Bloom regards Rousseau's philosophy as a threat to the hegemony of reason and therefore a betrayal of the Enlightenment.

According to Locke's philosophy there was no human nature, men did not have a soul—they were shaped by the regime in which they lived. No ethical imperative emerged from their being. In fact, reason delivered humans from their sense of dividedness, from the inner conflict between social solidarity and personal advantage. For Locke, humans were undivided: there was no call to altruism and solidarity—this was a myth to be discarded—there was only enlightened self-interest.

But Rousseau, Bloom laments, again divided the human being. Humans were indeed rational, but there was also a deeper longing in them. Returning to a concept of a deeper self, Rousseau opened the door to the irrational and prepared the way for all the modern errors. The idea that man remained alienated and unfulfilled in the rational society became the foundation for all the bourgeois-bashing modern philosophies: Marx's theory of alienation, Nietzsche's theory of the last men, Freud's theory of civilizational discontent, Heidegger's theory of inauthenticity, and other dangerous theories of 'roots,' roots in tradition, in nationhood, in religion. Rousseau's betrayal of reason spawned the modern errors of the left and the right. Bloom sees himself standing with John Locke at the very centre, holding on to rationality as the foundation of liberal democracy.

Bloom argues that Rousseau introduced a new language that was to become the tongue of modernity. Rousseau speaks of self, culture and creativity. Man is no longer a natural being, man is now a cultural being. Self-interest is no longer enough, man must be rooted in a tradition. Culture mediates patterns of behaviour and provides overall meaning and purpose. Rousseau here invites the return of myth. Thanks to his philosophy, the study of man has been withdrawn from science, which deals with universals. What are now emphasized are the differences among peoples, their cultures and self-definitions. But the move in this direction, Bloom argues, undermines the rational consensus, the social contract, upon which liberal democracy is based.

The University in America

Bloom sees himself as the defender of the United States. Since the American republic and, to some extent, all Western democracies are based on reason and its claim to universality, the present intellectual trend that makes concessions to openness, values, commitment and pluralism—the fashionable words— threatens the viability of the political order. The 60s represented a danger for America. 'The closing of the American mind' now threatens the well-being of the republic. Bloom deplores the contemporary obsession with pluralism. He regrets the recent emphasis on ethnicity in the United States. He makes fun of John Rawls, political philosopher and social ethicist, who argues that democratic society should exclude no one and respect all citizens, including their culture. By contrast Bloom holds that liberal society should allow others to enter only on condition that they accept the social contract and become assimilated into the rational society.

Similar reasoning leads Bloom to warn against the fashionable openness to non-Western cultures. No non-Western culture, he argues, has produced a transcendent rationality that criticizes traditional institutions and unmasks inherited myths. The philosopher's task is to defend reason and the rational society, especially the rational society par excellence, the United States of America.

A large section of *The Closing of the American Mind* deals with the entry of subversive ideas, derived in one way or another from Rousseau, into the American academy. The chief villains here are the German philosophers. They explored and developed Rousseau's irrational ideas in many directions. In a chapter I found hilarious, Bloom tries to show that the German immigrant intellectuals exiled by Hitler in the 30s, were the agents of irrationality in American universities. They brought along many sources of decline: the social sciences with their concern for culture, values and life-styles; phenomenology with its hostility to science; existentialism with its emphasis on commitment; psychoanalysis with its respect for the unconscious; Marxist philosophy and critical theory with their utopian imagination.

The task of the university, as Bloom understands it, is to initiate students to reason and the power of reason. The university is created by liberal society as a place of privilege where intellectually disciplined professors and students have the leisure to pursue the truth for its own sake. The university is meant to protect this intellectual adventure. The theoretical life, the *'vita contemplativa,'* which Bloom loves and claims our universities neglect, actually has long-range political consequences: it defends the foundation of liberal democracy. The intellectual elite formed at such universities will be the great defenders of the American republic.

According to Bloom, the great sin of American universities in the 60s was their willingness to yield to the pressure of the student movement and allow justice, solidarity and commitment to affect admissions policy, curriculum content, and the quest for truth. Moral indignation, he argues, is the great temptation the philosopher must resist (p. 278). Compassion can be sustained only by fables of human solidarity or love of neighbour, fables Enlightenment reason must reject. The truth, alas, is hard to take. The sin of American universities was to become involved in politics. They publicly expressed their opposition to the war in Vietnam; introduced courses based on commitment and solidarity, courses unworthy of the university such as black studies, feminism, or alternative consciousness; and, adopting affirmative action policies, admitted and graduated blacks and other minority students even if this meant lowering academic standards.

Universities must protect the highest intellectual norms. Universities also have the duty to remain uninvolved. Liberal society, based on enlightened self-interest, must create institutions for the full, untrammeled exercise of reason. Society needs greenhouses where thinkers, scientists and philosophers have the freedom to reflect, research, analyze and argue. Universities have the right to remain aloof, Bloom argues, even in times of conflict, poverty and injustice.

In this context Bloom laments the impact of utilitarianism on the university. Too many people want university education to be practical, to prepare students for a career. Bloom realizes that liberal capitalism creates people who love money and status. But utilitarian self-interest, because it is short-range, does not raise fundamental questions, nor does it protect the rational foundation of society. By contrast, enlightened self-interest is long-range: it deals with the entire human situation, it reaches for the truth. 'The theoretical life' does not have to prove itself by its practical consequences, except in the long run through its defense of reason against the myths that threaten it on all sides.

As we have seen, Bloom is critical of contemporary self-indulgence. Enlightened selfishness recognizes the need for discipline. Bloom defends the traditional family and inherited sexual norms. Capitalist society, he argues, demands hard-working citizens with regular habits. He laments today's multiplicity of lifestyles. But lest anyone think that sexual conformity applies to the intellectual elite, Bloom approvingly recalls that "in the past there was a respectable place for marginality, bohemia, but it had to justify its unorthodox practices by its intellectual and artistic achievements" (p. 235).

Bloom realizes that the university depends on the approval of ordinary people and especially on support by the rich and powerful, none of whom have access to the theoretical life. To please them, the philosopher must practice the gentle art of deception and pretend that there are answers to the urgent questions people ask. Since most people live by myths and legends, they should not be frightened by the bitter truth, the great Enlightenment insight, that by nature we are all enemies of one another.

Refutation Unnecessary

There is hardly any need to refute Locke's philosophical anthropology. The atomistic theory of man has no basis in anthropology, sociology or psychology; the theory contradicts our human experience of sympathy and solidarity, explored by phenomenology; it is at odds with the wisdom tradition derived from Scripture and Greek philosophy; it makes sense only as the ideology of the competitive, liberal capitalist society, marked by what C.B. Macpherson has called 'possessive individualism.' What Bloom does not mention is that the Enlightenment went beyond John Locke. The name of Kant alone suggests that Enlightenment thought had much to say about ethics and human solidarity.

We notice that Bloom makes no effort to challenge with reasoned argument Rousseau's analysis of human existence. If I understand his book correctly, Bloom tries to disprove Rousseau's theory *a posteriori,* by way of its historical consequences. Bloom wants to show that once liberalism abandons its strictly rational basis and opens itself to sentimentality, it inevitably generates nihilism and invites the collapse of civilization.

Bloom's endorsement of Lockean thought impresses one as singularly out of date. We are accustomed to philosophers who repudiate classical metaphysics, but to couple this with the rejection of history and the social sciences is a most unusual combination. Where does Allan Bloom come from? Despite his rage against the impact of German immigrant intellectuals on American universities, Bloom himself is a student and disciple of an important rationalist thinker, the German immigrant Leo Strauss, who regarded the universal truth which philosophers love as frightening and even dangerous for society, and who rejected all modern philosophies as relativistic, designed to flatter people's wishes and desires, thus unwittingly courting nihilism and the collapse of civilization. To gain a better understanding of Bloom's intellectual background, I recommend Shadia Drury's excellent book, *The Political Ideas of Leo Strauss.*

This is not the place to discuss the important question whether, to what extent, and in what manner universities should be committed to justice and solidarity. There can be no doubt, however, that Bloom's abstract and aloof intellectualism, his total separation of knowledge and love, his elitism, his opposition to affirmative action, his closed-mindedness in regard to other cultures, his stubborn opposition to feminism, and his encouragement of a capitalist society whose values he simultaneously despises—that all these are devoid of rationality once the Lockean basis has been found wanting. Bloom's book has turned out to be a fashion-piece encouraging the 'neo-conservative' culture of our day that tries to undermine the human bonds of solidarity, compromise us with social inequality, and make us hard-hearted in the face of the suffering of others.

6

Emil Fackenheim and Christianity

Dialogue with Christianity is an abiding dimension of Emil Fackenheim's religious thought. Even after the turning-point, when he recommends that Jewish thought distance itself from the Christian tradition, he remains in constant dialogue with Christian theology. Because Fackenheim's philosophical home is German Idealism, with its Christian connection, a thorough analysis of his relationship to Christianity would demand a critical examination of his entire philosophical work. How does he interpret the German philosophers? Fackenheim's reading of Hegel, which rescued Hegel for Christian orthodoxy and made his thought relevant for the present, has been enormously influential among Christian theologians. Yet, since I am not a philosopher, I shall not undertake such an ambitious task.

What I shall do, instead, is examine the relation to Christianity in Fackenheim's theological writings before and after the turning-point. I shall do this not as a detached scholar interested in the history of ideas, but as an engaged theologian wrestling with Fackenheim's thought and responding to him. After the turning-point, Fackenheim's religious reflections have become deeply disturbing to Christians, and to Christian theologians in particular. They are disturbing because they reveal how deeply the negation of Jewish existence has been inscribed in Christian teaching and hence how much Christians must change if they want to engage in constructive dialogue with Jews. Yet Fackenheim's later writings are also disturbing in an altogether different sense: they seem to provide theological legitimation for what in all honesty I must call 'right-wing' political positions, that is to say, for a politics of indifference in regard to peoples and groups oppressed by Western empire.

Beginnings

In his early writings Fackenheim sees himself allied with Christian theologians in the task of 'bringing the word of God to the modern world' (*QPF*, 275). Both Jews and Christians are witnesses to God's revelation. Together they stand against the secularizing and relativizing trends that characterize modernity. While Jews and Christians should expose themselves to the critical challenge of the Enlightenment, they must hold fast to the God of the Scriptures. Fackenheim acknowledges his affinity with neo-orthodox Christian theology, especially the thought of Karl Barth and Reinhold Niebuhr (*JRH*, 8). These men believed that 19th-century liberalism and subjectivism had interpreted Christianity as the highest expression of contemporary culture, a high-minded humanism, and therefore lost the sense of God's otherness and paved the way for the 20th-century ethical breakdown in European fascism and German Nazism. Barth in Europe and Niebuhr in America revealed the power of the neo-orthodox return to God's transcendence in their resistence to trends in Christianity that favoured Nazism or were unwilling to fight it. Still, in 1968, after the watershed, Fackenheim was able to write: 'It is fruitful for Judaism to establish contact with Christianity. The Christian like the Jewish faith is irreconcilable with secularism' (*GPH*, 46). Jews and Christians stand together as witnesses.

In his early writings Fackenheim defines faith—faith in God's word—as the essential mark of Jewish existence. Reflecting on the human condition in light of this revealed faith was the task of theology (cf. *QPF*, 104). Unlike Martin Buber, Fackenheim did not feel the need to distinguish between Jewish faith as *Du-Glaube* and Christian faith as *Dass-Glaube*. Nor was he uncomfortable, as some Jewish thinkers were, in applying the category of theology to Jewish religious reflection. More than any other Jewish thinker, Fackenheim recognized a community of faith between Jews and Christians.

The two great Jewish philosophers admired by Fackenheim, who had worked out an equivalent neo-orthodox critique of liberalism, were Martin Buber and Franz Rosenzweig. They had insisted against the trend of Jewish liberal thought, that God was the ineffable, transcendent mystery who encountered human beings in their lives. In his early writings, Fackenheim still followed Martin Buber's analysis of the darkness that had come over the modern world, humans' metaphysical homelessness, and the eclipse of God. Fackenheim wrote: 'The catastrophes of our times, however great, cannot by themselves account for the contemporary crisis of religious belief' (*QPF*, 231). The absence of God cannot be ascribed to what Fackenheim then called 'Auschwitz and Hiroshima.' Furthermore, 'Biblical faith—and I mean both Jewish and Christian—is never destroyed by tragedy but only tested by it, and in the test it both clarifies its own meaning and conquers tragedy' (*QPF*, 229).

What then accounts for the absence of God in modern times? At fault is a reductionist tendency: from religion to religious feeling, from the objective order of God to the subjective order of religious experience, from transcendent values to the historically relevant. Buber called this 'subjective reductionism' (*QPF*, 236). In modern times, subjectivism has won the day. The world has been delivered over to people's personal and collective dreams and desires, without boundaries set by God and without an objective moral order. Everything has now become possible. Subjectivism has led to the decline of ethical culture and the emergence of one-dimensional secularism. Neo-orthodoxy, Jewish and Christian, stands against this trend. 'The biblical faith has been restated in our times, both by Jews and Christians, with a purity perhaps unmatched in centuries; and this restatement has fully risen to the challenge posed by subjective reductionism' (*QPF*, 238).

Faith in the givenness of the divine presence is the answer to the question that has been 'forced upon Jewish and Christian believers by the Nazi experience (and not it alone)' (*QPF*, 274). Why have the Jewish people survived discrimination and persecution throughout the centuries? Their survival cannot be explained by a purely earthly attachment to their inherited identity, their ethnicity or their cultural values; nor can it be explained by resistance to oppression. Fackenheim argued that 'to account for Jewish survival is possible only in terms of Jewish faith' (*QPF*, 114). It is because of faith in the biblical God that the Jews still exist—a source of wonder to others and to themselves. In this context, faith refers not to a milk-and-water assent to religious ideas, but, Fackenheim writes, to a total commitment, a commitment based either on an all-consuming experience in the present or on the memory of such an experience in the past (ibid).

While Fackenheim acknowledges his affinity with Protestant neo-orthodoxy, the Catholic reader finds in his writings an emphasis absent in Catholic neo-orthodoxy. For neo-orthodox Christians, God as totally Other is encountered in certain significant moments of life, especially in reading Scripture and preaching the Gospel message. For Fackenheim, by contrast, the transcendent divine mystery is encountered in all significant experiences of life, including the quest for truth, love and justice. For those who listen to God's scriptural word, life itself becomes the locus of the encounter with God. Fackenheim endorses a sense of divine immanence, found in Buber and Rosenzweig and reminiscent of Jewish mysticism, that has a strong affinity with Catholic theological tradition. For the neo-orthodox, God is ever the Word that stands over against us, never the ground that supports us, or the light that enables us to see, or the matrix out of which we are alive, or the vector along which we move forward. The Catholic theologian finds in Fackenheim's early writings a sense of divine immanence that is absent in neo-orthodoxy. Fackenheim's vocabulary reveals the in-and-throughness of God. He speaks of the gracious presence, the nameless mystery, the commanding presence, and even of Grace spelled with a capital 'G,' which is at work in people's lives and in their history (*GPH*, 60). Even in his later writings, he refers with approval to Hegel's immanentist theology of transcendence and argues that the same position is held in Judaism: even conversion (*Teshuvah*) and mending (*Tikkun*) are possible only because divinely enabled (*MW*, 253).

Despite this sense of fellowship with Christian theologians, Fackenheim was not naive about historical Christianity. He recognized the plural structure of Christianity as he acknowledged the plural structure of Judaism. He did not think it was possible to search for 'the essence' of a historical religion. Religion is alive, it responds to historical challenges, it is always existential; hence it flourishes in distinct trends or currents that relate to one another and interact at certain times. There were Christian trends hostile to Judaism. In his *Paths to Jewish Belief*, a book addressed to young people, Fackenheim explained the great diversity in Christianity that prevented one from making generalized statements about it (145-54). Fackenheim saw Christianity and Judaism as spectra of various currents, and he recognized the possibility that currents in Christianity and currents in Judaism might overlap.

This means that Christians faithful to their beliefs and Jews faithful to theirs may actually experience themselves as brothers and sisters united by the same trust in the biblical God, even though the currents in which they move flow from different histories and hence react to different logics. In his later writings Fackenheim does not repudiate this perception. He becomes more aware that Christians and Jews, even when experiencing fellowship, follow different trajectories and hence are likely to be moved apart again by historical developments. As we shall see, Fackenheim believed that the Nazi period not only brought Jews and Christians closer together, but also created conditions for widening the gap between them (*QPF*, 20).

Because of this dynamic understanding of religion, Fackenheim addresses his theological writings to Jews and to Christians, and he formulates his message to the latter in a language consonant with Christian theology itself. Right to his most recent publications, even after the watershed, Fackenheim occasionally speaks to Christians as if he were a Christian theologian. Not that he is a crypto-Christian or in any way disguises his Jewish faith! But his knowledge of Christian theology and his empathy with Christian faith are so great that he can make constructive proposals to Christians in concepts and in a language that emerge in a creative way out of Christian theology. We shall see that he does this in his later book *To Mend the World*, where he specifies what repentance and reparation must mean for Christians after the

Holocaust. In fact, the paradoxical conclusion of this essay will be that Fackenheim is a brilliant theologian for Christians but an uncertain guide for Jewish believers.

Because of Fackenheim's later change of perspective, it must be said very clearly that, in his early writings up to 1967, he did not recognize that faithful Jewish self-understanding included the memory of the Holocaust or identification with the Jewish state. The young people for whom he wrote *Paths to Jewish Belief* in 1960 were not told these things. In later years, Fackenheim was puzzled and grieved when he recalled a symposium on the future of Jewish theology, organized by *Commentary* in 1961, at which next to no attention was paid either to the Holocaust or to Israel (*JRH*, 129). Prior to 1967, Fackenheim himself spoke of 'the catastrophes of the 20th century' and 'Auschwitz and Hiroshima,' and he trembled that these catastrophes might culminate in what he then called 'the nuclear Holocaust.'

After the turning-point, Fackenheim repented of his silence. Aware of his own development, readers of Fackenheim's later writing are surprised at the vehemence with which he condemns thinkers, Jewish, Christian or secular, who engage in reflections as if the Holocaust had never taken place. Making the Holocaust invisible is 'blasphemous.' Yet readers wonder whether such strong language is justified when even important Jewish thinkers only gradually came to recognize Auschwitz as the never-to-be-by-passed sign of discontinuity.

Fackenheim is equally severe with the silence of the churches, in particular with the Christian partners in Jewish-Christian dialogue, during the Six-Day War of 1967. Fackenheim believes that Christians did not cry out in protest against the aggression because a deeply rooted, possibly unconscious antisemitism made them wish on some level that the Jewish state might disappear from the earth. Not all Jewish commentators share this opinion. Rabbi Balfour Brickner has suggested that most Christians who were close to Jews and honoured their religion looked upon the conflict in the Middle East with great anxiety, but considered it a political matter, unrelated to Jewish religion or Jewish identity, just as they regarded the conflict in Northern Ireland as political and unrelated to the religious self-understanding of their Protestant or Catholic neighbours. If Christians had learnt what it meant to be Jewish from the early writings of Emil Fackenheim, they would have had no inkling of Israel's importance to Jews. Fackenheim's extraordinary inner turmoil during and after the turning-point seems to be related to his own previous prolonged inattention.

The Conversion

In a paper entitled 'The 614th Commandment,' (*JRH*, 19-24), presented shortly before the Six-Day War in 1967, Fackenheim revealed an entirely new perspective which deeply affected his philosophical thought and radically transformed his theology. He argues that, from the singular event of the Holocaust, organized to extirpate the entire Jewish people, the commanding Voice addresses the remainder of the Jewish community, ordering them 'to survive.' The 614th commandment given to the Jews is to survive, that is, 'not to grant Hitler a posthumous victory.' In the present situation, this means to stand behind the state of Israel and support it in its as yet uncertain struggle for survival. Auschwitz, historically unique in its irrationality, is seen as part of a revelatory event or 'root experience' (*GPH*, 8-14) that defines Jewish identity before God. Auschwitz is revelation: the commanding Presence at the Holocaust summons Jews and all humanity to confront the discontinuity, the radical rupture, which this event has produced in human history. After Auschwitz everything is different. The idea of humanity has broken to pieces, the idea of God has collapsed, reason itself has become null and void. To think and act as if Auschwitz had not taken place is to reject the divine Voice, and hence in some sense to blaspheme.

What does fidelity mean after Auschwitz? What does it mean for Jews? What does it mean for Christians? What does it mean for the philosopher? These are the questions Fackenheim pursued in his later writings. These writings have had an extraordinary impact on a significant number of Christian theologians. The October 1984 issue of *Concilium* (an international Catholic theological review that appears in seven languages) is entitled

'The Holocaust as Interruption.' The introduction, written by Elisabeth Schüssler-Fiorenza and David Tracy, begins this way: "As Christian theology moves past the concern for historical consciousness alone or even historicity alone into concrete history, it finds itself facing the frightening interruption of the Holocaust. 'History' can no longer be understood as linearity nor continuity much less as evolutionary. Theologically construed, history is concrete: here the concrete suffering of peoples trapped in the horrors of the Holocaust. When facing that event, history becomes theologically interruption."[2] Whether Christian theologians interpret the Holocaust as does Fackenheim remains to be seen.

Fackenheim's influence on Jewish religious thought is also enormous. It is my impression, however, that although Jewish theologians learn from him are challenged by him, and move to a higher level of reflection, only very few actually follow him.[3] Fackenheim has chosen a singular path.

Obedience to the 614th commandment leads Fackenheim to two paradoxes that invalidate the theological approach of his early writings. First, obedience to the commanding Voice at Auschwitz transcends the difference, important in his earlier theology, between religious and secular Jews. Religious and secular Jews are faithful to the 614th commandment when they bring up their children as Jews, when they wrestle against the forces that seek to destroy them, when they support and defend the state of Israel. Here it is no longer faith in God's revealed word that defines Jewish identity, but obedience to the 614th commandment. The eclipse of God and the threat to Jewish (and Christian) religion can no longer be ascribed to the secular spirit and subjective reductionism: it is antisemitism manifest at Auschwitz that threatens the state of Israel and endangers Jewish life. The reason I call this position paradoxical is that the commitment to survive is the reply to the commanding Voice, hence an act of obedience to the Nameless One. The struggle for survival is therefore theological. Committed Jews, whether religious or secular, belong to God.

Second, obedience to the commanding Voice transcends the religious commitment, important in Fackenheim's theology, to a dialectically conceived universal ethics. Jews are now summoned to be concerned with themselves, to struggle for their own survival, even to remain indifferent to a world that has abandoned them, if getting involved would weaken or interfere with their own effort to survive. In the past Jews were famous for their commitment to social justice and the solidarity they extended to all groups that suffered discrimination and oppression. The Holocaust event has made them discover that not only did the world not reciprocate this solidarity, but they, the Jews, had failed over their universal concern to fight wholeheartedly for their own right to exist and to have a state of their own to protect them. Commitment to a universal ethics is an expression of a liberal philosophy that does not survive the rupture of the Holocaust. Again, I call this position paradoxical because Fackenheim's turn to Jewish particularism is an act of obedience to God, and hence has universal meaning. Not only is the survival of Israel ultimately for the world, but unless all groups and peoples confront the rupture of the Holocaust, they will not escape the evil that threatens them (*QPF*, 310; *JRH*, 54; *MW*, 262).

These two positions, the relativizing of faith and the abandonment of a universal ethics, do not come easily to Fackenheim.

They go against convictions deeply rooted in his heart. They shatter the dialectical thinking that characterized his earlier writings. Dialectics is here replaced by paradox. Fackenheim speaks of 'enduring intolerable contradictions' (*JRH*, 24). He follows this new theological orientation, despite personal disinclination, out of obedience to the 614th commandment. Because the Jewish people have been betrayed and deserted by the world, and because the state of Israel remains threatened in its very existence, he feels that, by following his own ethical universalism, however dialectical, he would give Hitler a posthumous victory. Fackenheim obeys the commanding Voice with anguish and spiritual torment.

Fackenheim often recalls Kierkegaard's fear and trembling. According to Kierkegaard's famous analysis of Abraham's sacrifice, Abraham was ready to obey his God, even though he knew that to kill a child, especially his own child on whom God's blessing rested, was unethical. Kierkegaard spoke here of 'the theological suspension of the ethical' (*JRH*, 48). Curiously enough, speaking of Abraham's sacrifice is not part of the rabbinical tradition. In a lecture at the Toronto School of Theology in January 1985, Rabbi Dow Marmur showed that the rabbis spoke not of 'sacrifice' but of 'the binding of Isaac.' They argued that Abraham knew from the beginning that God did not intend him to kill the son of promise. Abraham was willing to bind Isaac as he waited for a new manifestation of the divine.

Fackenheim believes that Jews are called upon, in anguish and inner torment, to perform the theological suspension of the ethical. That is why Fackenheim himself was willing to be silent in the face of oppression caused by Western Empire, such as apartheid in South Africa and the mass killings by military regimes in Central America, and did not extend his solidarity to struggles for justice in Canada, such as the land claims of the Native peoples. That is why Fackenheim was able to publish a book in 1982 entitled *To Mend the World* without once referring to the threat of mass destruction by the ever-escalating nuclear-arms race. The only crimes he mentions, with very few exceptions, are those committed by powers more directly hostile to Israel and harmful to the Jews.

The commanding Voice at Auschwitz produced a turning-point in Fackenheim's Jewish self-understanding and his intellectual engagement. He kept wrestling with an appropriate response to the Holocaust. Sometimes themes from his earlier writings re-emerge, but they are quickly invalidated by a return to the 614th commandment. Fackenheim has continued his intense dialogue with the great German philosophers and the important Jewish religious thinkers of the past, but he now deals with them in a new and original way. In his *To Mend the World,* he outlined in a formal way the orientation philosophy, Christianity, and Judaism must follow after the Holocaust. Unless the rupture of the Holocaust is recognized, thinking, whether religious or secular, has no valid future. A gulf has opened up. The idea of humanity has been invalidated. The idea of God no longer holds out. What then is truth after the Holocaust?

To reply to this question Fackenheim engages in a study of two Jewish theological concepts, *Teshuvah* (turning or conversion) and *Tikkun* (mending or reparation) (*MW*, 250-62), concepts that have Christian equivalents. After the Holocaust, truth becomes available only through *Teshuvah*, through conversion. Confrontation with the Holocaust reveals the discontinuity of history: we may not continue doing what we did before, we may not return to thinking that seemed valid to us before, we must be converted. And second, since the rupture took place in the order of concrete history, the conversion of the mind must express itself in public witness. Truth after Auschwitz does not remain in the mind; it flows over into action, resistance, reparation. Thought must participate in the mending of the rupture. This mending, Fackenheim insists, will of necessity remain fragmentary. History will not be healed, the millions who were murdered will not be forgotten, the Holocaust will never be *aufgehoben*. But, however fragmentary, *Tikkun* must go on.

How do we know that, after Auschwitz, *Tikkun* is possible at all? Here Fackenheim gives an original and deeply moving theological reply. *Tikkun* is possible because there were men and women during the Holocaust event who gave witness and tried to mend the rupture. Fackenheim resonates with Adorno's despair that, after Auschwitz, poetry has become impossible, as well as with his later remark that poetry is still possible because some people wrote poetry during those years of terror (*MW*,198). Fackenheim also mentions Johann Baptist Metz, the Catholic theologian, who said that it was possible to pray after Auschwitz only because there were people who prayed at Auschwitz.[4] Fackenheim agrees. Mending is possible and necessary because the witnesses resisted during the Holocaust.

Future thought must be guided by the testimony of the victims and the survivors. Fackenheim has derived his own language of the 'commanding Voice' from the witness of a courageous woman, Pelagia Lewinska, whose memorable words he quotes many times. Appalled by the disorder and confusion in the concentration camp to which she had been sent, she suddenly saw clearly:

> And then I saw the light! I saw that it was not a question of disorder or lack of organization but that, on the contrary, a very thoroughly considered conscious idea was in the back of the camp's existence. They have condemned us to die in our own filth, to drown in mud, in our own excrement. They

wished to abase us, to destroy our human dignity, to efface
every vestige of humanity . . . to fill us with horror and contempt toward ourselves and our fellows . . . From the instant
when I grasped the motivating principle, it was as if I
had been awakened from a dream . . . *I felt under orders
to live* . . . And if I did die in Auschwitz, it would be as a
human being. I would hold on to my dignity . . . And a terrible struggle began which went on day and night. (*MW*, 25).

The Jewish woman felt under orders to live. She heard the commanding Voice. Pelagia Lewinska laid the foundation for post-
Holocaust Jewish philosophy and theology.

Who laid the foundation for rational thought and Christian
theology after the Holocaust? *Tikkun* is also possible and necessary for these. Fackenheim remembers two witnesses. Kurt Huber,
a philosophy teacher, defended before a Munich court the civil
disobedience of the 1943 protesters, Inge Scholl and her fellow
students, with arguments drawn from German philosophy. He
paid for this with his life (*MW*, 267). And Bernhard Lichtenberg,
rector of Berlin's Catholic cathedral, was arrested, tried, and condemned to prison because he daily offered public prayers in his
church for the persecuted Jews and other citizens sent to the
concentration camps. Outspokenly unrepentant, he died in
prison (*MW*, 289). Because of these two, Fackenheim argues,
there is today *Tikkun* for philosophical thought and Christian
theology. By focusing on these two heroic Germans, almost un-
known to his North American readers, Fackenheim offers a theological foundation for German *Tikkun*, for the future of German
philosophy and theology. The reader marvels at this. Despite
Fackenheim's passion, there is nothing anti-German in his
thought. Because of Huber's and Lichtenberg's *Tikkun*, Emil
Fackenheim is able to remain in conversation with the great German philosophers who have always been his main partners in dialogue.

Post-Holocaust Dialogue

We now turn to Fackenheim's directives for Christianity after Auschwitz and his message regarding the future of Jewish existence. Should I confine myself to the former and disregard the latter as being none of my business? I do not think so. To do my task properly, I must respond to Fackenheim's Jewish religious thought as a Christian theologian. He himself demands that Christians engage in theological dialogue with Jews. Christians should no longer do theology, he argues, unless they do it in solidarity with Jews.

After 1967, Fackenheim feared that the Holocaust, which had brought Jews and Christians together in a common resistance, was also creating a new distance between them. Fackenheim was overwhelmed by a feeling that the Jews had been abandoned by their friends, including their Christian partners in dialogue, who seemed to retain hesitations and suspicions vis-à-vis the State of Israel. What was at work here, Fackenheim believed, was unacknowledged antisemitic sentiment. The traditional Christian antipathy towards things Jewish was still operative. More than that, Fackenheim argued—more convincingly—that the more deeply one moves to the core of the Christian faith, the more clearly emerges the anti-Jewish structure of the classical proclamation.

This second point has been made in much greater detail by many Christian scholars. The anti-Jewish elements of the Christian tradition are not simply a few hostile liturgical references and a few quotations from Christian theologians, elements that could easily be corrected; the anti-Jewish thrust belongs to the very structure of the Christian proclamation, almost from the beginning. The New Testament is already marked by the conflict between church and synagogue. Rosemary Radford Ruether, a Christian scholar, to whom Fackenheim himself refers, has demonstrated in her *Faith and Fratricide* the theological roots of antisemitism.[5] According to the early Christian witness, the biblical promises were fulfilled in Jesus; he was the one who ushered in the Messianic age; he and his followers constituted the holy remnant of Israel; the church to which he called the believers was to be the true people of God, replacing the ancient Israel; and the Jews who did not receive his message excluded themselves from the divine plan of salvation. The Jews appeared as a historical anomaly. If the equation had been resolved evenly, they would have disappeared in the Christian church. Rosemary Ruether calls this anti-Judaism 'the left hand of Christology': every proclamation of Christ is accompanied by a negation of Jewish existence. Related to this is an interpretation referred to in theological literature as 'the theory of supersession': Israel is here superseded by the Christian church.

The Christian scholars who have uncovered the theological roots of the oppression and marginalization of the Jews in Western civilization believe that it is possible to interpret the Gospel differently. The Christian message can be proclaimed so as to make room for Jewish religion and present Jesus as the divinely sent protector of all human beings and their dignity, including especially the Jews, his own kin. Some Christians have undertaken this reinterpretation by separating themselves from Christian orthodoxy, while many others, including myself, have insisted that such reinterpretation is possible within the orthodox Christian tradition.[6] Still, Fackenheim is correct. We have discovered that the distance between Christians and Jews is much wider than well-meaning Christians and Jews believed when they first began their dialogue after the Second World War. A greater conversion than was anticipated is necessary on the part of the Christian church.

What then are Fackenheim's proposals for post-Holocaust Christianity? What do Christian *Teshuvah* and *Tikkun* mean after Auschwitz? (*MW*, 278 94).

First, conversion for Christians means to recognize that, without the anti-Jewish bias of the Christian message and the Jew-hatred associated with it, Nazi antisemitism and the Holocaust would have been impossible. Fackenheim acknowledges the gulf between Christian anti-Judaism, which aimed at the conversion of the Jews, and Nazi antisemitism, which aimed at mass murder. But he argues that, without the anti-Jewish symbols of the Christian tradition and the anti-Jewish sentiment derived from them, Nazi antisemitism would not have spread so quickly or found such wide support. Without the anti-Jewish heritage, Hitler may never have chosen the Jewish people as the great scapegoat for the ills of German and Western civilization.

Many Christian theologians have accepted this and live in a state of repentance. Fackenheim says that there are too few of them. He is correct. But the few are influential writers with considerable impact on the church.

Second, Fackenheim demands that turning and mending for Christians means the giving up of the theory of supersession. Christians may no longer look upon Jews as people destined to become Christians. They must recognize Judaism as a biblical religion in its own right, a sister religion of the church, which Christians honour and with which they seek dialogue. Christians need this dialogue for their own theology.

Again, Fackenheim knows that there are a good number of Christian theologians who have gone through this turning and mending. He thinks there are too few. He is correct: those converted are too few. Still, it is important to show how influential this new approach to Jewish religion has been and how much it has already influenced the official teaching of the churches, the catechisms used by children, the religious instruction given to adults, and the textbooks used in schools and colleges.[7] While Vatican Council II (1962-5) did not produce the statement on Jewish-Christian solidarity that many of us had hoped for—and Fackenheim rightly points to its many shortcomings—what the council did say represents none the less *Teshuvah* and *Tikkun*, even though as yet too fragmentary. The Vatican Council recognized the Jews as the irremovable people of the divine election, *populus secundum electionem carissimus propter patres*, even in the Christian dispensation; it recognized Jewish worship as the locus of the divine Word; and it encouraged Christian-Jewish dialogue, friendship, and cooperation.[8]

Third, Fackenheim demands that, in response to the Holocaust, repentance becomes a permanent dimension of Christianity, repentance over the negation of Jewish existence and its long-range historical consequences, however unintended. Christians must let go of their triumphalist style, modify their all-too-rapid claim that Good Friday has been overcome by Easter joy, and acknowledge the unredemption in which they are still immersed. Fackenheim recognizes that a new sense of unredemption has taken hold of certain sectors of the church. He acknowledges what he calls 'the leftward move' (*MW*, 285) of contemporary Christian thought. Here the Christian message is promise and beginning rather than declaration of victory already granted. Fackenheim is willing to entertain that there is a relation between response to the Holocaust and liberation theology. He warns Christians, however, not to extend their solidarity to the poor struggling for justice as a way of escaping the challenge of the Holocaust: for then they will worsen the situation of the Jews and unwittingly join the secular left in its biased perception of Israel.

Fourth, Fackenheim demands that Christians stand in solidarity with Jews and that for this reason they must be lovers of Israel. Doing Christian Tikkun demands that, in their political evaluation of the Middle East conflict Christians do not forget that, for Jews, in J.-B. Metz's words, Israel is 'a house against death.'[9] Even though the Vatican had not yet officially recognized the State of Israel, the Catholic bishops of Canada and the United States, as well as national hierarchies in Europe, following the good example of the major Protestant churches, publicly committed themselves in support of Israel and its right to exist in safe boundaries. Christians involved in dialogue with Jews have learnt since 1967 that the relation to the Land has become part and parcel of Jewish religious and secular identity, whatever may have been the opposition or indifference to Zionism of various religious and secular Jewish movements prior to the 1960s. To honour Jewish religion, Christians must be lovers of Zion.

Finally, Fackenheim proposes that the Holocaust raises the question whether there is any Good News at all. Can the sentence 'God is love' be repeated before the suffocating men, women, and children in the death camps without sounding like a taunt? Is the confident proclamation of Christ's victory an insult to the millions who found themselves delivered to the forces of hell? Many Christian theologians have been deeply impressed by Rabbi Irving Greenberg's statement that after Auschwitz there is room only for a 'troubled theism.'[10] An untroubled theism would be the sign of a lack of religious sensitivity. Whether Christians have gone as far, or are able to go as far into the believing anguish embraced by Emil Fackenheim, I do not know. But at least a great number of Christian theologians have recognized that, after Auschwitz, the traditional manner of dealing with the problem of evil and explaining the ways of God will no longer do. Fackenheim resists Whiteheadian process theology, which tries to account for the power of evil by seemingly abandoning the biblical understanding of God's omnipotence. After Auschwitz, Johann-Baptist Metz writes, theodicy must be relinquished: the only theological response we have are the stories of the great witnesses.[11] Even at Auschwitz, Pelagia Lewinska heard the commanding Voice. So did vast numbers. But even after their stories are told Christian theologians are not at rest. They do not want to engage in theological thinking without being challenged by Fackenheim's question 'Is there Good News?'

Fackenheim's message to Christian theologians is formulated from within the possibilities of Christian theology. Such are his knowledge and empathy—we saw this above—that he is able to think as if he were a Christian theologian. What he outlines as *Teshuvah* and *Tikkun* for post-Holocaust Christianity is fully acceptable to those who listen to God's judgment at Auschwitz, even within Christian orthodoxy. The church will not do theology without Fackenheim.

It should be said, however, that the Holocaust as interruption is likely to have a different meaning for Christians from the one assigned to it by Fackenheim. Christians do not ask whether Auschwitz is part of a revelatory event constitutive of Jewish identity, religious and secular. This issue is not for Christians to settle! For Christians, Auschwitz is a historical event of such shattering uniqueness that they can no longer reflect on Jesus Christ and his message without attending to this interruption. Christians may not repeat their inherited theology as if nothing had happened. In J.-B. Metz's words, Christians may not do theology 'with their backs turned to Auschwitz.' Radical reinterpretation is required, accompanied by public witness.

For Christians, the Holocaust is not the only historical event of the twentieth century that demands the reinterpretation of

Christian teaching. For instance, the collapse of colonial empire and the women's movement as response to the age-old subjugation of women are such events. Among these events of interruption, the Holocaust has an irremovable and qualitatively distinct pre-eminence, even though it does not make irrelevant the other historical events that call Christians to repentance and reparation. For Christians, Auschwitz is interruption not only because it has dismantled the idea of humanity and made ambiguous the idea of God, but because it reveals a distortion at the core of their own self-understanding. The Gospel has been revealed as source of hatred.

When the Finnish Lutheran theologian Aarne Siirala (who moved to Canada in the 1960s) visited the death camps in Eastern Europe right after the Second World War, he was shattered because he recognized what was here revealed was a sickness at the heart of Christianity and Western civilization.[12] What happened at Auschwitz, he sensed, was derived not from the worst, but from the best we have inherited. The Christian contempt for Jews and Jewish religion has exploded in history through forces that were no longer Christian and produced a mass murder of dimensions the world has never seen. What does it mean to be faithful to Jesus after Auschwitz? In the years that followed, Aarne Siirala devoted his theological effort entirely to this question.

In response to the Holocaust (and learning from Marx), Christian theologians have created the critical category of 'sacralism,' defined as the use of religion to legitimate domination, and demanded that the Christian proclamation must forever expose itself to ideology critique.[13] The prophetic tradition in the Scriptures assures us that God's Word delivers us, if we permit ourselves to be addressed, from the anti-Jewish element of our heritage and from the other elements that have sanctioned oppression. Fackenheim is correct when he sees a connection between the Christian response to the Holocaust and the emergence of liberation theology that understands the biblical message as God's promise to deliver people from domination. In fact, the 1971 Synod of Bishops held in Rome announced that, according to the contemporary understanding, the redemption Jesus Christ has brought included the liberation of people from oppression. This is true, as we shall see, only with an 'eschatological proviso.'

What Fackenheim calls 'the leftward move' of Christian theology at this time is related to the Holocaust. When Bishop Hunthausen of Seattle protested against the construction of the Trident—with the 'first-strike nuclear doctrine' it represented—in his diocese, he recalled the horrors of Auschwitz. The Trident, he said, can destroy as many as 408 separate areas, each with a bomb five times more powerful than the one dropped on Hiroshima. The Trident and the MX missile have such accuracy and power that they can be understood only as first-strike missiles. He was moved to speak out, Bishop Hunthausen said, because the Trident is being built in his own backyard. Remembering the Holocaust, he would not be silent.'[14]

The Christian churches have come to speak out on human rights and social justice as never before in their history.[15] Jews may well feel that this conversion is too late for them: more than that, that the churches' defence of human rights and self-determination for colonized people, including the Palestinians, now legitimates a critical, possibly a hypercritical and or even hostile attitude towards Israel. So asymmetrical is the Jewish situation to the course of Western history that things are often worse for the Jews when they get better for others. When Pope John Paul II travelled in Canada, he visited the Native peoples several times, he supported their land claims, he participated in their rituals, he respected their difference, and he regretted that the earlier missionaries had tried to suppress their rich spiritual tradition. In the context of Christian history, this was an extraordinary event. Who can blame Jews for feeling that John Paul II can do this for Native peoples, but neither Pius XI nor Pius XII visited a synagogue in the Germany of the 1930s, defended the human rights of the Jews, or told them how much he loved their spiritual tradition. I agree with Fackenheim when he says that, had Pius XII defended the Jews against Nazi terror, it might have been costly for the church but it would have produced a spiritual renewal of Christianity of the widest impact.

Despite the 'leftward move' of Christian thought at this time, the theologians who have consciously responded to the

Holocaust do not follow liberals or left-wing thinkers into any evolutionary theories. Pierre Teilhard de Chardin is not for them. The Holocaust as interruption renders impossible this sort of trust in history—or in God. These theologians take more seriously the apocalyptical passages of the Bible. They search for a theology of history that, on the one hand, summons Christians to join the struggle for social justice and, on the other, remains open to total defeat in this world. The possibility of defeat or deviation in a struggle for justice blessed by God, Metz includes in what he calls 'the eschatological proviso.'[16]

Since Christian theology has become more contextual and learnt to relate itself to concrete social analysis of oppression, Christian theologians may find that Fackenheim often arrives too rapidly at global statements. Thus, for Fackenheim, the Holocaust challenges the anti-Jewish inheritance as well as the Constantinianism of Christianity. While these two detrimental ideologies are related, they should be kept apart analytically. Christian preaching was anti-Jewish long before Christianity entered the Constantinian compromise with the Roman and the subsequent Western empires. It is, therefore, possible that today Christian churches in the former colonial world repudiate the inherited Constantinianism of Christianity and demand their own self-reliant development, while as yet remaining insensitive to the anti-Jewish ideology built into the Christian message. Such Christian communities may be tempted to follow the secular left in its hostility to Israel, especially if the Israeli government is selling arms to local dictators. At the same time, it is also possible that Jews who have successfully fought the humiliations inflicted on them in Western society themselves fall into Constantinianism, i.e., the identification with Western empire against the native peoples of the conquered world. One may think of the neo-conservative orientation adopted by *Commentary* in recent years.

A sociologically oriented theologian may also be ill at ease with Fackenheim's universal category of antisemitism. Is all hostility to Jews simply antisemitism? May it not be necessary to make a careful analysis in each place of the form this hostility takes and the causes that have produced it? Even if all forms of hostility to Jews have inherited the ancient Christian virus and a legacy of insanity, they also embody other historical elements. And if one wants to wrestle against a particular form of antisemitism it is important to have a more analytical grasp of the phenomenon. The creation of a universal category of antisemitism dispenses its vigorous opponents from critical analysis and prevents them from finding political measures that are most likely to be successful. It should be possible, for instance, to oppose the remnants of antisemitism in Quebec without adopting a language that reflects English-Canadian anti-French sentiment and is insensitive to the social experience of a people conquered by empire.

There is also a lack of distinction in Fackenheim's writings between opposition to Israeli political stances inspired by anti-Jewish hostility and opposition prompted by concern for Israel's future and justice to Palestinians. These two motivations may often be intertwined. But political realism counsels that one respect and take seriously criticism offered by one's friends and supporters.

Jewish Existence after the Holocaust

For Christians after the Holocaust, the overriding priority is the quest for a new theological self-understanding. The post-Holocaust Jewish response, Fackenheim writes, must be quite different. For Jews after the Holocaust, the overriding priority is simply the safety of their children (*WM*, 284). To understand the imperative of post-Holocaust Jewish existence demands a veritable leap. Jews have discovered that they are destructable: no divine providence protects them. That some have survived is simply an accident. If the war had not come to an end, all of them would have been murdered. The difference between Jews and the world is even greater. For Jews subjected to the machinery of humiliation could not, as could the Gentiles, become heroes and martyrs. It was no decision on their part that condemned Jews to death. They were killed simply because they were Jews. And some of them were subjected to such systematic humiliation that their conscious humanity was snuffed out before they were actually killed. So different was the interruption of the Holocaust for Jews that, for them, there is only one message, the 614th command-ment, the divine order to survive.

Despite the gulf between the Jews and the world, Facken-heim insists, *Tikkun* is possible and necessary. Why? Because this is what the victims' achieved under the Holocaust: to remain alive and do so with dignity in a day-and-night struggle. So must Jews struggle today. Jews must refuse to tolerate powerlessness, even though the world still wants to see them as a spiritual com-munity or in a situation of dependency. The world wants Jews to rely on the goodwill of others. Against this, the Jews must affirm and support the State of Israel, even though as *Tikkun* the state is inevitably fragmentary: it exists under extreme difficulties and re-mains in need of the solidarity of all Jews—and of the world, at least the sector of the world that has confronted the Holocaust. Survival here means, first of all, physical, biological survival. Fack-enheim is not ashamed of this, even though it differs from his earlier theology, which thought of Jewish survival as an ongoing witness to divine transcendence. After Auschwitz, it has become clear that, unless the Jewish people survives physically, it can not be a witness to God.

That Fackenheim, in his discussion of *Tikkun* for post-Holo-caust Jewish existence, says very little of faith and justice is no mere coincidence. It is related, as we shall see, to the special in-terpretation he gives to the Holocaust event. He does, however, say that Jews must not lose trust in the world altogether, even though they have been betrayed by it so many times. Jews may not despair of the world: they must seek cooperation with the world. For if they lived in segregation, Hitler would be given an-other victory.

Jews must have special concern for those who suffer. In a rare passage, Fackenheim mentions the hungry children of Af-rica, the prisoners of the Gulag, and the boat people drifting on the seas (*WM*, 306). But he does not mention the peoples who are made to suffer by systems ruled from, or dependent on, North America: not a word of solidarity with the Native peoples, with the persecuted in Latin America who try to get visas for Can-ada or the United States, or with the illegal refugees from Guate-mala and other Central American regions who live in hiding, deadly afraid of being sent back. The commanding Voice at Auschwitz orders survival. It demands that Jews remember the murder of the six million. But it does not call upon the Jews to help make visible the history of suffering of other humiliated peoples and extend solidarity to them. Fackenheim is tormented over this. 'The unredeemed anguish of Auschwitz must be ever present with us, even as it is past for us' (*WM*, 310). We return here to 'the theological suspension of the ethical.' Whatever their ethical feelings and ideas, Jews must obey the 614th commandment by giving all their strength to the struggle for their own survival. They will bless other struggling groups from afar, but they have no divine mandate to extend their solidarity to them.

While I have been deeply impressed by Fackenheim's guidance in Christian theology, I do not follow him as a reliable guide into Jewish theology. There are many Jewish religious thinkers today who have made the Holocaust foundational, possibly under Fackenheim's influence, and act as faithful Zionists, and who yet arrive at theological conclusions that appear to me, as an outsider, as more authentically Jewish.[17] There is a Jewish theology that differs from Fackenheim in the following three ways.

First, this theology holds that the words 'never again,' which the Jewish people are commanded to utter after the Holocaust, commits them to struggle against any new humiliation inflicted on them—*and on any other humiliated people*. We note that this conclusion is not an expression of liberal universalism favouring justice for people-in-general. It reveals, instead, the universality implicit in Jewish particularity, namely, the identification with particular peoples who suffer historically specific domination. Second, the Jewish religious thought that I find more reliable proposes that the existence of the State of Israel, the incarnate symbol of Jewish unwillingness to remain powerless, obliges Jewish thinkers to do what they never had to do before, namely, *to engage in ethical reflection on the use of power*. This theology does not admit theological suspension of the ethical. It holds that, without the ethical dimension, the public debate over policies and strategies to enhance the security of Israel will arrive at untrustworthy and even dangerous conclusions. And finally, I find more reliable the Jewish religious thinkers who, while refusing to forget the horror of Auschwitz, are willing to *let the Nameless One take over in their religious experience and at least occasionally allow justified protest and unredeemed anguish to be overcome in an inward gesture of surrender and peace.*

In accepting these three theological conclusions, I am willing to test them with Fackenheim's own criterion that *Tikkun* after the Holocaust is possible only if it has been initiated under the Holocaust. Here the witnesses are many. It is an honour for me to speak of a Jew from Poland living in Toronto, a survivor of the death camps, whose heart is bound in solidarity with his own people and extended to all oppressed classes and peoples struggling for justice. He has never known the theological suspension of the ethical. He even claims that it was his ethical faith, described by him in the secular language of the Bund, that kept him sane in the zone of terror through which he passed. And for mystical prayer as a form of resistance in a Nazi concentration camp, I turn to the witness of a Dutch Jew, Etty Hillesum, whose religious experiences are recorded in her diaries.[18]

Why does the important philosopher Emil Fackenheim, who has offered a trustworthy and influential program of Christian Tikkun, arrive at proposals for post-Holocaust Judaism that are accepted by few Jewish religious thinkers, even those who attach foundational importance to the Holocaust? Does Fackenheim think that it is strategically imperative for Jews at this time to concentrate on their own and Israel's survival, without distracting involvements in the struggles of other people? There are certainly Jewish political thinkers who hold this view. But there are also Jewish political thinkers who argue that an intelligent strategy for long-term peace and safety for Israel demands much greater sensitivity to the claims people in need have on Jewish support and Jewish solidarity. In my opinion, Fackenheim's proposals for post-Holocaust Jewish mending are related to certain unresolved questions in his theology.

Let us look for a moment at the kind of uniqueness Fackenheim ascribes to the Holocaust. He insists that the Holocaust is not an instance of wider species, such as genocide or mass murder. It is not the first on a long list of horrors. I agree with this. With many theologians, I ascribe to the Holocaust's unparalleled uniqueness because I see it as a culminating point of evil and ideological trends, linked in one way or another to every phase in the development of Western Christian civilization, brought about by Nazi ideology of empire and Nazi skills of technocratic control, and translated into humiliation and murder of six million by an extensive machinery of killing, involving the cooperation of vast numbers, a machinery flexible enough at each point to allow the brutal executioners to invent ever new humiliations for their victims. There is no parallel of this in history.

Yet in Fackenheim's theology, a historical uniqueness of this kind is not enough. For him, the uniqueness of the Holocaust has metaphysical dimensions. He tries to show that an analysis of this awful event touches upon the absolute. At first, he argued that, while other genocides were perpetrated by tyrants for military or other practical reasons in the establishment of empire, the Holocaust served no such purpose for the Germans. The Holocaust was unique because it, and it alone, was the exercise of evil for evil's sake (*QPF*, 18). Later, Fackenheim realized that, besides utilitarian purposes, governments also have ideological ends, and that, in the light of the Nazi philosophy of pollution and purification, the extirpation of the Jews had a certain insane rationality for their perpetrators. He then tried to show that an analysis of the many-levelled organization of genocidal destruction reveals a degree of cruelty beyond the possibility of what had hitherto been regarded as human nature. Auschwitz as 'a whole-of-horrors' makes the impossible possible. It touches upon the absolute (*MW*, 238-9).

Because of this metaphysical grounding, the Holocaust stands alone in history, it has no analogies, it may not be compared to other genocides or mass murders by nuclear weapons or organized famines. To link the Holocaust to Hiroshima or to the nuclear destruction, possibly on a universal scale, that was being prepared a decade ago, is not permitted. For this reason, the commanding Voice at Auschwitz, to which Fackenheim listens, had nothing to say of nuclear destruction, world hunger, or apartheid.

Yet, Fackenheim is unable to remain faithful to his own dis-course. He is unable to keep up the metaphysical unicity of the Holocaust, which allows of no analogy. Thus he repeatedly writes that, in June 1967, the Jewish people were threatened with a sec-ond Holocaust, even though the grave danger of that situation had an altogether different historical character. In a moving paragraph Fackenheim writes that Jews may not say, 'May the horror that has come upon us, never come upon you,' to accom-plices of the Holocaust or the silent bystanders, but Jews 'can and must say this to those upon whom *it, or something resembling it,* has come—starving African children, Gulag slave labourers, boat people roaming the sea' (*MW*, 306; emphasis added). Here Fack-enheim's discourse breaks down: the Holocaust has analogies. 'It, or something resembling it' takes place in the devastation of other peoples. At another place, Fackenheim tells us that 'when the bomb fell on Hiroshima . . . and when a shot killed Martin Luther King in Memphis, or for that matter, when Gomulka stirred Polish antisemitism against the pitifully few survivors of the Nazi slaughter, Hitler must have laughed in hell.' (*JRH*, 108). Here the 614th commandment not to grant Hitler a posthumous victory seems to be relevant to historical events that are not di-rectly related to Jewish survival. But, if this is true, does not si-lence and inactivity in regard to these events give consolation to Hitler?

Fackenheim has left unresolved the universal meaning of the Holocaust. He insists that, in its extraordinary uniqueness, the Holocaust has universal significance, it summons all people to conversion and mending, it affects the historical situation not only of Western civilization, but also of any and all other cultures and peoples (*MW*, 262). The rupture affects the whole of human history. But Fackenheim does not show us how this impact is me-diated. He cannot say that this impact is mediated metaphysi-cally, for then the Holocaust would be the highest manifestation of the demonic in general, thus violating the particular historical uniqueness Fackenheim ascribes to it. But if he thinks that the impact of the Holocaust is mediated historically, then he would have to show how a particular history of suffering of a particular people is historically interwoven with Western history, in which the Holocaust took place. What response to the Holocaust means for peoples beyond Western civilization would have to be worked out by them historically. What does post-Holocaust Tikkun mean for the Native peoples of Canada? What does it mean for the black people in South Africa? What does it mean for the Palestinians? I agree with Fackenheim that the Holocaust has meaning for all peoples and summons them to *Tikkun,* but the philosopher does not supply us with principles for working this out. When Fackenheim speaks of Christian *Tikkun,* and, as we have seen, he does so brilliantly, he is thinking of Christians identified with the major Western churches. But what does conversion and mending mean, for instance, for the Mennonites, pacifist Christians, who have been persecuted and chased across the map of Europe by empire and Constantinian church, Catholic and Protestant, since the sixteenth century?

One of the reasons why Fackenheim has not resolved the question raised by his understanding of Holocaust uniqueness is that he has not sufficiently unfolded the meaning of survival. What precisely is the commanding Voice ordering Jews to do? Fackenheim insists that what is meant here is the physical survival of the people. But the testimony of Pelagia Lewinska, with which Fackenheim legitimates his own theological language, has a much richer meaning. 'And even if I die in Auschwitz, it would be as a human being, I would hold on to my dignity . . . A terrible struggle began which went on day and night.' Fackenheim never tries to unpack the meaning of the divine orders received by Pelagia Lewinska. What does it mean to survive as a human being and to hold on to one's dignity? It is a mistake not to reflect on this important testimony in a more sustained way.

Occasionally Fackenheim's own discourse of survival breaks down. Thus he writes that, if Judaism ever forgot the six million who were murdered, it would 'not deserve to survive' (*JRH*, 27). What does this mean? Fackenheim claims that, by forgetting the Holocaust, Judaism would have disobeyed the commanding Voice and reversed God's message, and thereby forfeited the inner reason for its existence. Fackenheim's judgment is here strictly theological. But he does not question whether the 614th commandment contains other messages, such as 'survival as human beings, holding on to human dignity,' that also define the inner reason for Jewish existence and also demand fidelity.

Because he leaves these questions unattended, Fackenheim does not supply the Jewish community with appropriate norms for the important debates going on at this time about social responsibility, in general, and concrete public policies, in particular. His theology does not help Jews in North America who look for ethical guidance in the important policy debates, including those regarding nuclear weapons and economic justice, and it does not supply Jews in Israel with principles useful for the debate in their country in regard to strategies and national objectives. These unresolved questions, in my opinion, explain why Fackenheim has moved on a path in Jewish theology which few have followed. What he demands of Christians is the renewal of their theological self-understanding—and we have found his proposals brilliant—what he asks of Jews is a day-and-night struggle accompanied by Kierkegaardian anguish.

Emil Fackenheim's books quoted:

GPH – *God's Presence in History*, New York, NY: New York University Press, 1970.

JRH – *The Jewish Return to History*, New York, NY: Schocken Books, 1978.

MW – *To Mend the World*, New York, NY: Schocken Books, 1982.

QPF – *Quest for Past and Future*, Bloomington, IN: Indiana University Press, 1968.

Notes

1. This article was written before the publication in 1987 of Emil Fackenheim's *What is Judaism?* (New York: Summit Books).

2. E.S. Fiorenza and D. Tracy, eds., *The Holocaust as Interruption*, Concilium no. 175 (Edinburgh: T. & T. Clark 1984), xi.

3. Among the Holocaust theorists, themselves representing only one current of contemporary Jewish theology, E. Fackenheim seems to be singular. Cf. E.B. Borowitz, *Choices in Modern Jewish Thought* (New York: Behrman House 1984).

4. E. Fackenheim (MW, 293, 294) quotes an important passage from J.-B. Metz's article, "Ökumene nach Auschwitz," in *Gott nach Auschwitz* (Freiburg: Herder 1979), 121-44. In English, see J.-B. Metz, "Facing the Jews: Christian Theology

after Auschwitz," in Fiorenza and Tracy, eds., *The Holocaust as Interruption*, 26-33. For Metz's statement on prayer after Auschwitz, see ibid, 27.

5. R.R. Ruether, *Faith and Fratricide* (New York: Seabury Press 1974). For the subsequent debate, see Alan Davies, ed., *Antisemitism and the Foundations of Christianity* (New York: Paulist Press 1979).

6. For an analysis of these various theological attempts, see J. Pawlikowski, *Christ in the Light of the Christian-Jewish Dialogue* (New York: Paulist Press 1982). Also see E. Fleischner, ed. *Auschwitz: Beginning of a New Era?* (New York: KTAV Publishing House 1977).

7. There are studies that have examined the impact of the new approach. See J. Pawlikowski, "Judaism in Christian Education and Liturgy," in *Auschwitz: Beginning of a New Era?*, 155-78.

8. See J. Oesterreicher, "Declaration on the Relationship of the Church to Non-Christian Religions: Introduction and Commentary," in H. Vorgrimler, ed., *Commentary on the Documents of Vatican II*, vol. 3, 1-136 (New York: Herder and Herder 1969).

9. Metz, "Ökumene nach Auschwitz," 143

10. I. Greenberg, "Cloud of Smoke, Pillar of Fire: Judaism, Christianity, and Modernity after the Holocaust," in *Auschwitz: Beginning of a New Era?*, 33

11. This forceful expression was used by J.-B. Metz in a lecture he gave at Boston College in January 1985.

12. Aarne Siirala, "Reflections from a Lutheran Perspective," in *Auschwitz: Beginning of a New Era?*, 135-48.

13. Matthew Lamb, *Solidarity with Victims* (New York: Crossroad 1982), 10

14. Jim Castelli, *The Bishops and the Bomb* (Garden City, NY: Doubleday 983), 28.

15. In his speech at the United Nations on 2 October 1979, Pope Paul mentioned the memory of the extermination camp at Oswiecim (Auschwitz) as summons and starting-point for a new dedication of humanity to protect human rights and stand against genocide, oppression, domination, and torture, physical and spiritual. Complete text in *Origins* 9 (1979), 257, 259-66.

16. J.-B. Metz, *Theology of the World* (New York: Seabury Press 1973), 114.

17. It is not my intention to line up a list of critics against Emil Fackenheim, the great Jewish philosopher of our time, who despite differences is loved and honoured in the Jewish and Christian communities. In the Canadian context, I wish to refer to two books, David Hartman, *Joy and Responsibility* (Jerusalem: Ben Zvi-Posner 1978), and Dow Marmur, *Beyond Survival* (London: Darton, Longman and Todd 1982).

18. *An Interrupted Life: The Diaries of Etty Hillesum, 1941-1943* (Toronto: Lester & Orpen Dennys 1983). Cf. G. Baum, "The Witness of Etty Hillesum," *The Ecumenist* 23 (Jan.-Feb. 1985), 24-8.

Part II

Theology
and
Social Analysis

7.

Do We Need a Catholic Sociology?

This essay offers an interpretation of the contribution to sociology made by Catholics in the United States over the last fifty years. It is not a historical study that names Catholic sociologists and evaluates their work. What I wish to do instead is to outline an intellectual development among American Catholic sociologists over half a century. My thesis is—and this may be controversial—that there have been three types of Catholic involvement in sociological studies, where each type corresponded to a particular phase of the American economy. In the 1930s and 40s, American Catholics promoted their own Catholic sociology; from the 50s on they welcomed the ascending functionalist sociology and dropped the idea of a Catholic sociology; and in the 80s, some of them, at odds with liberal capitalism, moved beyond functionalism to examine society from the perspective of its victims. This essay pursues a point of view. The statement it wants to make is ultimately a theological one.

Catholic Beginnings

From its beginning in the early 20th century, American sociology was guided by a mechanistic, evolutionary concept of society. The spirit of Auguste Comte and Herbert Spencer was alive and well. This is how Gibson Winter describes the mechanistic model that underlay the sociology of the American scholar Graham Sumner, whose work set the tone for more than a generation:

> The mechanistic model postulates a set of instinctive forces playing upon one another in an environment; these forces move against one another within the limitations set by the environment; various resolutions of force furnish modes of adaptation, and the most suitable moves lead to survival; hence the construction of laws which express these suitable modes of adaptation enables the scientist to discern the order inscribed in the process.[1]

Winter suggests that this paradigm of the social process corresponds to the mechanism of the free market. Here competing parties, seeking their own interests, create conflicts that necessitate modes of adaptation, that are resolved by the most suitable moves leading to victory, and that are ruled by what scientists discover as the law of supply and demand operative within it.

American pragmatism tried to free social science from the mechanistic model of externally related forces and reinstate the human being as an active, responsible subject, but this perspective was never fully integrated into American sociology.[2] Sociology remained positivistic.

As Catholic higher education developed in America and sociology was introduced into Catholic colleges, Catholic professors found it impossible to join mainstream sociology. They were keenly aware that their study of society was guided by a different understanding of the human being. They engaged in what they called Catholic sociology. In 1937 they founded the American Catholic Sociological Society (ACSS) and in 1940 began publishing the *American Catholic Sociological Review* (*ACSR*). While these professors recognized that there could be no Catholic mathematics, they strongly defended the need for a Catholic sociology. None of these scholars were great theoreticians, yet their insights were often profound.

The first volumes of *ACSR* contained papers that offered arguments to explain why the dominant American sociology deserved to be rejected and why Catholics should pursue their own sociology in keeping with the Church's social teaching.[3] I wish to summarize these arguments under three headings.

First, Catholic scholars criticized the concept of the human being presupposed by the secular sociology of their day. They rejected its implicit determinism and evolutionism. For theological reasons they believed that people were free to make responsible decisions and that the future of society depended on these decisions. They also affirmed the religious dimension of human existence: people had ears to hear the call of God. They thus repudiated the dominant sociology which held a reductionist view of religion and tended to interpret religion as a pre-modern phenomenon to be left behind by the evolutionary process.

Second, Catholic sociologists objected to the perception of the social process implicit in the dominant sociology. The positivists regarded society as an interacting system of atomistic individuals, which they tried to understand scientifically, using the inductive method, taking into account only external, quantifiable factors and disregarding inner, non-measureable ones such as people's intentions. Catholic sociologists, relying on the concept of society derived from Catholic social teaching, recognized the spiritual dimension of society, the social bonds that united its members, and the symbols that defined their identity and common vision.

Third, Catholic sociologists found fault with the dominant sociology because of the absence of an explicit social ethics perspective. What did they mean by this? Catholic sociologists regarded their own work as scientific. They fully embraced the inductive method and defended the relative autonomy of sociology against conservative members of their college communities who opposed the presence of social science in the curriculum. They loved what they called 'the facts' and did not totally overcome their own positivistic prejudice. They made an excessively simple distinction between 'the facts' obtained by empirical research and 'the social philosophy' derived from an intellectual tradition that interpreted the facts and brought them together in a synthetic perspective. They repeatedly complained that American sociology was strong on facts but weak on philosophy: American sociology had no explicit social ethics perspective. For Catholic sociologists the social ethics perspective was defined by the philosophy derived from the Church's social teaching.

What did this social ethics mean in practical terms? In the 30s and 40s, Catholics who took papal social teaching seriously,

and this included the Catholic sociologists, were ardent supporters of the New Deal. Catholic sociologists were reform-minded.
They engaged in social studies to arrive at a better understanding
of society's ills, and they hoped that by their teaching they would
contribute to the reform of American society.[4] For them Catholic
sociology was value-laden and action-oriented.

We note that despite their criticism of American sociology,
the mood of the Catholic sociologists was upbeat and optimistic.
They shared in the vigour of American society. Thus they had
little sympathy for the pessimistic analyses offered by Pitirim
Sorokin who assigned American society to 'the sensate phase' of
civilization and described the tragic symptoms of its pervasive cultural corruption.[5] Sorokin's article in the second volume of the
ACSR found no echo among Catholic sociologists: in subsequent
issues the only reference to it was critical.[6]

The Catholic sociologists were reliable, but not brilliant. Today we read with them great sympathy. They saw themselves as a
minority of believing intellectuals swimming against the stream of
the dominant culture. But belonging to what was then the Catholic subculture, they lacked the training and self-confidence to
take on mainstream American sociology directly and refute its
theories and presuppositions in a rational, systematic way. Had
they been able to do this, they might have discovered that even
without reference to divine revelation and Catholic tradition it
would have been possible to offer a rational defense of their
three demands: an alternative concept of the human that recognized the spiritual core, a paradigm of the social process that
took into account values and symbols, and the need for an explicit social ethics dimension.

One more remark before we leave these Catholic sociologists: their sociological studies had no impact on their theological
ideas. Their work was guided by Catholic theology, but did not
spark new reflection in the field of theology. For them the relation between theology and sociology was a one-way street.

Varieties of Functionalism

In the 50s, America was steadily moving in the direction of welfare capitalism. During those years a new sociology achieved wide recognition in the United States. The new approach was called 'structural functionalism' because it assumed that the various subsystems (structures) of the complex interaction system (society) exercised specific functions, functions that enabled society as a whole to adapt to the changing environment and preserve social equilibrium whenever challenged and acted upon by historical forces. Here society was seen as a cybernetic, self-adaptive, self-correcting system. In this process the cultural subsystem, which included ethical values and religious symbols, exercised an important function in stabilizing the social order and aiding individuals to integrate smoothly into roles assigned by society.

Talcott Parsons, the most famous structural functionalist[7], provided a sociological theory that reconciled positivistic, quantitative research with an appreciation of cultural and religious factors. In light of his sociology, the conflict between science and religion appeared to be overcome.[8]

It is no wonder that Catholics were greatly impressed by the new sociology. Here the image of the human being included the spiritual dimension; the paradigm of the social process assigned an important role to values and symbols; and because functionalism saw expanding differentiation and integration as an evolutionary drift, it represented—in the American context—a reformist social philosophy supporting the move toward welfare capitalism and a more just income distribution.

Under these conditions Catholics became increasingly uncomfortable with the idea of a Catholic sociology. They were now able to join the dominant sociology without compromising their religious convictions. In the early 60s, the ACSS became the Association for the Sociology of Religion (ASR) and the quarterly *ACSR* took the name *Sociological Analysis*. In his 1962 presidential address, John Hughes paid tribute to the impact of functionalism: "Sociologists have a professional preoccupation with the functional utility of human activities. They are engaged in a constant search for purposes, manifest and latent, which are served by social behaviour."[9] This statement actually reveals, beyond the intention of its author, the ambiguity of functionalist theory: its implicit utilitarianism and the absence of transcendence despite the affirmation of religious values.

Before examining the limitations of functionalism, I wish to recognize the intellectual creativity it released among Catholic sociologists. As an example let me mention Thomas O'Dea, who occasionally wrote from a specifically Catholic perspective while most of his work represented the sociological science universally accepted at American universities. Thus he was invited by Prentice-Hall Publishers to write a textbook on the sociology of religion for their multi-volume college series on sociology.[10] In this volume O'Dea initiated the reader into functionalist theory, without disguising its unresolved questions and possible shortcomings. Human life, O'Dea observed, is marked by contingency and death. For most people life is also painfully affected by powerlessness and scarcity. It is religion that enables people to cope with these challenges, persevere in the roles they play in their social setting, and thus become instruments serving the equilibrium of society. Religion protects society from breakdown.

O'Dea mentions six functions of religion.[11] Religion offers support and consolation to people during times of disappointment; communicates a sense of security under conditions of uncertainty; confirms the accepted norms of society as religious duties and thus stabilizes the social order, despite the unequal distribution of rewards; expresses a social vision that at times fuels reformist impulses in society; provides people with a collective identity; and helps people as they move through the phases of their life cycle and teaches them how to die. Thus, because religion makes people peaceful, resourceful and stable, it fulfills an irreplaceable function in society.

In line with functionalist theory, Andrew Greeley offered a more concrete analysis of the power of religion in American society. He followed the inspiration of Alexis de Tocqueville who in the 1830s observed that under the impact of American egalitarian society, the Christian religion underwent a significant transformation.[12] While the religion of established churches in Europe undergirded the unity of their respective countries and thus exercised a certain political function, the religion of the many churches in the United States, none of which was established, exercised a very different function, one that affected people's personal lives more directly.

Tocqueville saw America as an individualistic, egalitarian and market-oriented society, characterized by an extraordinary social mobility, vertical and horizontal, that detached people from the communties in which they were born and set them on the lonely path toward success. In this social context, the denominational network of small congregations, spread over the whole country, provided people with a sense of community and social identity and offered them a message of love that restrained their ambition and self-preoccupation. This humanizing function of religion, Tocqueville believed, was the reason why Americans were so faithful in their religious practice.

In line with Tocqueville's analysis, Greeley praised 'the genius of American religion': religion in America responded creatively to the needs of the emerging modern, industrial society. While industrialization fostered the secularization of society in Europe, this was not the case in America. Pluralistic, denominational religion supplied people with what Greeley called 'a sense of belonging' and 'a source of meaning.'[13] Belonging—because being at home in a church gave them something resembling a tribal identity. And meaning—because the transcendent message gave their life a purpose beyond the short-range preoccupations generated by the business-oriented culture.

It is interesting to compare the functionalist interpretation of American religion offered by Greeley, the Catholic, with that given by Parsons, the Protestant. Parsons also rejected the theory of secularization defended by many European sociologists, according to which industrialization was inevitably accompanied by the waning of religion. What was taking place in modern society, Parsons argued, was a process of differentiation, of specialization and integration in all large institutions, including the churches.[14] Thus many functions exercised by the churches in the past—such as community-building, commemorating great events, teaching, counseling and providing recreation—were increasingly fulfilled by secular institutions, thus allowing religion to exercise its one unique function, namely 'the formation of conscience.' Parsons believed that the formation of conscience, the will to do the right thing at all times, was the essential personal motivation that made modern society work effectively. Complex institutions of government, industry and business depended on the reliability of each person working in them at whatever level; and since it was impossible to supervise every person's work, it was on the conscience of each, on their will to do the right thing, that the entire society, with its many interacting organizations, depended. Parsons argued that religion flourished in America because the Christian and Jewish traditions created the motivation that constituted the heart of the American system.

We note that the Protestant Parsons located the power of religion in the shaping of the mind while the Catholic Greeley, heir of a more communitarian and more mystical tradition, defined the function of religion in America as creating community and providing transcendent meaning beyond one's daily work.

To prepare us for the critical observations to be made further on, I wish to contrast Greeley's functionalist approach with the analysis of two other social thinkers. Tocqueville, we saw, believed that religion was important because it allowed people to integrate in the American republic. This was the line of thought Greeley explored. But Tocqueville also argued that religion was important for another reason: it rooted people in an ancient tradition and enabled them to resist the pressure of public opinion and thus escape the cultural conformism which characterized egalitarian societies.[15] For Tocqueville, religion was therefore a social source of freedom. Because it transcended society, it empowered believers to stand against the received set of values. In fact, Tocqueville feared that if the increasingly powerful government ever acquired the skills to manipulate public opinion, American democracy, despite its liberal philosophy, could become despotic. In such a system the people, bent on complying with public opinion, would accept government policy and obey official regulations willingly and joyfully, all the while believing themselves to be free and unconstrained. Tocqueville was afraid of the perfectly balanced social system in which people had internalized public norms. He regarded religion as a bulwark of independent thought.

It is also instructive to contrast Greeley's positive interpretation of American denominational religion with the more negative view of Richard Niebuhr. Greeley assigned the formation of denominations to the genius of American religion adapting itself creatively to meet the needs of a modern society. By contrast, Niebuhr argued that the denominational structure came into being because American churches were unable to bridge the social tensions produced in them by the complexity of American society: tensions between the towns of the East coast and the moving Western frontier, between North and South, between white and black, between rich and poor, and between immigrant groups and established elites. For Niebuhr, the proliferation of denominations was the social product of the churches' failure to transcend, in the name of Christ, the tearing conflicts created by a sinful world.[16]

Structural functionalism, we have noted, concentrates on the unifying and interconnecting elements of society and tends to interpret conflict and social struggle as temporary strains produced by society's effort to adapt itself to new historical circumstances. This American sociology understands differences of power largely in terms of the different functions exercised by various sectors of society in the service of increasing social equilibrium. Cultural values, including religion, make people readily accept their role and the roles of others in society. Legitimate power is thus not experienced as domination but as an aspect of differentiation, the division of functions promoting the well-being of society as a whole.

The functionalist understanding of hierarchy has a certain affinity with the organic, corporatist idea of society proposed by the Church's social teaching—at least until the early 70s. It also reflects the traditional self-understanding of the Church as a hierarchical body, an 'unequal society' in which the members know their place, and through the interplay of authority and obedience serve the well-being of the whole. In my opinion it is an abiding Catholic intuition—shared even by today's egalitarian Catholics—that a cooperative society in which the aspirations of individuals are fully reconciled with the requirements of the common good is an historical possibility. By nature and by grace this is the destiny of society.

The question remains whether this image is a useful paradigm for interpreting existing social orders or whether it is a 'utopia' serving as a guide for social action in the world and the reform of ecclesiastical institutions.

*

While the Catholic sociology of the 1930s and 40s made no impact on Catholic theology, functionalist sociology offered many opportunities for creative dialogue with Catholic theology. If it is true that religion stabilizes, pacifies and humanizes society and that religious symbols guide the social order and influence individual behaviour, then it should be possible to express the meaning of divine revelation in a language that accounts for its impact on social and personal life. Such an approach to theology has a certain affinity with Karl Rahner's transcendental theology which sought to articulate the meaning of dogma in terms of its revealing, saving and sanctifying power. Seen in this perspective, the symbols of religion are not 'weak,' images calling forth feeling, but 'strong,' essential elements in the self-constitution of society and its members.

Andrew Greeley has pursued this approach in an imaginative way. In several books he has explored the Christian message in terms of its transformative impact on people living in America.[17] To this end Greeley made ample use of the six functions of religion outlined by Thomas O'Dea. If the role of religion is to serve the well-being of men and women in society, then sociological reflection can make an important contribution to defining the Church's mission in the world. In his *The New Agenda*,[18] published after Vatican Council II, Greeley used this method to define and contrast two pastoral projects of the Church, the preconciliar and the conciliar one; and in several subsequent publications he employed the same sociological reasoning to make proposals for the Church's pastoral policies.[19]

What is presupposed in this interchange between sociology and theology is that divine revelation is God's saving and sanctifying Word addressed to this society in order to rescue its members from their anomie and to perfect the social order for the well-being of all. The perspective here is incarnational. Further on we shall ask what happens when God's Word is heard first of all as judgment on the world—the eschatological perspective.

It is of interest that Parsons makes religion disappear in the formation of conscience, a purely this-worldly function, while Greeley defends divine transcendence and human ecstasy. For him, America is a nation of mystics.[20] Yet these experiences of otherness make people more truly human and hence serve the well-being of the entire nation. In this perspective, divine otherness does not interrupt the well-tempered society.

*

Parsons's functionalism was vehemently attacked in the late 50s and the 60s by sociologists who perceived society in more conflictual terms. They provided a critique from the political left. C. Wright Mills[21] and Alvin Gouldner[22] argued against structural functionalism in ways that are of special interest to theologians. They showed that Parsons' sociology never really moved beyond utilitarianism. While he appreciated non-utilitarian values, he recognized them only for their social utility. Even though Parsons took people's interior life seriously, he thought that their subjectivity was engendered by society's effort to adapt to new conditions and preserve the social equilibrium. Thus, people's experience of freedom was an illusion: acting within them was the cybernetic social system following its own necessity. The interacting harmony of society was theoretically assured by eliminating human freedom. Parsons never escaped the assumptions of positivism and determinism. He believed that objective and value-free sociological research could uncover the laws operating in society that accounted for social development and people's personal behaviour.

Catholic sociologists who followed the functionalist approach, such as O'Dea and Greeley, did not endorse Parsons' presuppositions,[23] just as Christian thinkers who make use of Marxist paradigms do not accept Marx's ontological presuppositions. With Parsons the Catholic sociologists acknowledged society's trend toward differentiation, integration and social equilibrium, but they did this not because they accepted the evolutionary, determinist thrust of the social system (and the elimination of personal freedom), but because they shared what I have called 'the Catholic intuition,' the belief that a cooperative social order reconciling personal aspirations with service in the common good was an historical possibility and the high destiny of society.

Mills and Gouldner criticized Parsons' structural functionalism also because of its political implications. The focus on social harmony and interaction tended to make invisible the social conflicts and struggles initiated by groups and classes disfavoured in society. In presenting society as a self-correcting, cybernetic social system and dismissing discontent and disruption as temporary strains during periods of adaptation, structural functionalism exercised an ideological role. It provided a social theory that legitimated the existing order.

Arguing against Parsons, Mills and Gouldner defended a conflictual view of society. Karl Marx had pointed to the class-divided nature of feudal and capitalist society; and according to some even Max Weber, who had no sympathy for socialism, saw society divided between the dominant structures defended by the elites and the countervailing movements supported by the underprivileged. Mills and Gouldner argued that it was more rational, more faithful to social reality, to abandon the functionalist perspective in favour of a 'conflict sociology' of one kind or another.

A careful reading of Talcott Parsons' entire work reveals that he designed his social theory with its cybernetic, evolutionary thrust as an alternative to the Marxist theory of history that exercised such a strong appeal to classes, peoples and nations situated at the margin.[24] According to Parsons, the principle of differentiation, the application of reason to social development and adaptation generated an evolutionary trend in human history that culminated in industrial, capitalist society, ever moving self-correctively toward greater social cooperation and harmony. This evolution reached its high point in American society.

American sociologists became deeply divided over methodology. Functionalists and conflict theorists argued with one another. Conflict theorists were not united among themselves. Scientific Marxists, for instance, remained wholly within the positivistic, utilitarian intellectual tradition, while cultural Marxists and non-Marxist conflict theorists often defended a more humanistic understanding of the human being. Did these debates about conflict over values deserve serious attention by philosophers and ethicists, or were they politically inspired squabbles produced by ideological distortion on both sides? 'Yes' to the first question was said, among others, by theologians influenced by the emerging Liberation Theology. 'Yes' to the second question was said by certain sociologists who, in relying on phenomenology, tried to transcend the debate between right and left and find a value-free entry into the sociological analysis of social action.[25]

The work of these "symbolic interactionists," as they are sometimes called, is interesting. Some of their social theories, because of the claim to value-neutrality, have been employed by Christian thinkers in specifically Christian reflections. I am thinking especially of Peter Berger[26] and Gibson Winter.[27] Yet this article is not the place to examine whether symbolic interactionism really succeeded in providing an entry into a value-free analysis of social action, or whether the claim to value-neutrality actually trivialized the material inequality of American society and hence represented a value-laden theoretical strategy. In the rest of this article, I will argue that, under present conditions in particular, the truth about society is not available to the researcher who wishes to remain objective. Truth demands commitment, even in the social sciences.

*

In the late 70s and the 80s welfare capitalism entered into a severe crisis. The Keynesian economic policies that had been adopted by all developed capitalist countries no longer seemed to work. What began to take place as a response was a reorganization of capitalism on the global level, a process that has been evaluated in different ways. The topic is a controversial one.

I find convincing, for reasons that will become apparent later, the analysis of these changes offered in the ecclesiastical documents of John Paul II and the American and Canadian Catholic bishops. According to *Laborem exercens*, capitalism has passed, first, through an early 'free enterprise' phase that caused enormous suffering among workers, and later through a 'welfare state' phase, that was more willing to share the wealth produced with society.[28] At the present time, the Pope argues, capitalism is entering a new phase, one that threatens to widen the gap between rich and poor countries and between rich and poor even in the developed countries. Capitalism, according to the Canadian bishops, has become a new ball game.[29] The unwritten contract that existed between the capitalist elite and society, guaranteeing full employment, welfare legislation and respect for labour organizations, has been abrogated. Capitalism is being reorganized around privately-owned, giant, transnational corporations that are able to shift capital and relocate industries in parts of the world where labour is cheap, safety regulations minimal, and unionization forbidden by law. These transnationals are often strong enough to force a national government to serve their economic interests. Omnipresent international competition forces governments to adopt economic policies that will make the national economies 'lean and efficient,' competitive on the world market. What is demanded is a flexible and docile work force, the reduction of welfare spending, and governmental indifference to the growing sector of the deprived.

In their long pastoral letter on the economy, the American Catholic bishops analyzed the growing portion of the deprived, in some regions reaching into the middle class.[30] The Canadian bishops, in a series of shorter pastoral messages, have focused more directly on the systemic causes of these social developments.[31] They have provided an ethical critique of capitalism. And in his *Sollicitudo rei socialis* (1987), John Paul II has argued that the misery and the hopelessness of the Third World countries of the South is to a large extent the result of ideologies that determine the economic and political policies adopted by the capitalist and communist powers of the North.[32] The ideological and political competition between the two superpowers and the ensuing world-wide conflicts generate the nuclear arms race, arms production and the sale of arms; and the growth-orientation of capitalism, increasingly imitated by communist countries, unfailingly moves the global society toward a life-threatening ecological crisis. We are a civilization, John Paul II tells us, "oriented toward death rather than life."[33]

If this is true, if as a civilization we are indeed oriented toward death, then we must listen anew to the words of Jesus, "Repent, for the kingdom of God is at hand" (Mt 4:17). To articulate the meaning of this message for the United States and Western society as a whole is the task of a First World Liberation Theology.

If this reading of the signs of the times is correct, why are so few people aware of it? The new phase of capitalism is accompanied by a 'neo-conservative' culture that blesses and legitimates it. Thanks to the dominant cultural symbols, people become increasingly concerned with their private lives. In *Habits of the Heart* Robert Bellah has distinguished between 'utilitarian individualism' that makes people work for material success and 'expressive individualism' that makes them concentrate on their own subjectivity.[34] For both types, life is what you put into it. People reach the economic, social and cultural level they have merited. Society is an open playing field, and if people find themselves at the margin, it is probably their own fault. Neo-conservative culture tries to reconcile us with inequality. It wants to give society an untroubled conscience despite growing numbers of the deprived. The social passion so widely experienced in the 60s has come to be regarded as naive and unrealistic. Passionate concern for social justice, peace, disarmament, clean water, fresh air and a sustainable society is not viewed as a realistic response to the orientation toward death, but as a stubborn and irrational utopianism, even dangerous because it makes people yearn for what they can never have. Today's neo-conservative culture has little use for the Church's contemporary social teaching. Competition, not compassion and solidarity, is the rule of life.

The neo-conservative culture even mobilized religion to legitimate the existing order. Well-known are the spokesmen of the so-called 'New Christian Right' and, on a different intellectual level and appealing to a different part of society, the Catholic and Protestant academics hired by various neo-conservative research institutes. Yet there are even secular social scientists committed to neo-conservative politics who advocate a return to religion in order to make the present social order work more efficiently.

As an example, consider Daniel Bell's *The Cultural Contradictions of Capitalism.*[35] Bell argues that the decline of the American economy is related to the cultural tension between the hard work and dedication demanded by the capitalist economy and the pleasure and instant satisfaction offered to people by contemporary culture. Industry and hedonism do not walk hand in hand. Bell does not ask whether contemporary hedonism may be created by the capitalist economy in search of wider markets, transforming people into customers and consumers. For Bell culture is largely independent of the economic base. He believes that a new culture of self-sacrifice and self-limitation would make the American economy more productive and more efficient. Since people's desire for satisfaction is so great, it is only religion—the relation to the sacred—that can overcome the hedonistic, cultural trend. Thus, for the sake of American capitalism, Bell advocates a return to religion among the people.

What interests me here is the official reaction of the Catholic Church and other Christian Churches to this new situation. They have produced a reasoned, religiously-based critique of the present order. Catholic social teaching in particular has used as a guiding principle of thought and action the 'preferential option for the poor,' a principle that is theologically grounded and sociologically relevant. Where did this principle come from? And what does it mean?

Following the Vatican Council in the 60s, the Latin American Bishops tried to understand from a Christian perspective the situation of the people on their continent.[36] They realized that the Church's traditional social teaching with its organic concept of society was not very helpful. Latin American society was not organic. It was deeply divided between a small developed sector and the great masses living in destitution. During the 60s people in many parts of the continent organized in social movements and sought to liberate themselves from their plight. To interpret this situation some form of conflict sociology was necessary. To understand Latin America from a Christian perspective, the bishops argued, echoing here the call of the base communities and

Liberation Theology, it had to be looked at from the viewpoint of the poor and in solidarity with them.

The comfortable classes of Latin America, including the clergy, have tended to look at society from their own perspective. They recognized the presence of the poor masses, but felt that this was simply part of earthly reality, an unfortunate condition but one that could not be altered. What the Latin American Bishops Conferences of Medellin (1968) and Puebla (1979) demanded was a conversion of the Catholic people, including the Church, to the perspective of the poor. What precisely this conversion entailed we shall examine further on.

Did the option for the poor say anything to Catholics living in the United States and other developed countries? These countries were, after all, welfare societies: they were not split into two unequal sectors as were the Latin American societies. Still, liberation theologians in Latin America pleaded with their colleagues from the United States to develop a 'holistic' theological evaluation of their country.[37] By this they meant that Americans could not understand their own nation unless they were willing to look at the economic and political power it exercises in Latin America and, in fact, in the entire world. Marie Augusta Neal argued convincingly that one of the illusions fostered by Parsons' structural functionalism was that a national society was a self-contained social system that could be understood by analyzing its internal interactions alone.[38] In actual fact, Neal argued, a nation had economic and political links of domination or dependency to other parts of the world and could not be correctly understood apart from these links.

The World Synod of Bishops in 1971 adopted the preferential option with its sociological and theological dimensions.[39] The Synod recognized various systems of domination seeking ever greater power, and liberation movements that struggled to create conditions of justice. The bishops declared themselves in solidarity with these struggles for justice. Moreover, the Synod acknowledged that their critical perception of the world and their solidarity with the poor was their response to God's revelation in Jesus Christ. Why? Because the redemption which Jesus brought included the liberation of people from conditions of oppression.

As capitalism moved into its present phase, certain ecclesiastical documents began to adopt the preferential option even in the context of the developed world. John Paul II's *Laborem exercens* (1981) looked upon workers and other wage-earners as deprived of their human right to participate in ownership and decision-making. The encyclical proposed that this deprived sector was the historical agent of social reconstruction in the industrialized capitalist and communist societies, and called for the solidarity of workers supported by the solidarity of all who love justice, including the Church itself.[40] The Canadian and American bishops adopted the preferential option, even if not in identically the same sense.[41] The Canadian bishops defined the option as did Medellin and Puebla: "As Christians we are called to follow Jesus by identifying with the victims of injustice, by analyzing the dominant attitude and structures that cause human suffering, and by actively supporting the poor and oppressed in their struggles to transform society."[42]

The preferential option is centrally important to the Church's own self-understanding. The biblical basis for this option is presented in the American bishops' pastoral letter on economic justice.[43] This option, moreover, is in keeping with the Christian tradition. The Church has always advocated what may be called 'the compassionate option' for the poor: respect for the poor, almsgiving and other forms of assistance. The Church has also praised 'the ascetical option' for the poor: the option for the simple life, in solidarity with the poor and in total reliance on God. This option has found expression especially in religious life. In the 20th century, the Church has defended 'the missionary option' for the poor: priests and bishops should live simple, unadorned lives to support the credibility of their message. Puebla advocated 'the pastoral option' for the poor: it called upon dioceses and other church bodies to give priority to the poor in the use of their pastoral resources, including personnel, institutions and finances. Finally, Puebla also called for the conversion of the Church to 'the preferential option' for the poor.[44] This option was to orient the Church's social ministry. This option, it is worth mentioning, did not relieve people from the options previously mentioned; these retain their full validity.

At Puebla, the preferential option was defined as the double commitment, implicit in Christian discipleship, to look upon society from the perspective of the marginalized—the hermeneutical dimension—and to stand in solidarity with their struggle against oppression—the activist dimension.

Space does not permit me to defend the preferential option against certain misunderstandings. Elsewhere I have shown that the preferential option is not a patronizing gesture of the bishops bending down to the lower classes.[45] The option has meaning for all, including the poor: the poor are summoned to recognize God's presence among them, opt for themselves, overcome the false and degrading self-understanding communicated to them by the dominant culture, and discover their call to action.

Nor is the preferential option a commitment to populism. It does not imply a romantic idealization of the ideas and attitudes held by the underprivileged. Listening to the poor means looking at society from their marginal position, learning to take their plight seriously, and searching for the structural causes of their suffering.

It is also important to show that the preferential option is a transcendent principle. It remains operative in, through and after a radical social transformation: for as soon as other groups are pushed to the margin, the preferential option calls for solidarity with them. It is useful to compare the preferential option with the option for the proletariat or the option for the nation. The latter are both preferential options. Each expresses a double commitment: by creating a new perspective for seeing the social reality and generating acts of solidarity in the political order. There are undoubtedly historical conditions when it is right and just to opt for the emancipation of the proletariat or the free self-determination of a nation in bondage. But these two preferential options do not welcome critical self-reflection. If they are stubbornly clung to in new historical situations, they give rise to new forms of oppression and eventually become idols demanding even the sacrifice of human beings. By contrast, the preferential option for the poor is not an ideology: it is the bearer of a transcendent principle and hence generates ever new, critical historical judgments.

In the Puebla document, ideology was defined as a set of ideas and ideals that represented the aspirations of only one sector of society and hence could not claim to represent the totality.[46] Ideologies become myths when they forget their limited character and claim to speak for the whole. Yet the preferential option for the poor, Puebla insists, is not an ideology. Why? Because it represents a praxis that aims at the transformation of society and the promotion of its common good. The poor are not an 'interest group' in society whose claims should be weighed against those of other interest groups. The poor reveal the injustice inscribed into the whole social order. The poor bring to light the contradictions of society. Their marginalization harms them and, in a different way, damages all of society: it distorts society's perception of itself; gives an ideological twist to the dominant culture; and creates an insensitive, hard-hearted, egotistical, self-serving population deaf to the voice of God.

Thus, racism not only inflicts burdens on the despised race; but also promotes a culture of contempt, injustice and violence that spills over into every aspect of social and political life. Similarly, the subjugation of women not only inflicts injustice on the female part of the population, it also prompts men to adopt a false self-definition and embrace a love of domination that endangers society as a whole.

The preferential option for the poor, if I may repeat, serves the common good of society. It does not aim at the victory of one sector of society over another. Nor is it inspired by the illusion that a sinless society is an earthly possibility. What the option does reflect is what I have called the 'Catholic intuition' that the reconciliation of personal aspiration and service to the common good is society's high destiny—by nature and by grace.

*

In the context of this article it is important to emphasize that the preferential option is also a sociological principle: it calls for a reading of society from below. We have called this the hermeneutic dimension. Theologians who follow the preferential option are therefore bound to enter into dialogue with sociology. For their specific purposes structural functionalism has little to

offer. What interests them instead is some form of conflict sociology. But since the poor are not an economic class but include all
people pushed to the margin by economic, cultural, social and
political forces, theologians will be uncomfortable with conflict
sociologies that define oppression in economic terms and favour
quantification and positivism.

Theologians who embrace the preferential option have
great sympathy for the Catholic sociologists of the 30s and 40s
who for reasons of faith stood apart from the dominant model.
Following the Catholic social teaching of that time, they were re-
formists and supporters of the New Deal, intellectuals who studied and taught sociology to promote social justice. Because
Catholic social teaching also prejudiced them against Marxist
theories of any kind, they did not explore the usefulness of a
sociology of oppression. What puzzles the contemporary reader is
that despite their critique of positivism, they tended to believe in
'facts.' Sociology was for them fact-finding combined with social
philosophy.

In light of the preferential option, facts become somewhat
more problematic. There are of course situations where facts are
clear. For instance, how many cannons were used in this battle?
Here the correspondence theory of truth is perfectly valid. But
when we turn to important important historical events the situation is different. The American Revolution was certainly a fact,
but when answering questions about its contoures—when did it
begin and when did it end, what incidents were part of it—we
have to make use of a theory of revolution to carve the facts out
of the continuum of history. Facts already include an interpretive
key. Access to historical events is always mediated by theory.

Theologians who follow the preferential option also have
sympathy for the Catholic sociologists of the 50s and 60s who
turned to functionalist theory with some enthusiasm. They did
not endorse its positivist and determinist implications. In their
eyes, the cohesion that kept society together without violating
people's personal aspirations was not the cybernetic mechanism
of the social system but the destiny of society to reconcile personal aspiration with service of the common good. There are historical contexts for which the functionalist approach is appropri-

ate. The question whether it is appropriate or not is actually an ethico-political judgment.

Even Talcott Parsons did not make use of his own methodology when he studied the emergence of German fascism. He employed a conflict sociology which, following Marx, gave priority to economic factors.[48] In the 50s and 60s, when welfare capitalism promised to help the disfavoured sector of society and overcome excessive economic inequality, many Americans believed that the mild reformism implicit in functionalist theory was appropriate. Today, in the new phase of capitalism, this judgment has to be revised. This at least is the viewpoint of those who endorse the preferential option.

Functionalist sociology, as we saw above, defended the objective, value-free character of social science. This is contested by persons following the preferential option. They are keenly aware that looking at society from below, listening to the disenfranchised and interpreting social reality fom their perspective, makes an enormous difference. They realize that reading social reality is always guided by a certain pre-understanding. Social scientists must of course be truthful, respect the evidence available to them, and present their conclusions along with the arguments from which they are derived. Their work is scientific, their reasoning has to stand up under careful scrutiny, and in this limited sense their approach is 'objective.'

At the same time their work is inevitably guided by a particular stance. This stance may be influenced unconsciously by the scientist's social location or the dominant culture to which he or she belongs. But the stance may also be chosen deliberately, for instance, the preferential option.

Important historical controversies cannot be resolved by the scientific method alone. Thus we read in the first draft of the American bishops' pastoral on economic justice that scientists don't agree in their analysis of the causes of the growing misery in the United States and the world.[49] Some believed that fundamental structural changes were taking place in the American economy, linked to such forces as the internationalization of capital, the introduction of high technology, and new competition from other industrialized countries, all leading to a deepening crisis that will produce world-wide suffering. Other experts, using the same scientific tools of analysis, saw the situation in less dramatic terms. They recognized the existence of serious problems but took them as the result of particular policies that could be changed incrementally, rather than by a deep shift in the economy. Because the scientific method alone was unable to resolve this question, the American bishops decided to leave it unanswered.

The Canadian bishops decided to reply to the question left open by their American colleagues. Faced with conflicting scientific analyses, the Canadian bishops resolved the debate by attaching more importance to the scientists whose approach to social reality was close to their own.[50] The scientists whom they followed undertook their research guided by an 'emancipatory commitment,' a secular perspective analogous to the theologically-grounded option for the poor.

In the scientific study of historical processes in which we are involved, objectivity is not a possibility. Why not? Because we are in fact located within the process. We are free to relate ourselves to this process as we wish, to adopt a perspective that appears responsible to us and eventually decide upon the approach to be pursued. For some Christians, the option for the poor is the guide here. There are also secular social scientists who operate out of an emancipatory perspective: they too pay attention first to the victims, they wish to read society through its contradictions, they entertain a conflictual perception of the social order, they begin their analysis of society by asking for the causes of present suffering.

Even social scientific and historical studies of past events or of contemporary situations far away from us are guided by certain questions, pre-understandings, and chosen paradigms, and therefore despite their scholarly rigor are not strictly speaking objective. Our interpretation of the past will be influenced by how we relate ourselves to our own society, in other words by an ethico-political judgment. (Even listening to people speaking excitedly about a film they saw allows us to discern their political perspective on American society.) To enhance the scientific credibility of our research we must put our conceptual cards on the table, clearly articulate and defend our presuppositions, not to 'prove' them but to show why they appear to us well-founded.

If we endorse the preferential option for the poor, we recognize the subjective dimension in the quest for truth. Love enters into the process of knowing.[51] In an unjust society the love of God and neighbour transforms itself into a yearning for justice and an impulse to act so that the heavy burdens be removed from the shoulders of the victims. Truly to know society, therefore, is to recognize its contradictions and thus create the presupposition for its transformation. It has been the spiritual experience of many Catholics in the Americas that such transformative knowledge became available to them only after they had become engaged, after they had extended their solidarity to the poor.

Knowledge of the social world is truly circular: it begins with commitment, it is grounded in action, it adopts the perspective of the victims, it makes use of social scientific methodologies, and it generates commitment and action.[52]

Let us recall at this point that in the 30s and 40s Catholic sociologists decided, for strategic reasons, to advocate for a Catholic sociology. They objected to the sociology dominant at American universities because they disagreed with the image of the human being and the paradigm of the social process implicit in it, and missed an explicit social ethical commitment. Do Catholics who follow the preferential option in the 80s and into the 90s wish to reintroduce the notion of a Catholic sociology?

We note that the question of a Christian sociology has never disappeared among doctrinally conservative Protestants.[53] Protestants who defined themselves as evangelical were suspicious of secular humanism and contemporary rationality. In their campus ministry they warned university students against sociology. Yet over the last few years sophisticated Christian social philosophers who think of themselves as evangelical have engaged in a constructive criticism of contemporary sociology. They urge university students not to be afraid of sociology but to engage in a foundational dialogue with it. David Lyon's *Sociology and the Human Image* offers an introduction to sociology (including its classical authors) that pays special attention to the image of the human, the paradigm of the social process, and the social ethical perspective implicit in different sociological theories.[54] In this context Lyon is critical of the positivistic, deterministic and evolutionary trends in sociology and calls for a sociology in keeping with the vision and values contained in Scripture. As ethical perspective he advocates the biblical prophetic tradition, which in his interpretation resembles the preferential option for the poor. Still, Lyon does not defend the idea of a Christian sociology. What he proposes instead is a specifically "Christian contribution" to sociological science.

The reader will not be surprised to learn that I have a certain sympathy with this proposal. Yet when Lyon specifies the "Christian" perspective, it turns out that the same orientation could be pursued by Jewish thinkers who, following Buber and Heschel, identify with the biblical prophetic tradition. They too reject materialism and secularism, they entertain the same image of the human person open to God's call, and they share the same emancipatory commitment to justice and peace. But if this is true, does it make sense to speak of a "Christian" contribution to sociology?

Can secular thinkers, we ask, join the perspective of Christians and Jews? To answer this question let me compare 'the preferential option' with a purely secular emancipatory commitment. We note that human liberation can be understood in a variety of ways depending on the analysis of human oppression. A classical Marxist analysis is very narrow: it focuses on economic domination, and if it does pay attention to other forms of oppression, it interprets them in terms deriving from economic factors. There are other one-sided analyses that focus on a single factor, on national oppression, for instance, or the subjugation of women. A theologically one-sided analysis focuses only on the promotion of secularism and the repression of the spirit. 'The preferential option' assigns a certain priority to economic factors—especially after *Laborem exercens*—but in addition to this it recognizes all other causes of marginalization and cultural patterns of inferiorization. Thus, for instance, it also takes into account the burdens placed on the retarded and the handicapped. While a purely secular emancipatory commitment could produce an identical concern, it is likely that the theologically-grounded preferential option is more sensitive to cultural domination, including the repression of the spiritual.

Moreover, the preferential option sees itself as serving the common good. It does not anticipate the victory of one sector of society over another, nor does it envisage the destruction of all communal bonds. It aims at the qualitative transformation of the social order. It endorses the Catholic intuition of a reconciled society. For this reason those who follow the preferential option tend to shy away from social scientific analyses that generate disruptive or explosive action. Of course, secular emancipatory commitments may be inspired by the same vision.

The great difference between the preferential option and an analogous secular commitment has to do with a conscious relationship to the biblical God. For Christians the historical struggle for emancipation is not a Promethean project, not the salvation of the human race, not justification by works, but the human response to a divine initiative, a work of faith, an act of obedience, a form of discipleship. Here humans are not only actors or agents, but also and especially recipients or sufferers: they suffer divine grace, they are empowered from within, they are overwhelmed by a yearning for justice, they find it existentially impossible to be reconciled to a wicked world.

Secular people lack a discourse to articulate experiences of transcendence, but from many conversations with secular friends I conclude that many of them engage in the struggle for justice out of a passion they have not chosen, they do not fully understand, and they regard as a surprising gift or a precious inheritance.

What I conclude from these reflections is that the preferential option, theologically-grounded, defines an orientation from which secular thinkers are not necessarily excluded. While I have great sympathy for the position adopted by Catholic sociologists of the past and contemporary evangelicals such as David Lyon, I do not think it would be a useful strategy in the present to call for a Catholic or Christian sociology.

*

I cannot close this article without discussing the impact of the preferential option on Catholic theology itself. Catholics in the 30s and 40s did not think that their approach to sociology influenced their theology. By contrast, from the 50s on, Catholics sympathetic to functionalist sociology recognized that their sociological reflections could well affect their theology. Because the more recent preferential option is a theological and sociological principle, it clearly affects theological thinking. The preferential option actually transforms theological analysis. It has generated Liberation Theology in Latin America and an equivalent, Critical Theology, in the United States.

About these theologies I wish to make one observation. Since theologians of this orientation follow an eschatological perspective, since they hear God's Word first as divine judgment on the world, since they are deeply impressed by the message of Jesus, "Repent for the reign of God is at hand," they are compelled to analyze the structures of sin in which society finds itself. They cannot speak of Jesus unless they specify the sin and the death from which Jesus saves us. Thus theology itself calls for critical social analysis. Sociology here enters into the very constitution of theology.[55]

What is remarkable is that this form of theologizing has already affected the Church's magisterium. The Latin American bishops believed they could not express the meaning of divine revelation unless they first analyzed the structures of oppression in which the people of their continent were caught. The 1971 World Synod of Bishops recognized that the demand for social justice was an integral part of the message of salvation.[56] To announce the Gospel authentically one must articulate God's judgment on the given society. While personal sins also build the prison in which society is caught, they cannot be properly understood unless their relation to structural sin is clarified. The crimes of the poor in the ghetto cannot be understood apart from the structures of consistent and sometimes violent marginalization inflicted upon them. The notion of structural or social sin, until recently controversial in Catholic theology, was taken up and developed by John Paul II in his *Sollicitudo rei socialis*.[57] The orientation toward death in our civilization—world hunger, nuclear destruction, ecological disaster—is not blamed on individual sins; instead it is related to structural causes, to the powerful impact of economic and political institutions that are named—an impact that could be resisted, but in fact is not. Personal sin enters this equation principally as non-resistance to the powerful. The theological teaching on sin and redemption cyclical has integrated the outline of a global social analysis from a particular sociological perspective, the option for the poor.

At the end of this article I recognize that the Catholic Church's reaction to the contemporary situation, seconded by the World Council of Churches and many individual Protestant Churches, represents a minority in the Christian community. The preferential option goes counter to the flow of contemporary culture. The preferential option embraced by small Christian communities and endorsed by Catholic social teaching has called forth social justice committees in dioceses, parishes and religious congregations, and appealed to many individuals, including theologians, social scientists, priests, bishops and activists of all kind. Together these Catholics constitute a visible, definable network within the Church. The preferential option has affected new religious experiences and generated a new spirituality. This Catholic network cooperates with corresponding organizations in the Protestant Churches. The members of this network also enter easily into dialogue with the non-ideological Left and non-sectarian Greens and gladly cooperate with emancipatory popular movements, for peace, justice, gender equality and the protection of the earth.

Notes

1. Gibson Winter, *Elements for a Social Ethic,* New York: The Macmillan Company, 1966, p. 8.

2. Ibid., pp. 15-22.

3. Some of the Catholic sociologists publishing in the early volumes of *ACSR* were A.H. Clemens, James Connell, Francis Friedel, S.M., Paul H. Furfey, Ralph Gallagher, S.J., Howard Jensen, Robert Hartnett, S.J., Raymond McGowan, Franz Mueller, Remand Murray, C.S.C., Sr. Mary Consilia O'Brien, O.P., and Eva Ross. Confer also Paul H. Furfey, *The Scope and Method of Sociology,* New York: Harper, 1953, and Eva Ross, *Fundamental Sociology,* Milwaukee: Bruce, 1939.

4. See Robert Hartnett, "A Postwar Reconstruction Program for the American Catholic Sociological Society," *ACSR*, 4 (1943), 102-109.

5. Pitirim Sorokin, "Dualism, Chaotic Syncretism, Quantitative Colossalism, and Diminishing Creativeness of Contemporary Sensate Culture," *ACSR*, 2 (1941), 3-22.

6. See Leo Martin, S.J., "The Problem of War Causation," *ACSR*, 3 (1942), 231-243.

7. See especially Talcott Parsons' *The Social System*, New York: Free Press, 1951, and his article, "Systems Analysis: The Social System," *International Encyclopedia of the Social Sciences*, vol. 15, pp. 458-472. For a useful, critical introduction see Irving Zeitlin, *Rethinking Sociology*, Englewood Cliffs, N.J.: Prentice-Hall, 1973, pp. 17-60.

8. Rudolf Siebert, "Parsons' Analytical Theory of Religion as Ultimate Reality," *Sociology and Human Destiny*, ed. Gregory Baum, New York: Seabury, 1980, 27-53, 28.

9. John Hughes, *ACRS*, 24 (1963), 285.

10. Thomas O'Dea, *The Sociology of Religion*, Englewood Cliffs, N.J.: Prentice-Hall, 1966.

11. Ibid., pp. 13-15.

12. Alexis de Tocqueville, *Democracy in America*, New York: Vintage Books, Random House, 1945, vol. 2, pp. 21-33.

13. Andrew Greeley, *The Denominational Society*, Glenview: Scott, Foresman & Comp., 1972, pp. 102-107.

14. Talcott Parsons, "Christianity and Modern Industrial Society," in *Religion, Culture and Society*, ed. L. Schneider, New York: John Wiley & Sons, 1964, pp. 273-98.

15. Alexis de Tocqueville, *op. cit.*, p. 23.

16. This is the thesis of Richard Niebuhr's *The Social Sources of Denominationalism*, New York: Living Age Books, 1957.

17. Andrew Greeley, *The Jesus Myth*, Garden City, N.Y.: Doubleday, 1971, *What Modern Catholics Believe About God*, Chicago: Thomas More, 1971, *The Sinia Myth*, Garden City, N.Y.: Doubleday, 1972, *The Mary Myth*, New York: Seabury, 1977, *The Great Mysteries*, New York: Seabury, 1976.

18. Andrew Greeley, *The New Agenda*, Garden City, N.Y.: Doubleday, 1973.

19. Andrew Greeley, and Mary Greeley Durkin, *How to Save the Catholic Church*, New York: Viking, 1984.

20. Andrew Greeley, *Come, Blow Your Mind With Me*, Garden City, N.Y.: Doubleday, 1971, *Unsecular Man*, New York: Schocken Books, 1972.

21. C. Wright Mills, *The Sociological Imagination*, New York: Oxford University Press, 1959.

22. Alvin Gouldner, *The Coming Crisis of Western Sociology*, New York: Avon Books, 1970.

23. See T. O'Dea's critique of Parsons, T. O'Dea, *Society and the Study of Religion*, New York: Basic Books, 1970, pp. 221-34.

24. This theme is developed throughout Alvin Gouldner's *The Coming Crisis of Western Sociology*, for instance, pp. 176-85.

25. Developing an aspect of Max Weber's thought, Alfred Schutz produced a sociology of everyday life in which the world appeared as an intersubjective creation. People constituted their world, not through labor as Marx believed, but through meaning. The everyday life world, Schutz claimed, can be known objectively, and this knowledge provides the basic truth about reality, back to which every specialized science, including sociology, refers. Cf. Alfred Schutz, *The Phenomenology of the Social World*, Evanston, IL: Northwestern University Press, 1967. (German original, 1932.) Alfred Schutz's phenomenological sociology influenced many American sociologists, among whom Peter Berger and Gibson Winter.

26. Peter Berger and Thomas Luckmann, *The Social Construction of Reality*, Garden City, N.Y.: Doubleday, 1967, Peter Berger and Hansfried Kellner, *Sociology Reinterpreted*, Garden City, N.Y.: Doubleday, 1981. For Berger's Christian reflections see, for instance, his essays in *Facing Up to Modernity*, New York: Basic Books, 1977. For a critical evaluation see G. Baum, "Peter Berger's Unfinished Symphony," *Sociology and Human Destiny*, ed. G. Baum, New York: Seabury, 1980, pp. 110-129.

27. In his *Elements for a Social Ethic*, New York: The Macmillan Company, 1966, Gibson Winter tries to transcend the debate between functionalism and conflict sociology by following Alfred Schutz into the sociology of everyday life. The world is created by meaning, and social conflicts are caused by the clash of meaning paradigms. Winter applies this theoretical approach in his *Liberating Creation*, New York: Crossroad, 1981. Thus, for instance, he interprets the conflict over the land between the transnational corporations and the Native peoples in Western Canada not as a case of domination, but as "a conflict between root metaphors of historical development." (p. 98) By contrast, conflict sociology is used in a statement on American society made by a Chicago Reflection Group, to which Winter himself belonged: see *Theology in the Americas*, ed. Sergio Torres, Maryknoll, N.Y.: Orbis, 1986, pp. 215-241.

28. *Laborem exercens* mentions the present turning point in sec. 1 and the preceding phases in sec. 8, *Origins*, 11 (1981), 227, 231. Cf. Gregory Baum, *The Priority of Labor: A Commentary on Laborem exercens*, New York: Paulist Press, 1982, pp. 31-35.

29. "Ethical Reflections on the Economic Crisis," (Dec. 22, 1982), *Do Justice! The Social Teaching of the Canadian Catholic Bishops*, ed. E.F. Sheridan, Toronto: Jesuit Centre for Social Faith and Justice, 1986, pp. 399-408.

30. "Economic Justice for All," the sections on employment and poverty, nn. 136-215, *Origins*, 16 (1986) 426-432.

31. Gregory Baum/Duncan Cameron, *Ethics and Economics: Canada's Catholic Bishops on the Economic Crisis*, Toronto: Lorimer, 1984.

32. Gregory Baum, "The Anti-Cold War Encyclical," *The Ecumenist*, 26 (July/Aug., 1988), 65-74.

33. *Sollicitudo rei socialis*, n. 24, *Origins*, 17 (1988), 649.

34. Robert Bellah, et al., *Habits of the Heart*, Berkeley: University of California Press, 1985, pp. 147-148.

35. Daniel Bell, *The Cultural Contradictions of Capitalism*, New York: Basic Books, 1976. Cf. G. Baum, "Religion and Capitalism According to Bell," *The Ecumenist*, 14 (May/June, 1976), pp. 59-62.

36. For the important documents of the Medellin Conference (1968), see Joseph Gremillion, ed. *The Gospel of Peace and Justice*, Maryknoll, N.Y.: Orbis, 1976, pp. 445-476. For the document of the Puebla Conference (1979), see John Eagleson, ed. *Puebla and Beyond*, Maryknoll, N.Y.: Orbis, 1979. An interpretation of these ecclesiastical texts is offered in Donal Dorr, *Option for the Poor: A Hundred Years of Vatican Social Teaching*, Maryknoll, N.Y.: Orbis, 1983.

37. See the report on the 1975 Theology in the Americas Conference at Detroit, *Theology in the Americas*, ed. Sergio Torres, Maryknoll, N.Y.: Orbis, 1976, p. 406.

38. Marie Augusta Neal, *A Socio-Theology of Letting Go*, New York: Paulist Press, 1977, pp. 36-37.

39. Joseph Gremillion, *The Gospel of Justice and Peace*, pp. 513-529, 514. For an interpretation see G. Baum, *Theology and Society*, New York: Paulist Press, 1987, pp. 14-19.

40. *Laborem exercens*, n. 8, *Origins*, 11 (1981), 231. See G. Baum, *The Priority of Labor*, pp. 41-56.

41. For a comparison between the perspective taken by the American and Canadian Catholic Bishops, see G. Baum, "A Canadian Perspective on the U.S. Pastoral," *Christianity and Crisis*, 45 (Jan. 21, 1985), pp. 516-518.

42. "Ethical Reflections on the Economic Crisis," *Do Justice!*, ed. E.F. Sheridan Toronto: Jesuit Centre for Social Faith and Justice, 1987, pp. 399-400.

43. *Origins*, 16 (Nov. 27, 1986), pp. 415-416.

44. Final Document, nn. 1134-1152, *Puebla and Beyond*, pp. 264-266.

45. G. Baum, "Option for the Powerless," *The Ecumenist*, 26 (Nov./Dec., 1987), pp. 5-11.

46. The Puebla Document, n. 536, *Puebla and Beyond*, pp. 198-199.

47. The interpretative dimension of 'facts' is a theme developed by the great critics of positivistic social science, including Frankfurt School Critical Theory. In this essay I do not refer to these authors but confine myself to the experience of Christians dedicated to social justice who wrestle for an appropriate understanding of their historical situation.

48. Cf. Irving Zeitlin, *Rethinking Sociology*, Englewood Cliffs, N.J.: Prentice-Hall, 1973, pp. 35-40.

49. The Bishops' Pastoral: First Draft, nn. 7-14, *Origins*, 14 (1984), 342.

50. Christopher Lind, "Ethics, Economics and Canada's Catholic Bishops," *Canadian Journal of Political and Social Theory*, 7 (fall, 1983), pp. 150-166, and "An Invitation to Canadian Theology," *Toronto Journal of Theology*, 1 (Spring, 1985), pp. 17-26.

51. This is one of the important themes of Matthew Lamb's *Solidarity With Victims*, New York: Crossroad, 1982. See especially pp. 82-88.

52. A liberating hermeneutical circle was defined in Juan Segundo's *The Liberation of Theology*, Maryknoll, N.Y.: Orbis, 1976, pp. 6-34. A similar analytical circle was adopted by the Canadian bishops as the pastoral methodology for their

ethical reflections. "Ethical Reflections on Canada's Socio-Economic Order," n. 4, *Do Justice!*, Toronto: Jesuit Centre for Social Faith and Justice, 1987, pp. 412-413.

53. David Lyon, *Sociology and the Human Image*, London: Inter-Varisity Press, 1983.

55. G. Baum, *Theology and Society*, New York: Paulist Press, 1987, pp. 157-170.

56. 1971 Synod Bishops, n. 6, Joseph Gremillion, *The Gospel of Peace and Justice*, p. 514.

57. *Sollicitudo rei socialis*, nn. 36-37, nn. 36-37, *Origins*, 17 (1988), 653. See also pp. 189-204 of this volume.

8.

Vatican II:
Critical Openness to Modernity

In this essay, the author wishes to interpret Vatican Council II as
an effort of the Catholic Church to respond to the challenges
and expectations of modern society, without losing its own identity in the process.[1] We shall show that the openness to modernity in the conciliar teachings was not accompanied by an equivalent effort to insert these modern values into the Church's own
self-organization. The contradiction between what is taught *ad extra* and what is done *ad intra* has caused confusion and frustration in the Catholic Church. This state of disarray can be overcome only when the ecclesiastical institutions come to embody
the Church's own social teaching.

Definitions and Implications of Modernity

At the outset we must offer a definition of what we mean by
'modernity.' By that term sociologists usually refer to the new society created by the two great social transformations, the Industrial Revolution beginning in England in the second half of the
18th century and the democratic revolution, symbolized by the
dramatic events of the French Revolution at the end of the same
century. Industrialization and democratization are distinct historical processes that have not always gone hand in hand. A democ-
ratizing revolution created the United States of America in 1776
while large-scale industrialization only took place in the second
half of the 19th century. Conversely, the industrialization of Que-

bec began at the turn of the 20th century while the democratic modernization of Quebec matured only in the 1960s during the celebrated Quiet Revolution.

In Europe an affinity existed between industrialization and democracy. The development of industry produced new wealth for the members of the burgher class, thus giving them more power for the political struggle to transform aristocratic society into democracy. There is a close link between industrial capitalism and political democracy if the latter is understood as a form of government that protects personal safety and property rights and interferes as little as possible in the societal process. Yet there is a tension between capitalism and democracy if the latter is understood as a form of government that serves the well-being of society as a whole and for this purpose encourages the participation of all the citizens. In such a situation, industrial capitalism stands out as non-participatory and hierarchically-organized. This complex, shifting interrelation between capitalism and democracy makes the word 'liberal' an ambiguous term. For some, 'liberal' refers to a free market economy, unrestrained by government intervention, while for others 'liberal' designates the political orientation toward greater equality and participation. *The concept of modernization used in the present essay refers exclusively to the political modernization that has produced modern, democratic Western society.*

The process of democratization includes values and institutions such as constitutional government, the division of powers, democratic participation, free elections, equality before the law, religious liberty, the secularization of the state, human rights, religious and ideological pluralism, respect for public opinion and the right to organize political parties. Also included are the assumptions that government is responsible for promoting the well-being of society and the expectation that democracy is the ideal for the whole world.

These modern values and institutions have come to define the democratic ethos of Western society. All Western democracies pay at least lip service to this ethos, even if this high ideal is not fully supported by the values and institutions created by industrial capitalism. We note, moreover, that the democratic ethos is an embodiment of 'the Enlightenment principle,' the intellectual foundation of political modernization, which affirms that 'human reason' empowers people to free themselves from the distorting and self-limiting myths of the past to become the rational subjects of their own social existence.

The process of political modernization is not free of ambiguity. It has problematic side effects, such as centralization, bureaucratization, and the enhancement of state power, developments analysed and criticized by the early sociologists from Alexis de Tocqueville to Max Weber. Still, the democratic values and institutions have retained their appeal.

The Catholic Church's Stance Toward Modernity

In the 19th century the Catholic Church vehemently rejected the emerging liberal, democratic society as well as the Enlightenment principle implicit in it. The most vehement repudiation, the Syllabus of Errors, promulgated by Pius IX in 1864, listed and condemned 80 erroneous opinions of modern society, including the rationalistic philosophical theories that legitimated the new social order. The 80th erroneous opinion condemned was that "the Roman Pontiff could and should reconcile himself with and adjust to progress, liberalism, and the new society."[2]

Throughout the 19th century papal teaching lamented the revolutionary character of modern society, the rejection of traditional authority, the hostility to religion, the blind faith in human reason, the all-pervasive individualism, and the manner in which modernity undermined the common good of society, including the demand for human rights and religious liberty. Identified with the inherited feudal-communal society, the Catholic Church, sensitive to the ambiguous side effects of liberal society, defended the position that the old institutions of solidarity, community and tradition protected ordinary people more effectively from the arbitrariness of state power than did the new, liberal society. The Church articulated a critique of modernity that was shared by many conservative or Tory social thinkers of Europe.

Leo XIII's *Rerum novarum* (1891) was the Church's first official reaction to the growing industrialization of society and the far-reaching effect it had on the people of all classes. In that encyclical, the emphasis was on social justice. Leo XIII lamented that unrestrained capitalism undermined the common good and split society into two antagonistic classes, the self-serving owners of industry and the exploited and oppressed workers. He called upon national governments, made up of selfless, spiritual men, to stand above the competing interests of the classes, promote the common good, restrain the liberal economy, legislate social justice and protect the workers and the poor. While the Pope condemned socialism, he defended the right of workers to organize their own associations, and he upheld the justice of their demand for a living wage, The Church here defended what is often called a 'red Tory' position, adopted by progressive conservatives in many parts of Europe and Canada, which maintained that it is possible to promote social reforms while remaining faithful to time-tested traditions in the realm of politics.

It is significant that papal social teaching did not say a single word in favour of political modernization, including democracy, electoral participation, human rights, and pluralism. The idea that people were the sovereign subject of their society and hence the source of the power their government exercised over them seemed irreconcilable with Catholic tradition. In *Quadragesimo anno* (1931) Pius XII even suggested a 'corporatist' organization of society as an alternative to political democracy.[3] Envisaging the creation of 'corporations,' made up of owners and workers belonging to the same industries, he recommended that representatives of these 'corporations' form a national council, steered by government, that would promote the national economy in favour of the common good. 'Corporatism' thus gave all men, be they owners of an industry or salaried workers, a certain voice in the making of economic policy.

The first positive statement upholding modern democracy is found in Pius XII's Christmas address in 1944.[4] Toward the end of the war, the Pope realized that on the one hand the Soviet atheistic communism was gaining ground and that on the other the conservative ideals, some of which were defended by Italian and Spanish fascism, were not destined to survive after the war. The Pope now recognized the Western democracies as the societies in which the Church had the best chance of flowering. Still, the teaching of Pius XII showed only the slightest opening toward pluralism, human rights, and religious liberty.

For Catholics living in modern, democratic societies this conservative aspect of the Church's teaching was difficult to grasp. In the United States, in particular, with its liberal culture and the absence of a strong Tory tradition, Catholics were puzzled by the Church's rejection of political modernization. Already in the 19th century, American Catholics wanted to participate on equal footing in building the liberal society, yet their adjustment to modernity and their turn to a spirituality more attuned to democratic values appeared to Rome as an 'Americanism' worthy of condemnation.

In 19th-century Europe, the Church remained on the whole identified with the conservative tradition. The efforts to make the Church respond more positively to democracy and pluralism were condemned. This embarrassed Catholics living as minorities in Protestant countries—in England, for instance.[5] It was only after World War II that Catholicism located in Western democracies, especially France and Germany, experienced a lively spiritual renewal and a new openness, sparked and defended by brilliant theologians, like Chenu, Congar, de Lubac and Rahner, who gave expression to the aspirations of Catholics educated in an Enlightenment culture. These theologians were occasionally censured by Rome. Rebuked by Rome was also the American theologian, John Courtney Murray, who defended religious liberty as a human right.

On January 25, 1959 John XXIII announced his intention to convoke an ecumenical council, to be called Vatican Council II. One of the aims of the Council was to deal in an innovative way with the Church's situation in the modern world. In his first encyclical letter of June 1959, *Ad Petri cathedram*, John XXIII specified: "The major aim of the council will consist in promoting the development of Christian faith, the spiritual renewal of the Catholic faith, and the adaptation of Church disciplines to the needs and methods of our times."[6] What the Pope wanted was, in his own words, "a wise modernization"[7] of the Church, so that its internal structure could find a renewed vigour.

An ecumenical council is an extraordinary event in the life of the Catholic Church. According to Catholic teaching, a general or ecumenical council exercises supreme magisterium and jurisdiction in the Church. While these supreme ministerial powers are normally exercised by the pope united with his bishops in spirit, at an ecumenical council this highest office is exercized by the legislative assembly, the gathered episcopate with the pope simply acting as president. An ecumenical council is one of the rare historical moments when the bishops from various parts of the globe are institutionally empowered to affect the teaching, the pastoral policy and the organizational structure of the Catholic Church.

Vatican II was such a rare occasion. Thanks to the influence of the bishops from the industrialized and democratic countries, especially from the lands along the Rhine (Belgium, France, Germany and Holland), a leadership that was eventually endorsed by the great majority of the bishops, the Vatican Council significantly modified the Church's relationship to the modern world.[8]

An important event occurred at the beginning of the Council when the conciliar assembly rejected a draft document prepared by an ecclesiastical commission controlled by the Roman Curia and demanded the election of new conciliar commissions to be charged with the task of preparing the conciliar documents. Throughout the four sessions of the Council, it was the set of progressive Western European bishops, later joined by the American hierarchy, that exercised the greatest influence on the shaping of ecclesiastical policy. Behind the outspoken bishops and cardinals stood the important theologians from these countries, theologians had over the years laid a theological foundation for an open approach of the Church in regard to modern society.

Before turning to the conciliar texts, we must look at the historical moment at which the Vatican Council was held. The early sixties was a time of great cultural optimism in Western Europe and North America. The interventionist Keynesian economics adopted after World War II in the North Atlantic countries was now producing enormous wealth under conditions that almost abolished unemployment and permitted working class families to improve their standard of living. Welfare capitalism seemed to be the answer to the problem of poverty. There was hope that if this economic system could be exported to the poorer countries of Latin America, Asia and Africa, these countries would also be able to develop, industrialize, produce wealth and overcome the conditions of hunger and misery.[9] In America, John Kennedy gave expression to this optimistic perspective, and in Europe, Pope John XXIII became the symbol of this evolutionary hope.

It is not surprising that Latin American Catholics, examining the conciliar documents in the late sixties, came to the conclusion that in its approach to modern society, Vatican II reflected the perspective of the middle class in the North Atlantic nations. The Latin American Bishops Conference of Medellin, 1968, pronounced a judgement on modern, Western society, that clearly articulated the oppressive and exploitative structures, at which Vatican II had only hinted in vague fashion. The Latin American bishops accounted for the marginalization and the poverty of their people in terms of neo-colonial exploitation and internal class oppression.[10]

Vatican II and Modernity

The conciliar documents that clearly express the Church's positive response to modernity are the Decree on Ecumenism (*Unitatis reintegratio*), the Declarations on Religious Freedom and on the Church's Relationship to Non-Christian Religions (*Dignitatis humanae* and *Nostra aetate*), and more especially the Pastoral Constitution on the Church in the Modern World (*Gaudium et spes*). In these texts the Catholic Church formally approves and recommends the values and institutions of political modernization, in particular, 1) religious pluralism, 2) human rights, 3) respect for personal conscience, even if in error, 4) democratic participation, and 5) universal applicability. These innovations, as we shall see, raise a number of theological questions.

1. In the conciliar texts the Church becomes reconciled with religious pluralism. In the Decree on Ecumenism, the Church acknowledges other (non-Catholic) Christians as Christians, as brothers and sisters in Christ through faith and baptism, and recognizes the other Churches as ecclesial communities used by the Spirit to save and sanctify humanity. The Decree praises the ecumenical movement as a Spirit-inspired effort to reunite the divided Christian family and recommends dialogue, cooperation, and even in special circumstances, common worship.

In the Declaration on the Church's Relationship to Non-Christian Religions, the Church expresses a profound respect for the great world religions, especially biblically-grounded Judaism. It acknowledges that present in these religions are the rays of God's own light that mediate saving wisdom to their followers, even if the fullness of this light is available only in Jesus Christ. The Church here recommends interreligious dialogue and cooperation.

In these two conciliar documents and in the important Declaration on Religious Liberty, the Catholic Church recognizes religious pluralism as the historical reality of God's world. Vatican II clearly and unambiguously affirms religious liberty as a human right. Social justice demands that religious pluralism be respected and protected by government. What is necessary, therefore, is a certain separation of the state from any particular Church, including the Catholic Church. A special legal arrangement between the Catholic Church and a national government is acceptable only if it guarantees the freedom of other religious organizations.

The conciliar documents are sensitive to the ambiguous underside of religious pluralism, namely the relativism of religious truth. While the Council recommends dialogue and cooperation among Christians and among members of the world religions, it still defends the Catholic Church's traditional self-understanding—albeit in a modified form—as the one, true community of Jesus Christ in the world. The ancient formula, *'extra ecclesiam nulla salus,'* is here given a new meaning: it is understood not as invalidating the other Churches nor even the great world religions, but rather as affirming that the divine grace variously present in these religious traditions, Christian and otherwise, has been mediated—in a hidden way—by the Catholic Church. What this non-historical, metaphysical mediation means is not made clear. It is a notion that continues to raise great theological difficulties.

2. The Pastoral Constitution on the Church and the Modern World, *Gaudium et spes*, is the principal conciliar document, and the most startling one, recording the Church's positive response to modern society. Here human rights, including the freedom of religion, are fully recognized. Because of the dignity of the human person and the essential equality of humans, "every type of discrimination, whether social or cultural, whether based on sex, race, colour, social condition, language or religion, is to be overcome and eradicated as contrary to God's intent."[11]

It is made clear that these personal rights include the equality between of women and men. According to the Council, part of the broader desires of humankind for human equality is "the claim of women for equity with men before the law and in fact."[12] And regretting that human rights are not yet universally honoured, the Council gives as example "the case of a woman who is denied . . . access to education or cultural benefits equal to those recognized for men."[13]

The Council admits that the emphasis on personal human rights has had an ambiguous underside, the promotion of individualism and the undermining of social solidarity—such as is found in the liberal political tradition from John Locke to Margaret Thatcher. Against this atomistic, liberal tradition, the Council insists on the social nature of human persons and their rootedness in communities. People are destined to belong to one another and to be responsible for one another. Concern for the common good is not imposed upon men and women by an external authority: concern for the common good is generated in people as they discover themselves. We note that Vatican II recognizes not only the personal rights against discrimination mentioned above but also the solidarity rights, foreign to the liberal tradition, such as the right to work and the right to the necessities of life.[14]

3. *Gaudium et spes* praises the excellence of liberty, the fruit of political modernization. "Only in freedom can human persons direct themselves toward goodness. Our contemporaries make much of this freedom and pursue it eagerly; and rightly so, to be sure. . . . Authentic freedom is an exceptional sign of the divine image in humans."[15]

The same document also recognizes the possible negative consequences of this freedom. "Often people promote freedom perversely as a license for doing whatever pleases them, even if it is evil."[16] Yet if these people explore their own conscience, we are told, they will hear a summons to do good.

In this context *Gaudium et spes* introduces an innovative theology of conscience, echoing the work of Karl Rahner, the theory that God is graciously present in the moral quest of individual people. The conciliar document tells us 1) that in conscience people are addressed by a law not of their own making, summoning them to do good and avoid evil (the natural law) and 2) that in conscience, "the most secret core and sanctuary of a person," people hear the echo of God's voice, summoning them to live up to "the law that is fulfilled by love of God and neighbour."[17] What is affirmed here is that the natural law is not as natural as it appears: it is in fact 'supernatural', i.e., an echo of God's redemptive summons. God is graciously present in people's inner struggle to find the truth and do the right thing. That is why *Gaudium et spes* is able to propose that "in fidelity to conscience, Christians are joined with the rest of humans in the search for truth, and for the genuine solution to the numerous problems which arise in the life of individuals and from social relationships."[18]

Here is the theological foundation for an open discussion among Christians and other citizens in regard to the great ethical issues of the day. What the Church here admits is that it does not have all the answers. At the same time, open discussion does not imply an ethical relativism. On the contrary, God's guidance becomes available and the discovery of objective ethical norms is rendered possible precisely through respectful dialogue involving the whole of society. In this process, we are told, the erroneous conscience does not lose its dignity.

4. According to *Gaudium et spes* a just society is one in which the citizens are responsible agents and participate in the decisions that affect their lives. Political modernization is here judged to be in keeping with the Gospel. The following passages summarize the new social teaching.

> From a keener awareness of human dignity there arises in many parts of the world the desire to establish a political-jurisdical order in which personal rights can gain a better protection. These include the rights of free assembly, of common action, of expressing personal opinions, and of professing a religion both privately and publicly. For the protection of personal rights is a necessary condition for the active participation of citizens, whether as individuals or collectively, in the life and government of the state.[19]

> It is in full accord with human nature that juridical-political structures should, with ever better success and without any discrimination, afford all their citizens the chance to participate freely and actively in establishing the constitutional bases of a political community, governing the state, determining the scope and purpose of various institutions, and choosing leaders.[20]

Not discussed in *Gaudium et spes* is the ambiguity of the democratic revolution, i.e., the trend toward increasing centralization and bureaucratization, an aspect of modernity examined by Max Weber and other sociologists. Nor, as we shall see, does *Gaudium et spes* raise the difficult question of how the right to participate in decision-making demanded by justice, can be implemented in the Catholic Church.

5. According to the Vatican Council, democratization is not simply a Western development that deserves praise; it is a development, summoned forth by reason, justice, and a growing sense of human dignity, that is destined to affect the whole of the human family. "Now, for the first time in human history, all people are convinced that the benefits of culture ought to be and actually can be extended to everyone."[21] "In every group or nation, there is an ever increasing number of men and women who are conscious that they themselves are the artisans and authors of the culture of their community. Throughout the world there is a

similar growth in the combined sense of independence and responsibility."[22] The summons to justice, freedom and responsibility is here presented as a universal vocation.

The strongest statement that democratic participation is the
ideal for the whole of humankind is made in the chapter of
Gaudium et spes that deals with peace. For here peace is defined
not as the absence of war, nor as the maintenance of the balance
of power, but as an enterprise of social justice. Peace is not a
static condition, a tranquil order, achieved once and for all, but
an ongoing political endeavour creating the conditions of justice
between nations and within nations. Only justice can overcome
the outbreak of violence. To work for peace, therefore, includes
the economic and political development of the nations that will
deliver people from economic exploitation, political and military
oppression and the violation of human rights.

We have emphasized that the openness of Vatican II to political modernization was not a concession to secular Enlightenment philosophy but an original development of doctrine which
recognized the presence of God, creator and redeemer, in the
whole of human history. At first the reader is puzzled by the
secular-sounding statement that "we are witnesses of the birth of
a new humanism, one in which humans are defined first of all by
their responsibility toward their brothers and sisters and toward
history."[23] But upon closer inspection, the reader discovers that
the Council recognizes God's gracious presence as the ground,
the vector, and the horizon of people's entry into their full humanity. Echoing the theology of Karl Rahner and Henri de
Lubac, the Council affirms that the mystery of redemption is active in the whole of history. The humanism of solidarity and responsibility is brought forth by God.

A Critical Remark

Before we move on to the Council's unfinished business, let
us briefly reflect on the optimistic perspective adopted by the
Council. *Gaudium et spes* vaguely recognizes, but does not analyse,
the grave injustices existing in society and in particular the mis-

ery and hunger in the less developed regions of the world. The conciliar document suggests that a universal consensus is emerging in contemporary society that grave social and economic disparities among people are no longer tolerable.

> Our contemporaries are coming to feel these inequalities with an ever sharper awareness. They are thoroughly convinced that the wider technical and economic potential which the modern world enjoys can and should correct this unhappy state of affairs. Hence numerous reforms are needed at the socio-economic level, along with universal changes in ideas and attitudes.[24]

Gaudium et spes is hopeful that the contemporary form of capitalism, with its Keynesian, interventionist orientation, can be extended, with the generous help of the developed nations, to the regions of the world that still suffer from hunger, oppression, and lack of economic development. What is needed is economic reform and magnanimity. Catholic social teaching has always disapproved of 'liberal capitalism' because it leaves the production and distribution of goods solely to market forces, but confronted with welfare or interventionist capitalism, the Vatican Council has reacted more positively. For while there is room in welfare capitalism for the free enterprise of groups and individials (in accordance with the principle of subsidiarity), the government is responsible for promoting the economic well-being of all and for adopting economic policies that will benefit society as a whole (in accordance with the principle of socialization.)

Vatican II did not analyse the economic forces that produced inequality and exploitation in the world, especially among the poorer nations of the Third World. Following a certain middle-class optimism, Vatican II looked with some hope to the extension of the Western economic system to the world as a whole. By contrast—we have mentioned this above—the Medellin Conference (1968) of the Latin American Bishops looked at the growing world system with fear since, in their judgement, it increased the dependency and powerlessness of their continent. We note that the World Synod of Bishops, held in Rome in 1971, decided to adopt the Latin American perspective rather than that of Vatican II: "We perceive the serious injustices constructing around the world a network of domination, oppression and abuses, that stifle freedom and keep the greater part of humanity from sharing in the building up and enjoyment of a more just and more fraternal society."[25]

This, more radical line of thought that has been developed by Pope John Paul II in the eighties, first in *Laborem exercens* (1981) which analysed the exploitative and alienating character of capitalism (and communism)[26], and then in *Sollicitudo rei socialis* (1987) which denounced the devastating impact of the international financial institutions on Third World countries. This, more radical approach represents the Church's response to the decline of Keynesian welfare capitalism in the eigthties and its replacement by Friedmanian monetarism with its trust in the logic of the market forces.

Modernity and Church Structures

Is the Church's institutional apparatus capable of modernization? The Catholic Church regards as of divine origin its basic ecclesiastical institutions responsible for teaching and ruling, *magisterium* and *regimen*. Still, the ecclesiastical organization has greatly developed over the centuries. The synodal structures that characterized the early Church have been largely replaced by organizational patterns derived from feudalism and the subsequent aristocratic age. Power is here strictly exercised from above. No clear distinction is made between the legislative, executive and juridical powers. Thus there exist no independent courts capable of judging whether bishops and popes have acted in accordance with the law. The concentration of power in the papacy, an ancient trend in the Catholic Church, has been further intensified in recent centuries. As in all aristocratic societies, the people play only a passive role in matters of ecclesiastical teaching and polity.

Political modernization has generated a new ethic of governance. Modern men and women have ethical objections against an exercise of authority that is not open to dialogue and participation and not limited by checks and balances. How should the Catholic Church respond to this ethical challenge?

This question was not clearly faced at the Vatican Council, even though the Council itself was one of the rare occasion in the Catholic Church when dialogue and participation were able to influence public policy. At an important moment, the Council decided to treat its ecclesiological concerns in two separate sections, one dealing with the Church *ad extra* and the other with the Church *ad intra*. The fateful decision encouraged the illusion that these two aspects could be separated without causing serious confusion. If the Church accepts on theological grounds the values and institutions of political modernization and at the same time refuses to democratize its own self-organization, then it inevitably generates frustration and dissatisfaction among its members. If openness and dialogue are recommended *ad extra*, Catholics expect, and demand on ethical grounds, a corresponding renewal of ecclesiastical life *ad intra*.

Vatican II introduced into the Church the ideals of equality, co-responsibility, participation and respect for personal conscience. It laid the dogmatic foundation for the democratization of the Church. Defining the Church as 'People of God' in which all members, by virtue of their faith and baptism, participate in the threefold office of Jesus Christ, as prophet, priest and servant-king, Vatican II recognized that all Christians—not just the hierarchy—are teachers in the Church, all are priests offering worship, all exercise ministry in and for the Church.[28] The ministry of the hierarchy is not intended to replace the participation of the baptised, but on the contrary to assure and foster their co-responsability. Moreover by emphasizing the variety of gifts or charisms, the Council acknowledges that the Spirit uses the faithful, freely chosen, whatever their rank, to guide the Church on its way through history. The term 'collegiality,' which the Council applied to the share of the bishops in the governance of the Church universal, became the symbol of a participatory Church open to the Spirit speaking in the people.

It is possible to introduce participatory institutions in the Catholic Church without betraying the traditional papal-episcopal structure. Such a participatory Church was in fact recommended by the Puebla Conference (1979) of the Latin American bishops.[29] And at the end of their pastoral letter on economic justice

(1986) the U.S. Bishops were willing to "commit the Church to become a model of collaboration and participation."[30]

Yet Vatican II introduced almost no institutional changes providing for the participation of priests and lay people in the decisions affecting their lives in the Church. Parish councils, priests's councils and diocesan councils were recommended, but they were defined as purely consultative bodies, depending on the generosity of the pastors who convoked them and were willing to learn from them. Vatican II only hinted at a greater respect for personal conscience in the Church. It did very little to protect the freedom of theological research and debate. No attempt was made to introduce independent courts in the Catholic Church. Bishops, including the supreme bishop, the Pope, continue to be simultaneously rulers and judges, a feature reminiscent of a precious age.

The contradiction between Church *ad intra* and *ad extra* has become even stronger in the decades since the Council. The ecclesiastical authoritarianism introduced in the eighties clashes with the bold social teaching of John Paul II which has defined humans, men and women, as 'the subjects' of their society and the other institutions to which they belong.[31] According to John Paul II, governments are unjust whenever they confine decision-making to an elite, to a small group of men, thus depriving the people of what the Pope calls 'their subjectivity,' that is to say their right of participation and their call to co-responsibility. Authoritarian governments, according to the Pope, create frustrations among the people, prompting them to emigrate, to leave society, or to seek refuge in withdrawal and interior immigration.

The contradiction between the Church's approval of political modernization and its refusal to institutionalize these values in its own life creates a dilemma. As Cardinal König suggested in November, 1989, the problems in the contemporary Church are largely caused by the fact that the de-centralization and participation recommended by Vatican Council II have as yet not been fully implemented. The issue involves far more than expediency. Since the Catholic Church regards itself as the *magnum quoddam et perpetuum motivum credibilitatis,*[32] it must regulate its own institutional life in such a way that the ecclesiastical community appears to the public as a perfect image of social values derived from the Gospel, faithful to its own teaching, and in keeping with the ethical demands of the age.

Notes

1. This is an essay co-authored with Jean-Guy Vaillancourt.

2. N. Denzinger, A. Schoenmetzer, *Enchiridion symbolorum*, 32nd edit., Barcelona: Herder, 1963, no. 2980, p. 584. (Our translation.)

3. *Quadragesino anno*, nn. 81-83, *Seven Great Encyclicals*, New York: Paulist Press, 1963, p. 148.

4. *The Major Addresses of Pope Pius XII*, ed. V.A. Yzermans, vol. 2, St. Paul: North Central Publishers, 1961, pp. 78-89.

5. Cf. Owen Chadwick, *The Victorian Church*, part II, London: Adam & Charles Black, 1970, pp. 416-422.

6. 'Ad Petri cathedram,' Documentation catholique, vol. 56 (1959), col. 907. (Our translation.)

7. Ibid.

8. The story of the progressive bishops, told in all accounts of the Vatican Council, is recorded with a certain bitterness in Ralph Wiltgen's *The Rhine Flows into the Tiber,* Chowleigh, Devon: Augustine Publishing, 1967.

9. The best-known theoretical statement of this optimistic developmentalism is W.W. Rostow's *The Stages of Economic Growth: A Non-Communist Manifesto*, Cambridge: Cambridge University Press, 1960.

10. See Medellin Documents, 'Peace,' nn. 2-13, *The Gospel of Peace and Justice*, ed. J. Gremillion, Maryknoll, N.Y.: Orbis Books, 1976, pp. 455-458.

11. *Gaudium et spes*, n. 29, *The Gospel of Peace and Justice*, p. 266.

12. *Gaudium et spes*, n. 9, *The Gospel of Peace and Justice*, p. 207.

13. *Gaudium et spes*, n. 29, *The Gospel of Peace and Justice*, p. 266.

14. Cf. *Gaudium et spes,* nn. 67, 68, *The Gospel of Peace and Justice*, pp. 303, 304.

15. *Gaudium et spes*, n. 17, *The Gospel of Peace and Justice*, p. 256.

16. Ibid.

17. *Gaudium et spes*, n. 16, *The Gospel of Peace and Justice*, p. 255.

18. Ibid.

19. *Gaudium et spes*, n. 73, *The Gospel of Peace and Justice*, p. 308.

20. *Gaudium et spes*, n. 75, *The Gospel of Peace and Justice*, p. 310.

21. *Gaudium et spes*, n. 9, *The Gospel of Peace and Justice*, p. 250.

22. *Gaudium et spes*, n. 55, *The Gospel of Peace and Justice*, p. 292.

23. Ibid.

24. *Gaudium et spes*, n. 63, *The Gospel of Peace and Justice*, p. 300.

25. *Justice in the World*, n. 3, *The Gospel of Peace and Justice*, p. 514.

26. Cf. G. Baum, *The Priority of Labor: A Commentary on Laborem exercens,* New York: Paulist Press, 1982.

27. Cf. G. Baum/R. Ellsberg, *The Logic of Solidarity: Commentaries on Sollicitudo rei socialis,* Maryknoll, N.Y.: Orbis Books, 1989.

28. Cf. *Lumen Gentium,* chapters 2 and 4, *The Documents of Vatican II,* ed. W.M. Abbott, New York: Herder & Herder, 1966, pp. 24-37, 56-65.

29. Cf. *The Final Document,* part 3, 'Evangelization in the Latin American Church: Communion and Participation,' *Puebla and Beyond,* ed. J. Eagleson/P. Scharper, Maryknoll, N.Y.: Orbis Books, 1979, pp. 203-262.

30. "Economic Justice for All," n. 358, *Origins,* 16 (Nov. 27, 1986), 447.

31. *Sollicitudo rei socialis,* nn. 15, 25, 44, G. Baum/R. Ellsberg, *The Logic of Solidarity,* pp. 13, 24, 48. For a commentary see *The Logic of Solidarity,* pp. 80-81, 123-124.

32. Vatican Council I, 'Dei filius,' 1870, *Enchiridion symbolorum,* Denzinger/Schoenmetzer, n. 3012, p. 590.

9.

John Paul II on Structural Sin

Social sin is a relatively new concept in moral theology. In this paper I wish to offer a critical analysis of John Paul II's concept of social or structural sin. I choose the Pope's encyclicals as starting point for theological reflection not because I wish to invoke the power of the magisterium but because I find the relevant papal texts bold, stimulating and provocative. At the end of the paper I shall raise certain questions of pastoral importance. Should we feel guilty, as we drink our morning cup of coffee, because we derive some benefits from an economic system that exploits the coffee-pickers in Third World countries? Should we ask pardon of God and the Native peoples for being the heirs of an oppressive system that has gravely damaged them?

Social Sin

It is no exaggeration to say that in the past, moral theology and Christian preaching focused almost exclusively on the personal dimension of sin. Even Catholic Social Teaching, following an organic understanding of society, interpreted the violations of social justice as the fruit of human greed and selfishness and put forth the idea that a just social order could be established if the people, rich and poor, owners and workers, underwent a moral conversion to greater love, if they accepted the norms of justice and willingly served the common good.

In the face of human exploitation the Church at that time appeared to 'moralize,' i.e., to call people individually to moral conversion. This tied in well with the main trend of Catholic preaching which emphasized the universal call to sanctity. Confronted with social evil of various forms, Catholic preaching only too often created the impression that if people became more loving and more generous, the problems of society would straighten themselves out.

In the Sixties, Latin American Liberation Theology and German Political Theology criticized the 'moralizing' of Christian preaching. Liberation Theology tried to recover the "the social dimension of sin," and insisted that "sin was evident in oppressive structures."[1] "Conscientization," a notion confirmed by the Latin American Bishops Conference at Medellin (1968)[2], referred to the process by which the oppressed become aware of the structures that accounted for their marginalization. Part of the Church's pastoral mission, according to Medellin, was the raising of people's consciousness in regard to the institutional obstacles that prevented them from assuming responsibility for their lives. The necessary moral conversion was therefore not simply to private virtue but to a new way of seeing the social reality and to a new way of acting.

German Political Theology adopted as its programme the 'deprivatization' of the Christian message. J.-B. Metz argued that the Good News was addressed simultaneously to individuals and to society. Since Christian preaching had advocated a highly private understanding of sin, conversion and the newness of life, it was the task of Political Theology to recover the social dimension of the Christian message.[3] Sin was not simply private malice: sin also resided in society, sin also referred to structural realities, produced by human beings, that inflicted exploitation and oppression on sectors of the population.[4]

Influenced by J.-B. Metz and carrying forward his project of 'deprivatizing' the Christian message, I proposed in a book published in 1975 that social sin is a reality existing on four different levels.[5] The first level is the structure or institution that following its inner logic gravely damages human beings; the second level is the ideology or set of ideas that legitimates the damage-inflicting structure and makes it culturally acceptable; the third level is the approving consciousness of the people caught in the ideology; and the fourth level is the sphere of freedom enjoyed by certain individuals who recognize the damage-inflicting nature of the structure and the bias of the public ideology. These individuals then become capable of committing the personal sin of reaffirming the evil structure or even of giving it a twist for the worse, or of living with their raised consciousness, communicating it to others, and disassociating themselves from the sinful institution in their hearts. According to this analysis the redemption from structural sin begins with graced individuals enabled to see clearly, to resist, to communicate and to organize.

The social dimension of sin has been acknowledged by several ecclesiastical documents. At Medellin (1968) the Latin American bishops spoke of situations that were so massively unjust, exploitative and repressive that they had to be called "institutionalized violence."[6] The 1971 World Synod of Bishops recognized sin "in its individual and social manifestation,"[7] spoke of the Gospel as freeing people "from sin and from its consequences in social life,"[8] and recognized "the network of domination, oppression and abuses,"[9] built around the world, that kept the greater part of humanity excluded from power and resources. The Canadian bishops, following John Paul II, spoke of the plague of unemployment as a "moral evil" and as "symptomatic of a basic moral disorder."[10] In their economic pastoral, the American bishops defined injustice as the structured exclusion of people from political, economic and cultural participation and acknowledged that since these structures were created by free human beings, "they can be called forms of social sin."[11] And the Vatican Instruction on Christian Freedom and Liberation (1986) also recognized that while sin in the primary sense referred to voluntary acts, it was possible to speak of "social sin" and "sinful structures" in a secondary and derived sense since unjust structures were created by sinful human beings.[12]

Some theologians had difficulties with this new theological development.[13] Since the traditional notion of sin (with the exception of original sin) always included consciousness and deliberation, they did not see how sin could be applied to structures and institutions. They wondered what the relationship between this social sin and personal sin was supposed to be. In the United States, the Catholic defenders of capitalism and American empire opposed the notion of social sin: they were well aware that Liberation Theology designated as social sin economic and political institutions that systematically marginalized people and pushed them into misery.

Sollicitudo rei socialis

This is the context in which John Paul II put an emphasis on the notion of structural sin. In chapter 5 of *Sollicitudo rei socialis* (1987), entitled 'A Theological Reading of Modern Problems,' the Pope argues that it is impossible to understand the troubled world of today without the theological category of structural sin. "A world which is divided into blocs, sustained by rigid ideologies, and in which instead interdependence and solidarity different forms of imperialism hold sway, can only be world subject to structures of sin." (n. 36)

This sentence becomes clear when we read the preceding chapters of this encyclical, written—we note—prior to the collapse of Soviet bloc communism. Here John Paul II explained in detail how the increasing impoverishment of the Third World, the growing gap between rich and poor in the developed countries, and the death-dealing militarization of the globe were produced by the hostile logic of the two blocs, the false human self-understanding created by the two competing ideologies, and the global economic mechanisms set up by the powerful to the detriment of the poor. According to the Pope, then, structural sins are institutional realities, such as colonialism and imperialism, that create an unjust distribution of wealth, power and recognition, and thus push sections of the population to the margin of society where their well-being or even their life suffers damage.

Since structures and institutions have no consciousness and hence no conscience, why can they be called sinful? The encyclical gives a brief answer to this that deserves careful analysis.

Sinful structures are "rooted in personal sin, and thus always linked to the concrete acts of individuals who introduce these structures, consolidate them and make them difficult to remove."(n. 36) In a footnote, the text refers to a previous papal

document, *Reconciliatio et paenitentia* (1984), which recognized social sin and amplified on the manifold ways in which it is related
to personal sin. There are

> the personal sins of those who cause and support social evil
> or who exploit it, of those who are in a position to avoid,
> eliminate or at least limit certain social evils but who fail to
> do so out of laziness, fear or the conspiracy of silence,
> through secret complicity or indifference, of those who take
> refuge in the supposed impossibility of changing the world,
> and also of those who sidestep the effort and sacrifice re-
> quired, producing specious reasons of a higher order.

These sentences emphasize personal responsibility in the
construction and reform of institutions. If structures generate injustices, i.e., reveal themselves as sinful, personal sin is committed
by people who refuse to listen to the critics, who resist social
change, or who fail to take measures to forestall the evil effects.

We note that the papal sentences cited above are not as sensitive as the teaching of Medellin to the unconscious, non-voluntary dimension of social sin, i.e. to the blindness produced in
people by the dominant culture, blindness that prevents them
from recognizing the evil dimension of their social reality. Exploitative institutions are successfully maintained because they
are made to appear legitimate to their participants. Even oppressed people learn to look at their social situation through the
cultural symbols supplied by the dominant classes. Sinful economic and political structures tend to create a culture of conformity and passivity. What is required before people can be mobilized for social action is their "conscientization," i.e., the raising
of consciousness so that the structure of society can be recognized for what it is. As long as there is ignorance or non-recogni-
tion, as long as the minds of people—on any level of the institution—are caught in ideological prisons, there is no critical freedom and hence no personal sin in the strict sense.

John Paul II recognizes the blinding caused by ideology. In
Sollicitudo rei socialis he suggests that the dominant ideology of
West and East, "liberal capitalism" and "Marxist collectivism," actually blinds people in the two blocs from seeing that their system does not work well, even in their own country. And he ac-

knowledges that economic and political institutions, following a logic of their own, function "almost automatically"(n. 16), so that responsible decision-making would require an antecedent critical analysis and a new awareness.

Sinful Institutions

In an above paragraph we saw that the Vatican Instruction on Christian Freedom and Liberation (1986), signed by Cardinal Ratzinger, argued that sinful institutions derive their sin from the evil intention of the architects that created them. But this is not always true. There are sinful institutions that were created with the good intention of serving the community and began only later to have damaging effects. Good institutions may become bad. In a new historical situation, an institution that has served the common good in the past may become a source of injustice and hence a structure of sin. What happens here is that hidden contradictions implicit in the institutional structure become visible under the new circumstances and produce irrational, wholly unintended consequences.

In his first encyclical, *Redemptor hominis* (1979), John Paul II offered an interesting example of such an institutional dialectic (n. 15). Here the Pope warns us of the ambiguity of modern instrumental rationality. We create technologies and bureaucracies as instruments intended to help us promote the rational interests of society, yet after a certain period of time, under new circumstances, the situation seems to reverse itself. While we still think of ourselves as masters of these instruments, they have actually escaped our control. Following a logic of their own, the instruments have become our masters and despite our good intention, produce effects in society that harm the common good and undermine the ethical consensus. We are then tempted to cling to the illusion that we are still in charge, we rely on our good intentions, and we attribute the evil things that happen to other causes. We note in passing that this process of inversion, dramatized in the story of the Sorcerer's Apprentice, has been recognized by sociologists such as Max Weber and the social thinkers of the Frankfurt School.

We conclude that John Paul II is aware of the unconscious, non-voluntary, quasi-automatic dimension of social sin. The Pope recognizes the power of ideology: at the same time, he puts the greater emphasis in his analysis on personal responsibility.

In the three social encyclicals, *Laborem exercens, Sollicitudo rei socialis*, and *Centesimus annus*, the Pope wrestles against the 'economism' or 'sociologism' on the left and on the right. He repudiates 'positivism' as the dominant scientific approach in Eastern Marxism and Western social science. He opposes all forms of determinism and all ideologies that deny human freedom. While in contemporary mega-institutions the space left to human freedom is indeed small, one must not allow deterministic social theories to deny this remnant of freedom and in doing so promote resignation and political passivity. Here again John Paul II's teaching has a certain affinity with the emphasis on personal agency found in the work of Max Weber and of contemporary sociologists such as Anthony Giddens.

Capitalism

The stress on personal agency affects the Pope's understanding of capitalism in his social encyclicals. In *Sollicitudo rei socialis* he argues that an economic system always operates through certain concrete institutions—banks, trade agreements, exchange rates, etc.—and that the effects of an economic system, therefore, do not simply flow from its inner logic in a deterministic way, but depend also on the institutions which individuals have set up and for which they are responsible. What follows is that an economic system does not operates in accordance with fixed laws. Human decisions and human responsibility are never totally excluded.

Thus, according to the Pope, capitalism can be looked at as 'an ideology' and as 'an economic system.' As 'ideology' liberal capitalism is a fixed, internally defined system, that deserves rejection (n. 21) But the 'economic systems' that calls itself capitalist operates through institutions that can be set up in a variety of ways and hence are capable of being transformed.

The same analysis is proposed in the recent *Centesimus annus*. If capitalism is understood as a system guided by the ideology of the free market, it is unacceptable. But if it is understood as a market system regulated by public authority, constrained by the labour movement, and guided by a culture of solidarity, then capitalism or—as the Pope prefers—'the market economy' could become an economic system that serves the common good (nn. 19, 42). The Pope's emphasis on personal agency convinces him that economic systems are not driven by inner necessity: to a considerable extent they always depend upon institutional decisions made on many different levels. What worries John Paul II at this time is that after the collapse of communism, people might glorify the capitalist ideology and leave the future well-being of society to blind market mechanisms.

> There is a risk that a radical capitalistic ideology could spread which refuses to consider these problems (the marginalization and exploitation of masses of people), in an a priori belief that any attempt to solve them is doomed to failure, blindly entrusting the solution of these problems to the free development of market forces (n. 42).

Here structural sin is related to the damage-inflicting institution and the ideological theory that justifies and blesses it.

Idolatry

We conclude from the preceding that structural sin has a non-voluntary and a voluntary dimension. Because of his emphasis on agency, John Paul II pays special attention to the voluntary dimension. He wants to show that structural sin is intimately related to personal transgression. Here the question emerges whether people living in culturally-legitimated, gravely unjust structures are personally guilty. According to the Pope, they commit personal sin only if they resist efforts to raise their consciousness, hide in indifference or secret complicity, refuse to support the forces of social transformation, or in other ways side-step the opportunity to lessen the burden placed on the shoulders of the victims.

What about the power elites in structurally sinful societies? Are they personally guilty? Because the human damage inflicted by communist empire (before its collapse) and by capitalist empire is so enormous and so visible, the Pope does not appear to believe in the good will of the power elites. He does not think that they follow the logic of their respective system simply because they hold this system to be founded on truth. According to *Sollicitudo rei socialis,* the economic and political structures of sin that cause the present poverty-producing and death-dealing orientation of the world are driven by special attitudes and choices that include "the all-consuming desire for profit" and "the thirst for power with the intention of imposing one's will upon others."(n. 37)

> Better to characterize each of these attitudes—*indissolubly united* in today's word—one can add the expression, 'at any price.' We are faced here with the *absolutizing* of human attitudes with all its possible consequences . . . Obviously, not only individuals fall victim to this double attitude of sin; nations and blocs can do so too . . . If certain forms of modern 'imperialism' were considered in the light of these moral criteria, we would see that hidden behind certain attitudes, apparently inspired by economics or politics, are real forms of idolatry: of money, ideology, class, technology. (n. 37)

From Liberation Theology and the Puebla Conference the Pope takes the idea that the voluntary power that drives the present world society includes the endorsement of an absolute and thus represents, in the strict theological sense, a form of idolatry. The idolatrous attitude exists most prominently in the decision-making elite, but it is shared by vast numbers of people who without fully realizing it, are brain-washed by the dominant ideology. It follows from this that today's massive unemployment, poverty, misery and hunger are not simply economic or political problems for which appropriate, technical solutions must be found. The present social crisis is a crisis of values. Because our civilization has fallen into idolatry, the crisis is, in the last analysis, a theological crisis regarding the identity of the true God.

Repentance and Mourning

After examining the texts from the papal encyclicals, let me offer a few systematic reflections. The first meaning of sin is personal transgression or personal infidelity. Sin is here voluntary and incurs guilt. The sinner is summoned by God's Word to repentance and conversion. Turning to God with a humble heart, ready to do reparation, if necessary, the sinner receives forgiveness. This is the classical biblical teaching reaffirmed by John Paul II.

But this understanding of sin is not sufficient to account for the dreadful things taking place in human history. The evil in the world transcends personal malice. Hence the need to introduce the notion of social sin or sinful structures. Certain institutions, created by people with bad will or even with good will, have built into them mechanisms that in the long run, possibly in an unforeseen way, humiliate, damage or even destroy certain groups of people or sectors of society. These are sinful structures. They remain operative through a process that includes involuntary and voluntary elements. On the one hand, people tend to be unable to recognize the sinfulness of the situation because they have been blinded by the dominant, ideologically distorted culture, and on the other, many people do choose with a certain freedom to cooperate on various levels with the dominant system or at least to shrug their shoulders and miss opportunities to offer resistance. The question that emerges is whether people living in sinful structures are guilty. Are they in need of repentance and divine forgiveness?

It seems to me that an easy, unnuanced notion of collective guilt should be rejected. After World War II, a debate took place in the German churches whether the horrors committed by the German government with the support of the state bureaucracy and vast numbers of individual Germans demanded that the German nation as such avow before God and the world their collective guilt. Many Christians believed that a more nuanced theological language was necessary, one that distinguished various levels of involvement in the mass crimes and various levels of resistance. This, I think, corresponds to John Paul II's position on structural sin and personal responsibility. At the same time, there are German theologians[14], too young to have participated in World War II, who have taken to heart the political history of their nation, who refuse to shrug off the horrors of the past as if they had nothing to do with them, and who make repentance and reparation an essential dimension of their theology and their political engagement.

The complexity of sin, guilt and repentance is such that for the sake of greater clarity I wish to propose a distinction between 'guilt by personal implication' and 'guilt by common heritage.' Guilt by personal implication is incurred by people who knowingly and voluntarily participate in the structures of sin or who refuse to make use of their freedom to resist these structures and mitigate their evil impact. This is principal emphasis of John Paul II. In the present situation, he holds, the decision-making elites and vast number of people are defending the existing imperialist institutions driven by certain idolatries. If this judgment is correct, these people are guilty: they are in need of repentance and conversion.

Yet if one takes a longer look at the involuntary involvement in structural sin, at the dominant ideology that blinds people, at the doubts and uncertainty from which people suffer, at the absence of freedom in their lives, and at the prosaic need to survive from day to day, then one wants to reject the idea that all these people, despite their involvement and lack of resistance, are guilty of sin. Even among the power elite, there are probably men of good will who recognize the evil that is being done, have abandoned the idol long time ago, and yet do not know what to do to replace the present structures.

Still, I wish to argue, that even if the people are not guilty by personal implication, they share a common heritage and are spiritually identified with their community or their nation and hence willingly share in the burden of guilt that lies on those who are personally responsible. I call this 'guilt by common heritage.' The German theologians mentioned above, too young to have experienced World War II, believe that spiritual solidarity with their community, their nation and their church demand that the people assume the heavy burden of past transgression.

Without grieving over the past, they argue, people cannot come to a truthful understanding of the present nor adopt a responsible orientation toward the future.

In the pastoral letter on peace and war, the US Catholic bishops ask the Catholic people to persuade one another and their compatriots "to grieve" over the decision made in 1945 to drop atomic bombs on Japan.[15] It is not enough to say that one had nothing to do with this decision and hence is personally innocent. Because of spiritual solidarity with their people and their entire nation, Americans will want to bear the common burden: they will want to recognize that in the fateful decision to drop the bombs culminated dangerous cultural currents, with roots in the past and still present today, cultural currents that in one way or another touch the souls of all Americans. The American bishops do not ask their compatriots to feel guilty; instead they demand that they sorrow or mourn. They explain that unless this mourning takes place Americans will not have the consciousness required for bannig atomic weapons altogether.

The term 'grieving' used in the American pastoral is very suggestive. What I have called 'guilt by common heritage' is not guilt in the proper sense at all: it is more aptly described as grieving or sorrowing. In my own writing, I have often suggested that the appropriate response to structural sin is not guilt feelings but the readiness to mourn.

This seems to me an important pastoral issue. When we try to raise the consciousness of a parish in regard to the subjugation of the Native peoples or the exploitative economic structures that impoverish the Third World, people often get the impression that they are being blamed or accused of sin. They resist the Church's social teaching because they refuse to be made to feel guilty. They know they did not participate in the imperialist project to subjugate the Native peoples nor in the extension of the capitalist economy to the nations of the Third World. In this situation it important to explain that we assume the burden of collective transgressions by spiritual solidarity. In my experience people are quite ready to mourn that we belong to a society that has damaged and is still damaging significant sectors of the population at home and abroad. Mourning of this kind is a mental preparation for social renewal and political action. The proper spiritual response to social sin then is mourning and a keener sense of personal responsibility.

A Repentant Church

What interests me at the end of this paper is whether the notion of structural sin could and should be applied to the Catholic Church itself. In the past, certainly since the Council of Trent, popes and bishops have refused to acknowledge that the Church is sinful and in need of repentance. The Church is made up of sinners, yes, and sinners, whether they be lay or ordained, must ask for forgiveness, but the Church as such, we have been told many times, cannot sin. The divine promises mediated by Jesus Christ and the power of the Holy Spirit offer us the guarantee that the Church will remain forever in the truth and not betray her mission in the world by sin. Even at the Vatican II, every effort made by different episcopal groups to summon the Council to confess the sins of the Church, to repent and ask God's forgiveness was curtailed. At the Council, the Church changed its teaching and its pastoral policies—on the topics such as religious liberty and ecumenism—without admitting that its previous stance had inflicted heavy burdens upon people and without regretting that the theologians who had, at an earlier time, defended the present policies were made to suffer unjust punishment. Even when Vatican II recognized that Christian language had created contempt for the Jewish people and demanded that these texts in liturgy and catechisms be changed, the Church was unable to say that it was sorry. Since the Vatican Council several regional churches in the Catholic Church have confessed their sins, especially their former alliance with the colonial powers[16], but the official documents coming from Rome have not acknowledged the Church's need of repentance.

In my opinion the theological concept of social sin and the distinction between guilt by personal implication and guilt by common heritage enables us to speak of the sins of the Church with greater precision.

When the Provincial of the Oblate Fathers made the now famous spiritual gesture of apologizing to the Native peoples for the collaboration of missionaries with the imperial forces of cultural assimilation, he was greatly admired by a wide sector in the Catholic Church. According to many Catholics, the biblical principle that without repentance there is no grace for renewal applies not only to individual Christians but also to the Christian community. For these Catholics, the renewal of Vatican II has largely failed because it was not preceded by repentance. Reflecting on the Church's past involvement in or cooperation with slavery, exploitation, discrimination, repression, colonialism, and other forms of structural inferiorization, there seems to be something outrageous about an unrepentant Church. Catholics who feel that way were grateful for the Christian gesture of the Oblate Provincial.

Other Catholics, among them many missionaries, were offended by the declaration of the Oblate Provincial. They greatly admired the faith, courage and spirit of sacrifice of the early missionaries and the love and dedication that have inspired the missionary movement since the early days. Some retired priests who had dedicated their lives to the mission felt that the public apology was an accusation addressed to them, robbing their lives of its deepest meaning.

Here the notion of structural sin and the distinction between guilt by personal implication and by common heritage reveal their usefulness. The Oblate Provincial acknowledged the structural sin built into certain facets of the traditional missionary movement. These facets produced contempt for the Native cultures and supported the forces of cultural assimilation. At the same time, the Oblate Provincial made no judgment whatever regarding the personal responsibility of individual missionaries. More than likely they were captives of the wider Western culture to which they belonged and acted in perfectly good faith. The missionaries loved the Natives people and intended to serve them and do them good. But, alas, our good will is no guarantee that we are not involved in sinful structures.

Since sinful structures are often blessed by an appropriate ideology and assimilated into the cultural consciousness, they become invisible. Love and good will alone will not reveal them. It is through moments of interruption, disturbing events that shatter our perceptions, that we discover the human damage done by our taken-for-granted world. When we do make this discovery, the first impulse is to insist on our innocence. We did not recognize the harmful impact of the system which we served, and hence we are not guilty by personal implication. But reflecting of this discovery as Christians, we realize that we cannot simply shrug our shoulders in regard to what happened in the past and—who knows!—is still happening in the present. Our common heritage and spiritual solidarity with our community, our people and our church, demands that we assume the burden of these transgressions. While not guilty by personal implication, we soon come to feel that as a community, as a culture, and even as a church, we are in need of conversion. We must say we are sorry, for without such mourning we shall not encounter the grace of renewal. The notion of structural sin enables us to say without contradiction that the Church in which the Holy Spirit dwells is a repentant Church.

Notes

1. Cf. Gustavo Gutierrez, *A Theology of Liberation*, Maryknoll, N.Y.: Orbis, 1973, p. 175.

2. Medellin Documents, 'Justice,' nn. 17, 23, 'Peace,' n. 18.

3. J.-B. Metz, *Theology of the World*, New York: Seabury Press, 1973, pp. 107-124.

4. Cf. G. Baum, *Religion and Alienation*, New York: Paulist Press, 1975, pp. 199-204.

5. Ibid., pp. 199-204.

6. 'Peace,' n. 15.

7. *Justitia in mundo*, n. 51.

8. Ibid. n. 5.

9. Ibid. n. 3.

10. "Ethical Reflections on the Economic Crisis," n. 3, G. Baum/D. Cameron, *Ethics and Economics: Canada's Bishops on the Economic Crisis*, Toronto: Lorimer, 1984, p. 3. Cf. John Paul II, Redemptor hominis (1979), n. 52.

11. "Economic Justice for All" (1986), n. 77.

12. *Instruction on Christian Freedom and Liberation* (1986), n. 75.

13. Cf. Hugues Paul, "Structure du péche," *Le Supplément*, 176 (March 1991), pp. 125-133.

14. A repentant recognition of German guilt and the Church's silence was an important dimension of Protestant theology in the former East German Republic. See, for instance, Bishop Albrecht Schönherr's *Abenteuer der Nachfolge*, Berlin: Wichern Verlag, 1988.

15. "The Challenge of Peace" (1983), n. 302, *Catholics and Nuclear War*, ed. Philip Marnion, New York: Crossroads, 1983, p. 329.

16. G. Baum, "Bussfertigkeit im kirchlichen Lehramt," *Mystik und Politik*, ed. E. Schillebeeckx, Mainz: Matthias-Grünewald, 1988, pp. 311-321.

10.

Liberal Capitalism: Has John Paul II Changed his Mind?

Some interpreters of papal social teaching have suggested that between promulgating *Sollicitudo rei socialis* in 1987 and *Centesimus annus* in 1991, Pope John Paul II changed his mind in regard to liberal capitalism. It is true that in 1987 the Pope still believed that the socialist economies of the Soviet bloc countries were reformable while in 1991, after the collapse of the communist regimes, he spelled out the important lessons to be learnt from this world-shaking event. But, as we shall see, he did not change his mind in regard to liberal capitalism. He put a new emphasis on the importance of markets and the function of free economic enterprise, but he demanded at the same time, in keeping with traditional Catholic teaching, that the market economy be constrained by government regulations, an organized labour movement and a culture of solidarity.

The Offensive Comparison

When *Sollicitudo* was published, many readers where disturbed by the Pope's critical treatment of Marxist collectivism and liberal capitalism as if these two systems shared certain common characteristics, on account of which both deserved to be rejected.

Writing during the Cold War, John Paul II lamented the division of the Northern part of the world into two blocs, organized around two superpowers, in political opposition and competition with one another.

> This political opposition takes its origin from a deeper opposition which is *ideological* in nature. In the West there exists a system which is historically inspired by the principles of *liberal capitalism* which developed with industrialization during the last century. In the East there exists a system inspired by *Marxist collectivism* which sprang from an interpretation of the condition of the proletarian classes made in the light of a particular reading of history . . . It was inevitable that by developing antagonistic systems and centres of power, each with its own form of propaganda and indoctrination, the *ideological opposition* should evolve into a growing *military* opposition and give rise to two blocs of armed forces, each suspicious and fearful of the other's domination. (n. 20)

The logic of the two blocs, the encyclical continued, generated a dynamics of hostility that created the 'cold war,' in some regions 'wars by proxy,' and even preparation for 'open and total war.' In his rhetoric, the Pope distanced himself from the ideological and political conflict between Marxist collectivism and liberal capitalism as two systems and two blocs, both of which were in error.

The Church's opposition to Marxist theory has been constant: it needs no further comment here. What calls for an explanation is the understanding of liberal capitalism in Catholic social teaching and in *Sollicitudo.*

Liberal Capitalism

Liberal capitalism, according to ecclesiastical teaching, refers to a particular economic system as well as to the theory or ideology that stands behind it and justifies it. An economic system is called liberal capitalism when the free market is the one essential mechanism for regulating the production and distribution of goods. Liberal capitalism, in other word, is the self-regulating market system. Of course, markets have existed for a long time. Catholic teaching, echoed in *Rerum novarum* (1891) and *Quadragesimo anno* (1931), has always appreciated the market as an enormously useful mechanism, but the same teaching also demanded that the market be embedded in a culture of generosity and selflessness, opposed to greed and the excessive desire for profit, and regulated by public norms specifying what could be bought and sold and where and when these exchanges could take place. Over the years papal social teaching also came to recognize the role of labour unions in constraining the market economy.

What theory justifies the self-regulating market system? The inventors of liberal capitalism at the end of 18th century, protesting against the control of economic activity by kings and princes, argued that the freedom of the market would greatly increase economic development, generate enormous wealth, and eventually raise the material well-being of the entire society.[1]

Why would the free market be helpful to all, rich and poor alike? To answer this question the liberal thinkers replied that the market, ruled by the law of supply and demand, made men give their very best and at the same time limited the profit each could make. If a merchant asked too much for his merchandise, customers would not buy it: they would turn to the competition that offered a lower price. The competitive market, the liberals argued, was the wonderful regulating device that transformed people's desire for gain into socially useful activity. The market liberated people from the restraints of the past. People could dispense with virtue; all they needed was enlightened self-interest. While each player reached for the best deal he could get, the market mechanism, responding to the rule of supply and demand, would regulate—like a hidden hand—the economic activity so that it benefited society as a whole.

According to the liberal ideology, human beings are defined by the 'conatus,' i.e., the relentless struggle for self-preservation. The constant effort to improve the material conditions of one's life is here seen as the essential characteristic of human nature. This concept of man is called 'economistic.' Liberal ideology looks upon the free market as the marvelous institution that transforms the material self-interest of each into a contribution to the material well-being of all. Interfering with the market mechanism by government or other social forces, even when inspired by the best of intentions, only upsets the careful balance and produces negative economic results in the long run. The self-regulating market can be trusted because like a hidden hand it makes the economy serve the common good.

This ideology, we note, looks upon economics as an exact science: for if people always act to increase their profit and comfort, if—in other words—they are utility-maximizers, then their economic behavior is predictable and scientists are able to discover the laws operative in the economic life of society.

The theory of liberal capitalism was thought out in reference to the commodity market. In actual fact, the theory was also applied to labour and land, which were not at all the work of human hands: they were commodities in a purely fictitious sense. This fiction, not surprisingly, was severely criticized by the opponents of liberalism, conservatives and radicals alike. From the beginning, Catholic social teaching condemned treating workers as if they were commodities as unethical.

Has this self-regulating capitalism ever existed? The answer is No. For many people in society, economic activity remained embedded in the ethical culture they had inherited. There also continued to exist certain laws that imposed limits on the market. According to Karl Polanyi's famous book, *The Great Transformation*,[2] reaction against liberal theory and practice began to take place in England already in the second half of the 19th century, through parliamentary bills protecting people from damage produced by the market and through pressure exerted by labour organizations.

But it was only during the great depression in the 1930ies that capitalism underwent a significant transformation. Relying on the economic theory of John Maynard Keynes and other economists like him, governments began to assume greater responsibility for the national economy: they helped the industries during periods of slow-down, they protected the unionization of labour and defined rules for collective bargaining, and they introduced welfare legislation to help the unemployed and the poor. What emerged, as we shall see further on, were various forms of modern welfare capitalism.

Liberal Democracy

After this brief look at the theory of liberal capitalism, it is interesting to note the affinity of this theory with the ideals of liberal democracy. Allan Bloom's best-seller of a few years ago, *The Closing of the American Mind*,[3] expounded and defended the political philosophy of John Locke which, according to Bloom, is to this day the theoretical foundation of the democratic state. According to Locke, human beings are by nature aggressive competitors, each man a threat to his neighbour. By nature, human beings are afraid of one another: they live in mortal fear that they be attacked and robbed of their property. Their overriding passion is to survive, keep their property, and pursue their own interests.

In the past, Locke argued, people believed in all sorts of fairy tales pretending that human beings were good, that they constituted a family of brothers and sisters, that they were destined to solidarity, or even that a kindly divinity watched over them. But believing these legends did not change the cruel reality: it made things worse because people did not take adequate care to protect themselves. War followed upon war.

It was only when people allowed themselves to be guided by enlightened self-interest did they recognize that the only rational way to overcome their fears and assure their safety was to create, by means of a contract, a democratic state that would protect the human rights of all, including their property. This was the great discovery of the Enlightenment. Here people were delivered from exhortations to virtue and solidarity and freed from guilt feelings that their selfishness neglected concern for the common good. It was precisely their individual self-interest, guided by reason, that prompted them to constitute the democratic state, affirm the rights to life and property, and create a political space of freedom where they could peacefully increase their property and pursue their happiness.

The democratic state, then, was the marvelous invention that transformed the enlightened self-interest of all into protection for society as a whole. Allan Bloom recognized the affinity between democracy thus conceived and liberal capitalism. Enlightened political reason, he writes, "wipes the slate clean of all the inherited theories and inscribes on this slate contracts calmly made in expectation of profit, involving the kind of relations involved in business."[4]

Catholic social teaching criticized these liberal theories of capitalism and democracy. As we mentioned earlier, Catholic social teaching appreciated the institution of the market and along with it, profit and competition, but it demanded nonetheless that the desire for material success be restrained by virtue and that the authorities responsible for the common good limit the market in its exercise. Commerce and industry must make a reasonable profit, but the maximization of profit was reprehensible. The popes believed that the free market allowed the rich, the powerful and the clever to triumph over ordinary people and that good government had to intervene to protect the poor from exploitation. While Catholic social teaching strongly defended private property of productive goods against Marxist theory, Catholic teaching on private property differed considerably from the liberal theory inasmuch as the Catholic viewpoint associated ownership with social obligations. Property was indeed private, but its use was to serve the whole society.[5]

During the depression, in *Quadragesimo anno*, Pius XI recognized that in certain situations the state was ethically entitled to nationalize privately owned corporations: such situations occurred, according to Pius XI, when corporations had become so powerful that they prevented the government from protecting the common good of society.

Still, Catholic social teaching continued to warn against excessive power attributed to the state. One argument against Marxist theory and practice was precisely that the state as the sole owner of property would end up as totalitarian master. Catholic social teaching sought a balance between the freedom of small enterprises and the government's responsibility for the well-being of all. The principle of 'subsidiarity' protected smaller groups, capable of taking care of their own concerns, from interference by a higher authority, while the balancing principle of 'socialization' demanded that higher authorities coordinate help from above whenever smaller groups were in fact unable to take care of themselves.

Catholic social teaching thus tended to favour a mixed economy. When liberal capitalism moved in the direction of welfare capitalism—we mentioned the impact of Keynesian economics above—Catholic social teaching looked with greater favour on the economic system of the West.[6] In the early 60s the Vatican Council expressed a certain hopefulness in regard to the humanizing possibilities of welfare capitalism.

An Alternative Definition

Before we turn to John Paul II's evaluation of liberal capitalism, let me say a few words about Catholic social teaching on democracy. The liberal theory, derived from John Locke and still passionately defended by Allan Bloom, was unacceptable to Catholics. They refused to define human nature in terms of the 'conatus' for self-preservation. They rejected the idea that human beings came into the world alone and unprotected and were by nature hostile to one another. Catholics defended the classical concept, derived from Greek and Christian tradition, that human nature was inwardly oriented toward the good and that humans were born into communities and had a natural inclination toward solidarity. Catholics also repudiated the idea that institutions could be beneficial for the wider community if they were simply guided by enlightened self-interest without a commitment to virtue. Papal social teaching repudiated liberal democracy defined in terms of maximizing personal freedom.

However in dialogue with a wider range of political thought, Catholic social teaching eventually developed an alternative concept of democracy. Here a regime is seen as democratic when it allows the participation of all in the important decisions that affect their lives. This idea was explored in John Paul II's encyclicals *Laborem exercens* and *Sollicitudo* (nn 15, 25, 44) and greatly emphasized in his more recent *Centesimus annus* (nn 46, 47). Human beings, created in God's image, are meant to be 'subjects,' i.e., responsible agents, of the institutions to which they belong. If they are not allowed to share in the important decisions that affect their lives, they are reduced to mere 'objects' and deprived of their human rights. Even when governments protect the common good and legislate in its favour, their measures are ethically acceptable only if they respect what the Pope calls "the subjectivity" of the people, i.e. their human right to share in the decision-making process. Democracy is here defined as maximizing participation, not as maximizing freedom—the liberal theory.

John Paul's theory of 'subjectivity' has important consequences even for his perception of economics. He argues that the dignity of workers is such that they are meant to be 'subjects', not 'objects' of production.[7] Workers are destined to participate in the decisions that affect the work process and the use of the goods they produce. If workers are excluded from these decisions, they become 'objects' of production and victims of injustice.[8] For John Paul II social ethics demands the extension of democracy (defined as maximizing participation) into the economy. Ultimately workers are to become the co-owners of the giant workbench at which they labour.[9] This radical critique calls for the reconstruction of the present-day economic institutions.

Welfare Capitalism

Under the impact of the labour movement and progressive political parties, from the second half of the 19th century on, capitalism slowly evolved. I have mentioned the influence of Keynes's economic theories during the great depression. After World War II the economic system in the Western countries moved in the direction of welfare capitalism. Governments regarded themselves increasingly responsible for the well-being of the national economy, the re-distribution of income and the creation of full employment.

Welfare capitalism can be conceived and justified in various ways. Liberal theory remains within a utilitarian perspective. Here the arguments in favour of the welfare system are simply drawn from enlightened material self-interest. These liberals argue that a commercial civilization can thrive only if there is social peace: it is thus important to avoid an excessive gap between rich and poor. Since poverty among the masses creates unrest governments must promote public welfare. It is, moreover, economically useful to allow workers to organize and fight for higher wages because then they will be able to buy more commodities, become devoted customers and consumers, and invigorate the economy.

Other concepts of welfare capitalism transcend the utilitarian perspective. While they respect people's rightful rational self-interest, they also invoke higher ethical principles such as justice, solidarity and the common good. Ethical theories of this kind also lead to different practices. Social-democratic theory, for instance, flows from an ethical vision of a just society. Improved income distribution and greater material equality are here seen as a requirement of justice. The greater participation of workers, the majority of the people, on all levels of political and economic life is an ideal derived from the vision of a fraternal (sororal), egalitarian, democratic society. Social-democratic theory relies on an ethical tradition and calls for ethical commitment.

After World War II, Catholic social teaching also recommend the creation of a form of welfare capitalism—even though the word was never used. Catholic social teaching demanded that governments contain and stear the capitalist economy so that it served the well-being of the entire nation. Government were also held to introduce welfare legislation and laws protecting labour from exploitation. This Catholic social theory, based on an ethical tradition and calling for virtue, was adopted by the Christian Democratic Parties of Italy and several other European and Latin American countries. Christian Democracy at first presented itself as 'a third way' between liberal capitalism and Marxist socialism.[10] Christian Democratic governments favoured welfare capitalism in one form or another, yet in the long run always became the defenders of capitalism *tout court* against the socialist parties.

The New Phase

In the late 70s and 80s, or possibly already before that, welfare capitalism based on Keynesian economic principles seemed unable to cope with the economic problems of Western society. The reasons for this are still disputed among economists. The group of economists who became influential at that time, Milton Friedman among them, argued against Keynesian economics and welfare capitalism in favour of a return to the principles of liberal capitalism or the self-regulating market system. Their theory, called 'monetarism,' has been applied with more or less consistency in Britain and the United States, and, following them, in most of the nations of the West. What we have witnessed since then is increasing deregulation, new free trade agreements and a previously unheard-of globalization of the economy. The power of the corporate actors in this global economy has become so great that national governments must curry their favour and as a result have become unable to protect the economic well-being of their own people.

Capitalism has entered a new phase. Harsh critics of present-day economic globalization are not only economists with socialist sympathies but also defenders of welfare capitalism, especially those who have vindicated it on ethical grounds. They have provided us with a literature that documents the tragic human consequences of monetarist economics. Catholic social teaching itself has become more critical of the Western economic system. In *Laborem exercens* John Paul II declared that the capitalist economy had entered a new and cruel phase after the more benign period of Keynesian welfare capitalism. This new phase guided by the principles of 'liberal capitalism,' he predicted, would be characterized by dislocation and widespread human suffering.[11]

Following the lead of *Laborem exercens*, the pastoral letters of American and Canadian bishops have offered a detailed criticism of the monetarist economy. They claim that it produces structural unemployment, creates spreading pockets of poverty, leads to growing insecurity of employment, increases economic inequality, produces dramatic housing shortages, marginalizes people of colour and women in particular, and widens the gap between a shrinking economic elite and the majority of the people.

The Canadian bishops have analysed the change in the structure of capital.[12] The free-market philosophy and the corresponding public policies, they argued, have encouraged the reorganization of the economy around privately-owned, internally diversified, giant corporations, operating on the global level without ties of loyalty to the societies to which they belonged. What is presently taking place is the widening of the gap between rich and poor nations, and between rich and poor within these nations, and the surrender of decision-making power affecting the well-being of society, to an ever shrinking economic elite. Governments help this process through privatization and deregulation and by removing institutions designed to constrain the market to protect the common welfare. Relying heavily on *Laborem exercens* and its principle, 'the priority of labour over capital,'[13] the Canadian bishops have raised serious ethical questions regarding the very foundation of capitalism.

The bishops of the United States, we note, did not question the capitalist system as such. They did not deal with the foundational issues raised in *Laborem exercens*.[14] The American pastoral simply criticized liberal or monetarist capitalism in the name of a Catholic commitment to an ethical form of welfare capitalism. It is not surprising that the bishops were vehemently attacked by those who defend and justify the economic policies of the Canadian and American corporate class.

To defend this liberal or monetarist economic orientation on ethical grounds, some apologists of the *status quo* praised the present system as an example of 'democratic capitalism.' But what does this term mean? Here democratic capitalism does not refer to any particular quality of the capitalist economy. It does not designate, for instance, the entry of democracy into the organization of the economy—which is John Paul II's proposal mentioned above. Nor does democratic capitalism refer to a capitalist economy constrained by a democratic government elected to serve the welfare of society. Democratic capitalism here refers to any form of capitalism that is located in a democratic society. The term therefore allows apologists to praise contemporary capitalism in the Western democracies without having to ask any questions about its impact on society, such as income distribution, rate of unemployment, spread of chronic poverty and deterioration of the environment.

To strengthen and dramatize his critique of the new phase of the global economy in *Sollicitudo*, the Pope proposed that a certain similarity existed between liberal capitalism and Marxist collectivism. Many Western commentators were greatly displeased by this even-handedness. Yet the Pope argues that both theories, liberal and Marxist, attach value only to enlightened material self-interest, in liberal capitalism to the personal self-interest of individuals and in Marxism to the collective self-interest of the working class. Both theories entertain an 'economistic' concept of the human being, both look upon economic behaviour as following certain laws and hence as determined, both regard economics as an exact science, and both reject the entry of traditional values, such as justice and solidarity, into the logic of the economy.

Written during the Cold War, *Sollicitudo* observed that the two economic systems and their ideologies had defined themselves against one another.

> Each of the two ideologies, on the basis of two very different visions of man and of his freedom and social role, has proposed and still promotes, on the economic level, antithetical forms of the organization of labour and of the structures of ownership, especially with regard to the so-called means of production. (n. 20)

The logics of the two competing blocs, the encyclical argued, tended to make both sides cling to their ideology in an inflexible manner. Indoctrination prevented the people on both sides from discovering that the system they regarded as superior actually did not work so well in their own countries. The people caught in these ideologies did not recognize the danger in which they lived: the endless production and sales of arms, the relentless preparation for nuclear war, and the ongoing race to increase production irrespective of the damaging impact on the environment. What we presently have, the Pope wrote, is a civilization "oriented toward death rather than life." (n. 24)

At the same time, the Pope recognized that it was the Western free market system, not Marxist socialism, that dominated the world economy. The Western bloc controlled the flow of money. The Pope lamented that the poorer nations of the Third World were unable to escape from their underdevelopment because the international trade agreements, the world monetary system and the global financial institutions have been put into place by the powerful in the Western bloc to the detriment of the Third World. "These mechanisms, maneuvered directly or indirectly by the more developed countries, favour by their very function the people manipulating them."(n. 16) "Through these mechanisms, the means intended to assist the development of peoples has turned into a *brake* upon development, and in some cases has even *aggravated underdevelopment.*" (n. 19)

Writing at that time, John Paul II believed that both the Western and the Eastern economic systems could be reformed. He argued that economic systems are never subject to a strict internal logic, even though this is what the ideologues claim. Economic systems always operate through concrete mechanisms and institutions that have been designed by individuals and that could be changed. What is needed first, therefore, is a new spirit, the virtue of solidarity. Guided by the logic of solidarity, the Western system could be made to serve the well-being of all the people—some form or other of ethically-steered, mixed economy welfare capitalism—and the Eastern European system could change by becoming more responsive to the economic initiative of individuals, or—to use the Pope's terminology—more respectful of the people's subjectivity.

A special paragraph (n. 15) offered a harsh critique of the economic control exercised by communist governments and defended the right of people to economic initiative or free enterprise. The paragraph analysed the paralyzing and alienating effects produced by the bureaucratization of the Marxist economies and in fact by any "bureaucratic apparatus that wants to be the only ordering and decision-making body . . . thus putting everyone in a position of almost absolute dependence." Such bureaucratization, the Pope argued, kills the spirit of economic initiative and "the creative subjectivity of the citizens."

Catholic social teaching, as we noted above, has always recognized the need for markets. Needless to say, praising markets and economic enterprise does not mean approval of liberal capitalism. What *Sollicitudo* envisages is an economy where free markets and economic enterpise are regulated by governments and other social institutions so that the economy comes to serve the common good of society. Despite his rejection of liberal capitalism in *Sollicitudo*, the Pope believed that Western societies could and should create an ethically-guided mixed economy, a welfare-serving market society—in other words, a capitalism with a human face.[15]

Centesimus annus

The encyclical *Centesimus annus*, published in 1991, celebrated the collapse of the Eastern European communist regimes and the unexpected rescue of the world from the dangers of the Cold War. In Poland the Marxist government collapsed, the Pope argued, i) because the labour movement demanding the rights of workers, supported by a majority of citizens, was able to exert increasing power, ii) because the national economic performance failed, excluding as it did all individual entrepreneurship, and iii) because a false, atheistic and materialistic anthropology built into the entire social system prevented it from ever being fully embraced by the people.

What should we learn from the collapse of the communist regimes? The Pope mentions several lessons: the significance of the labour movement as an agent of social change, the importance of the virtue of solidarity in the struggle for social justice, and the success of social movements committed to non-violence that remain open to honest negotiations and are guided by ethical values rather than an inflexible ideology.

Among the lessons to be learned in the field of economics is the need for markets. The Pope writes, "It would appear that, on the level of individual nations and of international relations,

the free market is the most efficient instrument for utilizing resources and effectively responding to needs" (n. 34). If this sentence is removed from its context in *Centesimus annus*, it does
suggest that the Pope has changed his mind in regard to liberal
capitalism. Is he not here advocating the free market system? Yet
reading the sentence in its context, we discover that the Pope
praises the free market only if it is appropriately regulated by
society.

Already the next sentence tells the reader what "resources"
and what "needs" are efficiently taken care of by the free market:
only "resources" that can obtain a price deemed satisfactory and
only "needs" for which customers are able to pay. But there are
resources the market does not distribute to people who need
them because the owners or producers would not make enough
money. There are also needs that are not met by the market because people are unable to afford them. The text here adds that
"it is a strict duty of justice and truth not to allow fundamental
human needs to remain unsatisfied, and not to allow those bur-
dened by such needs to perish."

The encyclical recognizes that "the modern business economy has positive aspects: its basis is human freedom exercised in
the economic field as well as in many other fields"(n. 33). Yet it
is

> still possible today, as it was (at the turn of the century), to
> speak of inhuman exploitation. Inspite of the great changes
> that have taken place in the more advanced societies, the hu-
> man inadequacies of capitalism and the resulting domination
> of things over people are far from disappearing. In fact, for
> the poor, to the lack of material goods has been added a lack
> of knowledge and training which prevents them from escap-
> ing their state of humiliating subjection (n. 33).

In today's world the struggle for social justice must continue. Addressing trade unions and other workers' organizations,
the Pope explains that

> it is right to speak of a struggle against an economic system,
> if the latter is understood as a method of upholding the abso-
> lute predominance of capital, the possession of the means of
> production and of the land, in contrast to the free and per-

sonal nature of human work. In the struggle against such a system, what is being proposed as an alternative is not the socialist system, which in fact turned out to be state capitalism, but rather a society of free work, of enterprise and of participation. Such a society is not directed against the market, but demands that the market be appropriately controlled by the forces of society and by the state, so as to guarantee that the basic needs of the whole society are satisfied (n. 34).

It is difficult to see how these passages could have been overlooked by the commentators who claimed that John Paul II had changed his mind in regard to the capitalist economy. The Pope insists on the limits of the market system.

It is the task of the state to provide for the defense and preservation of common goods such as the natural and human environment, which cannot be safeguarded simply by market forces. Here we find a new limit on the market: there are collective and qualitative needs which cannot be satisfied by market mechanisms. There are goods which escape its logic and by their very nature cannot and must not be bought and sold. (n. 34)

Despite the enormous usefulness of market mechanisms for facilitating the exchange of products, for offering the opportunity of economic initiative, and for bringing resources to customers and respecting their wishes and preferences, "nevertheless, these mechanisms carry the risk of an 'idolatry' of the market, an idolatry which ignores the existence of goods which by their nature are not and cannot be mere commodities"(n. 34.)[16]

This, then, is the question posed by the Pope: "Can it perhaps be said that after the failure of communism, capitalism is the victorious system, and that capitalism should be the goal of the countries now making efforts to rebuild their economies and society?"(n. 42) The Pope's answer has two parts. If by capitalism is meant the self-regulating market system of liberal capitalism, the answer is simply No. But the answer is Yes if by capitalism is meant an economic system defined by personal enterprise, the free market, business and private property, all situated within a juridical framework that assures that they serve the common good as well as freedom in its totality, the core of which being ethical and religious.

While putting greater emphasis on business and the market, John Paul II has not changed his mind in regard to liberal capitalism. Catholic social teaching continues to regard the self-regulating market system as a moral evil. The Pope reminds us that while "the Marxist solution has failed, the realities of marginalization and exploitation remain in the world"(n. 42). Because of the collapse of the communist system in so many countries, "there is a risk that a radical capitalist ideology could spread which refuses to consider these problems (the marginalization and exploitation of people) . . . and blindly entrusts their solution to the free development of market forces" (n. 42).

Notes

1. A popular introduction to Western economic history is John Galbraith's excellent *The Age of Uncertainty*, Boston: Houghton Mifflin, 1977. For a more thorough look at this history and the contemporary economic debate, see Charles Wilber/Kenneth Jameson, *The Poverty of Economics*, Notre Dame: University of Notre Dame Press, 1983, which follows a perspective largely defined by Catholic social values.

2. Karl Polanyi, *The Great Transformation*, Boston: Beacon Press, 1957.

3. Allan Bloom, *The Closing of the American Mind*, New York: Simon & Schuster, 1887. Cf. pp. 96-107 of this volume.

4. *Op. cit.,* p. 167.

5. *Quadragesimo anno*, n. 114.

6. Joseph Gremillion, *The Gospel of Peace and Justice*, Maryknoll, N.Y.: Orbis Books, 1976, pp. 15-37.

7. *Laborem exercens*, n. 7.

8. Ibid., nn. 9, 14.

9. Ibid., n. 14.

10. Cf. G. Baum/J. Coleman, ed., *The Church and Christian Democracy*, Concilium no. 193, Edinburgh: T. & T. Clark, 1987.

11. *Laborem exercens*, n. 1.

12. G. Baum, "Toward a Canadian Catholic Social Theory," *Theology and Society*, New York: Paulist Press, 1987, pp. 66-87.

13. *Laborem exercens*, n. 12.

14. G. Baum, "A Canadian Perspective on the U.S. Pastoral," *Christianity and Crisis*, Jan. 21, 1985, pp. 516-518.

15. *Laborem exercens* presented a more radical vision. Emphasizing 'the priority of labour over capital' and the human right of workers to be 'subjects of produc-

tion' and therefore ultimately the co-owners of the industries, the encyclical of 1981 proposed that it was necessary to move beyond capitalism. See G. Baum, *The Priority of Labor*, New York: Paulist Press, 1982, pp. 80-91.

16. The thesis of the market system as idol, derived from Latin American Liberation Theology, has been taken up by John Paul II in *Sollicitudo* (n. 37). Cf. p. 197 of this volume.

11.

The Ethical Foundation of Workers' Co-ops

From its beginning in the 19th century the cooperative movement has been a self-help enterprise. Men and women unable to
make a living under the existing economic conditions organized
their economic activity on the basis of solidarity and cooperation.
The motivation here was people's material self-interest. At the
same time, from the very beginning the cooperative movement
generated an ethical critique of the social conditions produced
by capitalism and presented itself as a social enterprise that, if
widely accepted, could create an alternative order of society, a
cooperative commonwealth. The material self-interest that motivating the movement was accompanied by other, more universal
aspirations. Implicit in the movement was a commitment to a set
of values. Cooperatism had an ethical foundation.

These ethical values were woven into the principles worked
out by the Rochdale Pioneers in 1848. The Rochedale Principles,
with slight modifications, have continued to define cooperatism
right to the present.[1] Cooperatism defined a new socio-economic
vision of society. 'Open membership' rejected the barriers created by religious, ethnic and gender discrimination pervasive in
the social order. 'One member, one vote' repudiated the logic of
capitalism and introduced democracy in the economic order,
and related to this, 'democratic control' was an expression of the
Enlightenment ideal that people were meant to be the responsible agents of the institutions to which they belonged. 'Co-operative ownership' rejected wage labour that defined the existence
of workers under capitalism. 'Limited return on capital' repudi-

ated the greed implicit in capitalist maximization of profit, and 'distribution of surplus to the members' offered an alternative to the exploitation of labour. Finally, 'education of the members' intended to make the participants well-qualified cooperators and make the movement a source of social criticism. Another principle added in later years, 'cooperation with other cooperatives,' expressed the social aim of the movement, the transformation of society as a whole.

Where did these radical social values come from? Some were old, some were new. They were part of the people's response to the economic and cultural turmoil produced by industrial capitalism at the end of the 18th and the beginning of the 19th century. Cooperatism emerged as a movement as people wrestled against the oppressive conditions under which they lived, and for this reason cooperatism can only be understood in the context of the other social projects that were generated at this time.

The 'liberals,' we recall, welcomed the emerging society defined by capitalism, industrialization and democracy.[2] They accepted the new individualism as progress. They trusted in scientific rationality and believed in the perfectibility of society.

This emerging liberal or bourgeois society was resisted and criticized on ethical grounds by 'conservatives' and 'radicals.' The conservative or Tory critique of modern society lamented the loss of community, the emergence of individualism, the waning of solidarity, and the victory of personal greed or acquisitiveness. The Tories evaluated the new order in the light of an idealized image of the past.

The radicals, on the other hand, shared with liberals the belief that society could be reconstructed along rational lines. The radicals too anticipated progress. Yet with the Tories they lamented liberal individualism, the centrality of competition and the breakdown of solidarity. Radicals differed from Tories in their almost religious yearning for social equality: they were egalitarians. They repudiated the conservative vision of an organic society with its connatural hierarchy, and they opposed the liberal concept of a competitive society dominated by a new ruling class, the bourgeoisie. The radicals re-interpreted the liberal idea that humans were meant to be the subjects of their own lives by giving it a more social and historical meaning. By their rational nature, people were destined to become jointly responsible for their collective existence.

Among the radicals were socialist and anarchists. Among them were also cooperatists. In the early stages it is not always easy to tell these groups apart. The radicals criticized the present order in the light of an idealized image of the future. They analysed the alienation produced by liberal society and involved themselves in the creation of an alternative social order. Socialists focused on economic oppression: they believed that exploitation and alienation could be overcome once the industries and natural resources became public property. Socialists tended to think in centralizing terms. By contrast anarchists focused on bureaucratic oppression: they distrusted the state and all large organizations, including socialist political parties; they believed that through the creation of small communities, defined by sharing and mutuality, the whole of society may one day be reconstructed. Anarchists produced a de-centralizing imagination.

The reaction to liberal society and the ensuing debate among its critics was the context for the creation of cooperatism. The cooperative movement entertained an original vision that combined values derived from several sources. With conservatives they treasured social solidarity, community and coooperation, and with the radicals they distrusted hierarchy, defended egalitarianism, and called for co-responsibility. With conservatives they opposed centralization—as did the anarchists—and worried that class struggle was a strategy that undermined social solidarity. They shared the de-centralizing zeal of the anarchists, but differed from these in their concentration on economic reconstruction. Yet with both liberals and radicals, they endorsed the Enlightenment principle that people were responsible for their own history and hence that human progress was possible.

The cooperative movement was radical because it defined itself against the ethos and the practice of capitalist society: it sought to extend democracy to the sphere of economics. But cooperators were less combative than socialist and anarchists. They were culturally more conservative. They drew strength and inspiration from traditional sources, from the inherited religion and the memory of pre-industrial village society. Cooperators were willing to defend their vision in ethical terms. What they rejected of traditional culture was the elitism of class and the divisions created by ethnicity and religion. Yet they recognized themselves as heirs of an ethical tradition.

*

The ethical foundation of cooperatism—especially of worker co-ops—is a topic that continues to attract attention. What I wish to show is that the cooperative values have a pluralistic foundation: they have been defended by secular and religious thinkers coming from quite different philosophical traditions.

To begin with let me look at two famous ethico-philosophical texts that argue in favour of a cooperative commonwealth, even if the respective authors were not identified with the cooperative movement. We shall examine Karl Marx's 'Early Writings' and R.H. Tawney's well-known book, *The Acquisitive Society*.

In his early writings Karl Marx offered reflections critical of capitalism that promoted a cooperative vision of society. The young Marx argued that human emancipation called for i) the extension of democracy to the economic order and ii) the overcoming of wage labour through social ownership.

According to Marx's analysis, capitalist society—he called it civil or bourgeois society—obliged people to compete with one another, regard the neighbour as a means and degrade themselves as means as well. Thus people became the plaything of alien powers. Civil society produced an alienated population. Whether they were bourgeois or workers, people were ruled by the law of the market, unable to realize their true human nature.

The young Marx contrasted this 'civil society' with the 'political community' that was the emancipatory aim of the democratic revolution.[4] Here people were meant to be responsible citizens; here legal equality was to allow people to transcend the distinctions created by birth, social rank and personal property; here people were supposed to discover themselves as communal beings—species-beings, as Marx called them—collectively responsible for one another and in solidarity with the whole human family. Humans were essentially communal beings identified with the good of the species.

In reality, however, according to Marx's analysis, this 'political emancipation' existed only in theory. It did not produce 'human emancipation' because as members of civil society people continued to be caught in the alienation produced by the capitalist economy. Political democracy created a discourse of freedom and self-determination which actually disguised the alienating social conditions under which people had to live. "Political emancipation certainly presents a great progress," Marx wrote, "but it is not the final form of human emancipation: it is only the final form of human emancipation within the framework of the prevailing social order."[5] Ultimately people were destined to be the responsible subjects of their society, and this included their coresponsibility for the economic institutions in which they laboured.

For Marx there existed a profound contradiction between democracy and capitalism. People could become free and self-determining only through a bold social transformation that would extend democratic participation to the economic order, to the process of production and distribution.

The young Marx offered a very wide definition of alienation. He defined the alienation of labour in such a broad manner that it included not only the worker's separation from ownership but also the worker's exclusion from the decisions affecting the labouring process. "So far we have considered the alienation of the worker only from one aspect, namely his relationship with the product of his labour. However, alienation appears not merely in the result but also in the process of production, within productive activity itself."[6] Workers are meant to be the subjects—not the objects—of the productive process.

Following a detailed analysis of alienated labour Marx argued that wage labour, under any conditions, even if it should be well paid, prevented workers from realizing themselves as human beings. Wage labour deprived them not only of the product of their hands, it also made them into objects of production: it deprived them of their human dignity and kept them from assuming their 'species-life,' i.e., their self-realization through labour in solidarity with the entire human family. Human emancipation, therefore, demanded that the economic system based on private ownership and hired labour be replaced by a system of social ownwership shared by the workers.

In Marx's early writings, social ownership cannot be understood as state ownership since this would inevitably lead to wage labour. What the young Marx advocated was the overcoming of alienated labour through cooperative ownwership.

The young Marx's ethico-philosophical reflections advocate economic democracy and cooperative ownership—a cooperative commonwealth. It is well known that these ideas did not have a significant place in Marx's later, scientific writings, where he defined alienation in more narrowly economic terms and avoided ethical reflections on human beings and their destiny. It has been argued that his early humanistic ideas remained the philosophical horizon for his later, more strictly economic writings, but this was certainly not the way his followers interpreted him. Still, whenever Marxists did return to the early writings, they always arrived at a humanistic interpretation of their tradition.

Marx's early writings are a collection of essays and fragments that do not contain a unified and consistent social philosophy. They seem important to me because they provide ethical arguments that rely neither on religious ideas nor on classical metaphysics. Basic to Marx's argumentation is the Enlightenment conviction, derived from people's historical struggle against the inherited order, that reason is the organ of human self-emancipation. Reason is able to analyse human oppression and alienation, project a vision of society that promises emancipation, and guide the historical struggle for the new order. Emancipatory reason is not classical metaphysical reason seeking an abstract definition of human nature; it is rather a practical reason that interprets historical experience and seeks to deliver people from the concrete conditions of their bondage. Practical reason affirms itself as true because without it emancipated human life is impossible. The ethics of the young Marx, we note, is not deductive or 'idealistic,' not derived necessarily and a priori from a religious doctrine or a metaphysics of human existence. His ethics is rather inductive or 'materialistic,' derived from reflection on people's practical experience in their joint struggle for emancipation. Marx's ethics is a posteriori, generated by a historical struggle, and it is true precisely because it serves human emancipation.

Startling in the arguments offered by the young Marx is the notion of species-being and species-life. Against the individualistic presupposition of bourgeois philosophy, the young Marx argues that humans differ from the animal world in that they seek and constitute their identity in solidarity with the entire species. Here again, the ground for this is not metaphysics but practical reason. Marx argues historically that oppression and alienation inflicted on one class of human beings actually distorts the human reality of the totality, of the entire society. The oppressors and those in solidarity with them also become alienated human beings. The master/servant relationship damages the servant, but it also diminishes the master. Ultimately emancipation is indivisible. The contemporary reader finds this reasoning impressive, but also feels that behind such arguments stands great faith in human destiny.

*

With R.H. Tawney, the English historian and social philosopher, we enter a very different intellectual universe. He wrote his well-known *The Acquisitive Society* shortly after World War I.[7] In line with a Christian-Aristotelian philosophy widely respected in the Anglican and Roman Catholic traditions, Tawney looked upon the world as an ethical universe. He accepted the ethical status of human existence because God had created it thus and because it corresponded to people's rational intuition renewed and defended throughout the ages.

What follows from this is that every human institution must be justified in ethical terms. An economy must serve the well-being of the community. All rights in society, in particular property rights, can be ethically justified only if they fulfill a social function for the benefit of the community. Examining the capitalist market in the light of this philosophy, Tawney concludes that the existing economic institutions do not serve society as a whole: instead they serve the owners and exploit and humiliate the workers. Ethics demands that the capitalist order be changed.

Tawney summarizes his proposal in two principles that resemble those of the young Marx: (1) "The economy should cease to be conducted by the agents of property-owners for the advantage of property-owners and should be carried on, instead, for the service of the public," and (2) "Subject to rigorous public supervision, the responsibility for the maintenance of the services should rest upon the shoulders of those, from organizer and scientist to labourer, by whom in effect the work is conducted."[8]

Tawney argues that capitalism is based on a moral confusion. An economy is meant to serve the community, not to enrich the owner of the machinery. Essential to the Christian 'natural law' tradition is the distinction between ends and means. People are ends, things are means. People may never be used simply as ends. Since people are ends and since capital, whether it be machinery or natural resources, is always and inevitably a means, the latter must be subordinated to the former. Capital must serve people's needs. "A society is rich when material goods, including capital, are cheap, and human beings dear; indeed the word 'riches' has no other meaning."[9]

Yet the present economic order where capital holds priority over people "is preposterous in the literal sense of being the reverse of that which would be established by considerations of equity and common sense."[10] It gives rise, among other anomalies, to what has misleadingly been called 'the struggle between labour and capital.' It is as meaningless to regret 'ill feeling' and advocate 'harmony' between 'labour and capital' as it is to lament the bitterness between a man and his hammer or to foster reconciliation between people and the machines they use. Labour consists of persons, capital of things; and the only use of things is to be of service to persons.

Tawney argues that ethics calls for an alteration of proprietary rights. The Anglican philosopher distinguishes three main claims associated with ownership, the right to interest as the price of capital, the right to the profit of the enterprise, and the right to control, in virtue of which managers and workers are the servants of the shareholders. The first step towards a more ethical social order is to remove from capitalists the power to control. Control must be in the hands of people who will make capital serve the interests of workers and the community.

Ultimately the economy will have to be reconstructed so that labour, including managerial labour, employs capital, and not the other way around. Workers will be the owners of the industries: they may have to borrow the capital they need and pay a rent for it. But whether they are owners in the full sense or not, they will certainly be in control of the industries. Yet lest they run their industry to enrich themselves along capitalist lines, society must in some way supervise their governance and see to it that their industries actually serve the well-being of the community.

Tawney's organic view of society is derived from the Tory heritage: its deeper roots, as I indicated above, go back to the ancient Christian tradition that tried to bring together biblical wisdom and Greek philosophy. The understanding of labour and trade as services to the community was widely held in the Christian Church and the contempt for greed and avarice was a constant theme of Christian preaching. With the arrival of modern individualism and the spread of Protestant Christianity the Churches began to overlook the critical social concern of the biblical message and the Christian tradition. Religion became increasingly preoccupied with the interior journey of individuals; and by remaining neutral and indifferent in regard to the economic order, religion—wittingly or unwittingly—played into the hands of the capitalist class.

Tawney, we note, was not a lonely critic in the Anglican Church. He belonged to a socially concerned, progressive movement in the Church, dating from the middle of the 19th century, known under the name of 'Christian Socialism.'[11]

Still, we notice that in his argument Tawney did not invoke the whole of Christian doctrine. From the Christian tradition he only drew the profound conviction that we live in an ethical universe, that people have an inestimable dignity, and that organizations and institutions are ethically acceptable only if they serve the common good of the community. This conviction is shared by many, if not by all the world religions. There are also classical humanists, secular in outlook, who share this metaphysical intuition: they too believe in the ethical nature of the human project. They honour the dignity of persons, acknowledge human solidarity, and evaluate institutions, including the economy, in terms of the service they render to the community.

If my reading of Tawney's work and Marx's early writings is correct, then it is possible to distinguish two sets of humanistic arguments for cooperatism: there are the classical humanists who rely on a metaphysical understanding of human nature (often though not always derived from religious sources) and the radical humanists who derive their understanding of the human vocation from people's historical struggle against alienation and oppression.

*

The cooperative movement did not keep its early enthusiasm.[12] There are many reasons for this. Because it is a self-help movement cooperators were often tempted to forget the wider vision originally attached to it. Since the early cooperatives were for the most part consumer cooperatives, they offered advantages to people who did not see themselves as critics of capitalist society. When they became large and experienced economic success, they tended to become competitive and run their operations along capitalist lines. Because of their size they were often forced to hire trained managers, professional men with no sense or awareness of belonging to a radical movement. Instead of influencing and transforming capitalism, cooperatives were influenced and transformed by capitalism.

The cooperative vision, if my argument is correct, is not an abstract idea: it is always generated by people's struggle against the oppressive conditions produced by the capitalist revolution. Thus it was again during the depression of the 1880s that many worker cooperatives were founded in Britain, cooperatives that saw themselves to be at odds with the dominant economic order. But because they sought to promote cooperatism, the labour movement and the Fabian socialists criticized worker coops for undermining labour solidarity and lacking a political strategy to change the order of society. Socialist and social democratic political parties have on the whole been rather aloof from the cooperative movement.

Cooperatives had their ups and downs. In Canada the cooperative movement was often fueled by religious energies. This was true of the Dejardins movement in Quebec, of the farmers' cooperatives in Western Canada, and of the Antigonish Movement in Nova Scotia.

The Quebec movement is interesting because it combined Catholic ideas with nationalist interests.[13] Roman Catholicism with its social teaching in the Tory tradition, the same tradition interpreted by the Anglican, R.H. Tawney, had never fully reconciled itself to modern society, to capitalism and democracy. The Catholic ethos was at odds with the self-centredness and acquisitiveness implicit in the market society. Catholic social teaching, moreover, affirmed the principle of subsidiarity, which claimed that if small communities were able to look after their own needs no higher authority has the right to interfere in their activities. This principle was the traditional expression for 'small is beautiful.' Subsidiarity was understood as a principle of de-centralization in the economic and the political order. In the past Catholics used this principle to defend the formation of cooperatives, just as today radical Catholics in the Third World use this principle to justify their struggle to escape from world capitalism and create their own self-reliant economy.

In Quebec the cooperative movement, especially the setting up of credit unions, was also fueled by nationalist sentiment. French Canadians were economically disfavoured in Canada. Capital was mainly in the hands of 'foreigners.' To promote their own economy, to help themselves as a people, they needed their own capital. The cooperative movement, supported as it was by church organizations, became the instrument as well as the symbol of the national quest for greater self-determination.[14]

In Western Canada it was the Protestant Social Gospel that produced wide-spread support for the farmers' cooperative movement.[15] Here it was the egalitarian, democratic tradition of British Protestantism that provided the values for the cooperatist vision. In Free Church Protestantism, co-responsibility and self-determination have always been religious principles. Moreover, the special historical conditions under which the Western farmers had to make their living forced them to take a critical look at the exploitative structures of the Canadian economy. As a consequence many of them became socialists, religiously motivated socialists. This joining of cooperative and socialist activity in the Prairie provinces was perhaps the most important historical development responsible for the creation of the Cooperative Commonwealth Federation (CCF). The Regina Manifesto of 1933 that committed the new party to an original, Canadian form of socialism included a paragraph pledging support for the cooperative movement.[16] The call of Canadian socialism for centralized, democratically controlled economic planning was to be balanced by the de-centralizing role to be played by cooperatism.

The Antigonish Movement in Nova Scotia, founded in the late 20s, was of Catholic inspiration.[17] Because the movement was regarded as radical and controversial in the culturally conservative world of those days, Father Moses Coady, one of its founders, was obliged to provide a theological defense of the cooperative principles. We are indebted to him for a literature that reveals vigour and originality.[18] Since the open membership and the implicit ecumenism of the movement offended many Catholics, Coady presented a reasoned yet passionate plea for economic cooperation among people of different religious convictions. He was disgusted by religious prejudice. Coady tried to show that the cooperative philosophy of the Antigonish Movement was in keeping with the official papal teaching of the time. Cooperatism, he argued, was as critical of liberal and socialist economics as were the Popes. For tactical purposes he exaggerated the affinity between cooperatism and papal social teaching. In fact, at that time Pope Pius XI proposed 'economic corporatism' as the solution for the crisis created by the depression and only made the slightest hint in favour of the right of workers to 'co-determination.'[19] Co-ownership was not envisaged in papal teaching at that time.

Religious members of the cooperative movement have always shown more theoretical interest in its ethical foundation than have the secular participants. We note that the values of the cooperative movement were also attractive to people of religious traditions other than Christianity. Many Jews, secular and religious, have supported the principles of cooperatism. It is interesting to note, however, that in Israel religious Jews did not invoke their own religious values as motivating force for cooperatism: they participated in the movement on the basis of rational, secular convictions.[20] Cooperatism has also appealed to Hindus and members of other Asian religions.[21]

*

If it is true that cooperatism as a radical movement is always created as practical response to economic oppression produced by capitalism (or state socialism), then it is not surprising that the last decade has seen the rebirth of worker cooperatives in many parts of the world. We are witnessing at this time the reorganization of corporate capitalism along international lines, a process that is widening the gap between rich and poor nations and between the rich and the poor classes in these nations. The important economic decisions that affect the fate of the nations are made by an ever shrinking elite unaccountable to any societal body.

During and after World War II capitalists were increasingly forced to enter into an unwritten contract with their society, an agreement that upheld full employment, promised welfare legislation, and assured respect for labour organizations. This Keynesian phase of capitalism produced great wealth in the industrial countries of the West. But this phase has come to an end. What has been taking place for a decade now is a new internationalization of capital. Everywhere the unwritten contract with society is being abrogated: we have massive unemployment, increasing reduction of welfare, and an undeclared war against labour and labour organizations. The new information technology enables transnational corporations to keep control of their empires even as they de-centralize production, automate their factories, introduce new flexibility, serve a global market, and relocate in places where human labour is cheap. National governments are obliged to comply with the new trend by removing trade barriers and tariffs, reward the industries for remaining at home, and create a social climate attractive to foreign investment.

In response to this new economic development the movement of worker co-ops has come to life again in many parts of the world. The movement wants to offer people work. It is critical of capitalism and state socialism and opposes the power of all highly centralized bureaucracies. Its aim is to enable people to regain the economic power that has been taken away from them, and in doing so to become the sign and harbinger of a more democratic, participatory society.

Allow me, then, to examine two contemporary ethico-philosophical approaches that offer a theoretical defense of worker cooperatives. The first one is found in the writings of David Ellerman, an American social thinker committed to worker co-ops; the second is drawn from the encyclicals of Pope John Paul II.

*

David Ellerman makes an effort to derive the ethical foundation for cooperatism from the liberal tradition, the dominant philosophical trend in Western society.[22] Foundational for him is the dignity of the human person and his or her inalienable rights. Because if this great dignity, he argues, people are entitled to live in institutions characterized by self-government. Democracy is thus the only ethical form of government. In fact, ethics demands that even economic institutions be self-governing. The capitalist organization of production, which excludes the democratic participation of workers, is at odds with human dignity. Against the objection that people join capitalist institutions voluntarily and hence freely consent to the rule from above, Ellerman argues, in line with the socialists of old, that people do not act freely but are forced by poverty to become workers in the industries and enter into legally valid and binding contracts. As a robber uses a gun to obtain the free, voluntary surrender of the victim's purse, so do capitalists use the legal system to rob the workers of their right to share in decision making. Ellerman speaks of "the tyranny of the workplace."[23]

Human dignity, moreover, demands that people are responsible for what they do and for what they make. People can never abdicate this responsibility. If an entrepreneur hired a few men to break into a bank for him—this is Ellerman's example—the judge would regard them as guilty, as accomplices of a crime. The judge would not blame the instruments used in the break-in, but he would accuse the hired men. He would not accept their argument that they too were simply instruments and that the entrepreneur alone is morally at fault. Persons cannot abdicate their responsibility for their own actions, even if they try.[24]

Ellerman argues that this is true not only for what people do, but also for what they make. People have ownership rights over the work of their hands. While this is not legally recognized in modern society, whether it be capitalist or state socialist, it is nonetheless a natural and hence a moral right. Workers are meant to be the owners of the fruit of their labour. Against the objection that workers are treated justly when they are rewarded for their contribution to production by their wages, Ellerman argues that a person's right to own what he or she produces is inalienable and hence that an economic system based on wage labour is intrinsically at odds with human dignity. What we have at present is "institutionalized theft."[25]

He writes, "If a legal property system is not to violate these moral norms, then it must recognize and guarantee in law: (1) that the work force is an enterprise that has collective legal responsibility for its productive activities, i.e., the workers have the right to self-management, and (2) that the work force is an enterprise that has the legal right to appropriate its whole product."[26] Worker cooperatives constitute the only ethically defensible economic arrangement.

But is it really possible to derive the ethical foundation for worker ownership and self-management from the liberal tradition? We notice that in contrast with Marx's early writings and Tawney's social philosophy, Ellerman does not mention people's collective responsibility for one another and their society. He argues simply from the entitlement of individual persons. Marx and Tawney went further: they invoked the principle of human solidarity. According to Marx, people struggling for emancipation make the rational discovery that humans are species-beings and hence the collective subject of the historical process, and according to Tawney, people who acknowledge the ethical nature of the universe—because of their religious belief or their humanism—

recognize the preeminence of the common good, the well-being of all, to which the quest for personal well-being must be subordinated.

Ellerman does not mention universal human solidarity. His ethical defense of worker co-ownership, therefore, does not exclude the possibility that worker co-ops imitate capitalist profit maximization and engage in brutal competition with one another. It is impossible, in my opinion, to draw arguments for social solidarity from the Anglo-American liberal tradition, a tradition in which Ellerman wants to stand.

And what does Ellerman mean by 'natural rights'? Since he is not a philosopher, he does not feel the need to offer a clear definition of his terms. To convince his reader he presents instead interesting and suggestive examples. But one has the uncomfortable feeling that by 'natural right' he refers to John Locke and traditions derived from him which defend the rights of humans on the basis of 'reason.'[27] But what reason? Not the metaphysical reason of the classical philosophical tradition, but the empiricist reason that defines good and evil in terms of a calculus of pleasure and pain. Rationality is here essentially individualistic. The human rights derived from this intellectual tradition—primarily property rights—are those that protect individual citizens from the encroachment of the community and the claims of outsiders.

David Ellerman writes with great passion. His moral intuition transcends the intellectual tradition with which he wants to be identified. He may think that it is strategically important to show that Anglo-American liberalism brings forth its own critique and is capable of moving beyond itself. Yet in my opinion David Ellerman has moved beyond the liberal tradition: he believes in the human vocation as a collective enterprise. He is haunted by the conviction, beyond the letter of his arguments, that human beings are meant to build their world co-operatively and that the responsibility of each is related to the responsibility of all the others. This conviction, we noted above, is shared by many classical humanists who derive it from a religious or secular metaphysics, and by many radical humanists who derive it from people's historical struggle for emancipation.

*

The second contemporary author I wish to examine is Pope John Paul II. The historical context in which this man's social thought has emerged is the shift to the left that has affected the major Christian Churches over the last twenty years, first, as a positive response to the protest of Third World Christians and their liberation theology and, later, as a negative reaction to the contemporary re-orientation of global capitalism and the accompanying neo-conservative culture. This more radical social justice movement is strongly supported by the Geneva-based World Council of Churches[28] and by the Catholic Church's official social teaching.[29]

By the Churches' shift to the left I refer to the so-called 'option for the poor,' adopted by many Christian groups and ecclesiastical councils, which commits them (1) to reading their social reality from below, from the perspective of the powerless and marginalized, and (2) to giving public witness of their solidarity with the poor struggling for justice.[29] The social teaching that has emerged from this option includes an extended ethical critique of capitalism.

This is the context for John Paul II's encyclical on labour, *Laborem exercens,* which proposes two ethical principles of far-reaching implications.[31] First is "the priority of labour over capital." This phrase has several interrelated meanings. Since labour refers to people and capital to things (machinery and resources), the right order demands that capital serve the well-being of the workers and contribute to the common good of society. Whenever this principle is violated, we find ourselves in a system that deserves to be called 'capitalism,' even if it should present itself as state socialism. In fact, such is the worth and dignity of labour that workers are entitled to participate in the decisions affecting the work process and the use of the goods they produce. Workers are deprived of this right in Western capitalism as they were deprived of it in Eastern European socialism. John Paul II forcefully defends workplace democracy and workers' self-management.

Related to this first principle is a second one that affirms 'universal human solidarity.' What follows from this principle is that an economic system must serve the entire human community. An economic system has an end and purpose and cannot be left to the arbitrary, competitive game defined by the free market. Society as such is co-responsible for the production and distribution of goods.

The second principle also means that access to the goods of this earth is universal. Ownership may be circumscribed, but the use of these goods, especially those necessary for a dignified human life, is to be accessible to all. All people have to eat and be clothed, and not only those who can afford to pay for these goods. What follows from this is that ownership, whether private or public, is always conditional. What must be tested is the use of the goods owned. Does it serve the common good? The ownership question, according to this papal encyclical, cannot be solved once and for all. State ownership is no guarantee that capital will be made to serve the well-being of labour and the wider community. Both private ownership and various forms of social ownership are fully acceptable, but their entitlement is not an absolute: they remain essentially conditional.

John Paul II's position on ownership is a provocative formulation of traditional Catholic social teaching:

> Isolating the means of production as a separate property in order to set it up in the form of 'capital' in opposition to 'labour'—and even to practice exploitation of labour—is contrary to the very nature of these means and their possession. They cannot be possessed against labour, they cannot even be possessed for possession's sake, because the only legitimate title to their possession—whether in the form of private or public ownership—is that they should serve labour and thus by serving labour that they should make possible the first principle of this order, namely the universal destination of goods and the right to common use of them.[32]

John Paul II's teaching stands against the liberal tradition and against Marxism. According to him, there exists no form of ownership that guarantees the use of property in the service of the workers. He argues that the greatest likelihood that the priority of labour over capital will be respected is obtained when the industries are owned by the workers themselves. Ultimately, he argues, workers are meant to be the owners of the giant work-bench at which they labour. Only then will they be able to work for themselves and not for another; only then will they overcome the alienation of labour. And yet in doing so, they will at the same time serve the well-being of their co-workers and of society as a whole. John Paul II assigns worker ownership the highest place among the various ways in which industries can be owned. Yet even this ownership remains conditional, subject to the ethical test of whether the goods produced are made to serve the entire community.

The reader will have noticed that John Paul II moves in the same intellectual universe as the Anglican social philosopher, R.H. Tawney. Their arguments are very similar. What is presupposed is the ethical foundation of the human world. For Christians the doctrine of divine creation announces the destiny of people to cooperate in building a just society. In dialogue with Enlightenment philosophy, Christians have discovered the dynamic character of this world building process and following a modern terminology, they now affirm that people are divinely called to be 'the subject' of their own history.

R.H Tawney stood in the 'natural law' tradition, derived from classical philosophy and later confirmed by the Christian Church, a tradition verified by human reason reflecting on people's ethical experiences. As I mentioned above, there are also secular humanists who subscribe to this understanding of natural law.

It is worth mentioning that Protestants tended to have difficulties with the natural law tradition because (1) they were more aware of the distortion of reason wrought by the sinful world, and (2) they wanted to rely more exclusively on God's Word in the Scriptures. While until recently Catholic social teaching drew its arguments mainly from the natural law, over the last two decades it has paid more attention to the content of the biblical message. This is true especially for the above-mentioned, radical 'option for the poor,' the ultimate vindication of which is God's own bias for the poor as recorded in the Bible. John Paul II defends his social teaching not only with reference to divine creation but also to divine redemption exemplified in the liberation of Israel from Pharaoh's power and in the liberation of humanity through the death and resurrection of Jesus.

If one wanted to contrast the ideas of R.H. Tawney and John Paul II, one could say that the former remains more exclusively in the natural law tradition while the latter invokes more readily the specifically Christian biblical message. Still, while John Paul II quotes the scriptures and relies on the Christian message, he believes nonetheless—in keeping with the Catholic tradition—that the social values revealed in the Bible correspond to the aspirations of human reason, not the dominant rationality marked as it is by current ideology, but the deeper rationality by which people reach out for the meaning of their collective existence.

Studying contemporary Christian social ethics, we find that some authors defend 'a just, participatory and sustainable society' with reference to the natural law tradition while others, especially at the World Council of Churches, prefer to offer a moral justification for this position from the message and the historical experiences recorded in the Scriptures. This difference of theological methodology, however, does not lead to divergent conclusions. Left-wing Christians defined by the 'option for the poor' may belong to different theological traditions, but they are united in their support for a cooperative society.

*

The ethical foundation for worker co-ops, we conclude, is pluralistic. The values implicit in cooperatism, here understood as a radical movement, are affirmed and defended by people coming from various ethical traditions. Cooperatism is countercultural. It is at odds with the individualism and utilitarianism characteristic of contemporary capitalist society. The people who do endorse cooperative social values appear to do so either on explicitly Christian grounds, or on the basis of a less specific religious humanism, or on the basis of a secular humanism, classical or radical, that recognizes—beyond empiricism—the solidary unity of the human family and the social responsibility of people for one another. Many persons share these values without ever articulating them. These values are actually communicated more effectively by acting together than by talking about them.

Notes

1. George Melnyk, *The Search for Community: From Utopia to a Cooperative Society,* Montreal: Black Rose, 1985, pp. 5-9.

2. For the commonly accepted distinction between 'liberal,' 'conservative' and 'radical,' see Robert Nisbet, *The Sociological Tradition,* New York: Basic Books, 1966, pp. 21-42.

3. Marx's early writings, sometimes called his Paris Manuscripts, are available in many editions, among them T.B. Bottomore, ed., *Karl Marx: Early Writings,* New York: McGraw-Hill, 1963.

4. See the essay, "On the Jewish Question," idem, pp. 3-31.

5. Ibid., p. 15.

6. See essay, "Alienated Labour," ibid, p. 124.

7. R.H. Tawney, *The Acquisitive Society,* London: G. Bell and Sons, 1921.

8. Ibid. p. 111.

9. Idem, p. 112.

10. Ibid., p. 113.

11. W. Charlton and T. Mallinson, *The Christian Response to Industrial Capitalism,* London: Sheed & Ward, 1986, pp. 34-40, 65-68, 84-92.

12. Jenny Thornley, *Worker's Co-operatives: Jobs and Dreams,* London: Heinemann Educational Books, 1982, pp. 10-29.

13. G. Deschènes, C. Beauchamps et D. Lévesque, "La coopération québécoise des origines á nos jours," C.I.R.I.E.C., 1981, no. 14.

14. L. Labraque, "Le déclin des cooperatives de consommation et les mutations d'une culture économique," *Recherche sociographique,* 1986, no. 27.

15. Gary Fairburn, *From Prarie Roots,* Saskatoon: Western Producers Prairie Books, 1983.

16. Cf. 'Regina Manifesto,' section 6, in Walter Young, *The Anatomy of a Party: The National CFF,* Toronto: University of Toronto Press, 1969, p. 308.

17. G. Baum, Catholics and Canadian Socialism, Toronto: Lorimer, 1980, pp. 191-204.

18. Moses Coady, *Masters of Their Own Destiny,* New York: Harper & Row, 1939; Alex Laidlaw, *The Man From Margaree: Writings and Speeches of M.M. Coady,* Toronto: McClelland & Stewart, 1971.

19. G. Baum, op. cit., pp. 78-81.

20. Cf. Harry Vitales, *A History of the Co-operative Movement in Israel,* London: Vallentine, Mitchell, 1965, vol. I, p. xii.

21. P.R. Dubhashi, *Principles and Philosophy of Co-operation,* Poona, India: Vaikunth Mahta National Institute of Co-operative Management, 1970.

22. David Ellerman, "Capitalism and Worker's Self-Management," in *Workers' Control: A Reader on Labour and Social Change,* ed. Gerry Hunnius, New York: Random House, 1973, pp. 3-21; "Workers' Cooperatives: The Question of Legal Structure," in *Worker Cooperatives in America,* ed. R. Jackall, Berkeley: University of California Press, 1984, pp. 257-274.

23. "Capitalism and Workers' Self-Management," p. 10.

24. Ibid., p. 4.

25. Ibid., p. 10.

26. Ibid., p. 5.

27. For Locke's theory of rights, see Alastair MacIntyre, *A Short History of Ethics*, New York: Collier Books, 1966, pp. 157-161.

28. Ulrich Duchrow, *Global Economy*, Geneva: WCC Publications, 1987.

29. For the evolution of Catholic social teaching, see G. Baum, *Theology and Society*, New York: Paulist Press, 1987.

30. G. Baum, "The Option for the Powerless," *The Ecumenist*, 26, (Nov./Dec., 1987), pp. 5-11.

31. For the text of *Laborem exercens* and a commentary, see G. Baum, *The Priority of Labor*, New York: Paulist Press, 1982.

32. *Laborem exercens*, n. 14, *The Priority of Labor*, p. 123.